Parenting Your Infant/Toddler by the Spirit

*Yes, you can lay
the foundation for
a godly character*

Sally Hohnberger

Pacific Press® Publishing Association
Nampa, Idaho
Oshawa, Ontario, Canada
www.pacificpress.com

Cover design by Mark Bond
Cover design resources from istockphoto.com
Interior Design by Aaron Troia
Interior photos supplied by the author

Additional copies of this book are available by calling toll-free 1-800-765-6955 or by visiting http://
www.adventistbookcenter.com.

Unless otherwise noted, Scripture quotations are from the King James Version of the Bible.

Scriptures quoted from NKJV are from The New King James Version, copyright © 1979, 1980, 1982,
Thomas Nelson, Inc., Publishers. Used by permission.

Scripture quotations marked NLT are taken from the Holy Bible, New Living Translation, copyright
1996. Used by permission of Tyndale House Publishers, Inc., Wheaton, Illinois 60189. All rights reserved.

Scripture quotations marked NIV are taken from the HOLY BIBLE, NEW INTERNATIONAL
VERSION®. Copyright © 1973, 1978, 1984 by International Bible Society. Used by permission of
Zondervan Publishing House. All rights reserved.

Scriptures quoted from NASB are from The New American Standard Bible®, Copyright © 1960,
1962, 1963, 1968, 1971, 1972, 1973, 1975, 1977, 1995 by The Lockman Foundation. Used by
permission.

Library of Congress Cataloging-in-Publication Data
Hohnberger, Sally, 1948-
Parenting Your infant/toddler by the Spirit : yes, you can lay the foundation for a Godly character /
Sally Hohnberger.
p. cm.
ISBN 13: 978-0-8163-2283-1 (paperback)
ISBN 10: 0-8163-2283-X
1. Parenting—Religious aspects—Christianity. 2. Parenting—Religious aspects—Seventh-day
Adventists. 3. Parenting and infant. I. Title.
BV4529.H627
248.8'45—dc22

2008018460

08 09 10 11 12 • 5 4 3 2 1

Dedication

If you sense God calling you to raise your little one to follow Him; if you want your child to know God's voice, to learn how to work with Him; if you desire to cultivate Heaven's ways in your child's thoughts, feelings, and responses; if you are seeking to raise someone special for God to use, this book is dedicated to you.

Acknowledgments

First and foremost, I thank God for giving me the ideas to express the keys that will make infant and toddler training successful in your home. His endless inspiration never ceases to amaze me. He is there whenever I call upon Him—and I did often during the writing of this book. He was my Rescuer and "Idea-kindler" so very often.

I also thank the Lord for my personal assistant, Jeanette Houghtelling, for her faithful service as she works her pen right alongside mine, and for her strength and tenderness of heart to challenge me to take a different approach when I need to.

Contents

Lord, how do I bring up this infant to follow you?

Chapter 1

Wonderfully Wrought

*Before I formed thee in the belly I knew thee; and before thou camest
forth out of the womb I sanctified thee.*
—Jeremiah 1:5

Of all the wonders of God's creation, nothing exceeds the amazing possibilities found in the conception of new life. God bestowed upon humanity—made in His own image—the incredible ability to procreate. A man and his wife unite in love, and two cells, incomplete in themselves, merge to form a new person.

Because this new person is so small, helpless, and hidden away within its mother, we are prone to overlook the advantages of parenting by the Spirit before the baby is born. And yet, it is a reality, pressed home by inspiration and confirmed by modern science, that the foundation for both physical and psychological well-being begins at conception. The baby is built of, and within, the mother. Her health supports his. Her thoughts and feelings build his perception of himself and the world he is preparing to enter.

In the words spoken to the wife of Manoah, God speaks to all mothers in every age. The message, sent by an angel of God and twice given in the most solemn manner, shows that the prenatal period deserves our most careful thought. "Let her beware," the angel said. "All that I commanded her let her beware."[1] The well-being of the child will be affected by the habits of the mother. Her appetites and feelings are to be controlled by principle. God has a purpose in giving her a child—to mature him into the image of God. In order to cooperate with God in accomplishing this, there is something for the mother to shun, something for her to work against. If she is self-indulgent, selfish, impatient, and exacting before the birth of her child, these traits may be reflected in the child's disposition. Thus, many children have received as a birthright almost unconquerable tendencies to evil. But if the mother unswervingly adheres to right principles and is temperate and self-denying; if she is kind, gentle, and unselfish, she may give her child these same precious traits of character that will prepare him to fulfill God's purpose for his life.

The one essential key to successfully parenting your unborn child is a *connection with God*. God supplies the direction we need through His Word, through the impressions of His Spirit upon our hearts, through our own experiences, and by the experiences of others. He is the Source of strength, courage,

---

1. Judges 13:13.

hope, and love that empowers us to give to our child that which she most needs—the sense that she is wanted, loved, and welcomed.

Another useful key is understanding the physical, mental, and spiritual development of the unborn child. So let's take advantage of the "windows" provided to us by modern science into the dark world of the unborn, and seek after this wise Creator God who can change and recreate *our* life practices to follow Him. Then let's bring before Him our little ones to serve Him from their earliest beginnings.

The Creator at work

When conception takes place, a sperm cell penetrates an egg and creates a single set of forty-six chromosomes, forming the basis for a new human being. The fertilized egg spends a couple of days traveling through the fallopian tube toward the uterus, dividing into cells. Anywhere from six to twelve days after conception, this cluster of cells imbeds itself into the lining of the uterus.

The next six weeks are the most critical for the developing baby, because during this time all of the essential external and internal body parts are formed. Any disturbances that occur during this stage in the developmental process are likely to result in major malformations or malfunctions. During this time, the mother should avoid taking drugs or medications of any kind, unless it is absolutely necessary.

After only three weeks, the developing baby has a head and tail, swims in a fluid inside the shock-absorbing amniotic sac, and develops features that eventually will form the brain and spinal cord. In the fourth week, the beginnings of the heart, blood circulation system, and digestive tract have begun to grow. Arms and legs begin to bud out in the fifth week. The heart starts pumping blood even as it is undergoing construction from one chamber into four, complete with interconnecting valves, all of which will be in place at two months. The activation of the heart muscle demonstrates that the nervous system is beginning to function. Is there any doubt of our Creator God's power and wisdom?

While the mother may still be wondering if she is pregnant, the brain, eyes, liver, and ears are developing. Six weeks old and only three-fifths of an inch long, the embryo is floating securely in its silvery sac. At seven weeks the face, eyes, nose, lips, and tongue are visible, along with the earliest signs of teeth and bone. Electrical activity in the brain is now measurable. Every essential organ has begun to form, even though the baby still weighs less than an aspirin.

By the eighth week, fingers and hands are well defined, and toe joints are obvious. The baby is now sensitive to touch in all body parts, and muscle movement begins. He not only moves his head, arms, and trunk easily, but he also expresses his likes and dislikes with well-placed jerks and kicks. What he especially does *not* like is being poked. Push, poke, or pinch a mother's stomach and her two-and-a-half-month-old baby will quickly squirm away (as observed through various techniques).[2] He also moves his mouth, lips, and tongue in a swallowing motion.

By the tenth week, everything that is present in an adult human is now present in the tiny preborn—and the mother is still less than three months pregnant! The bones are beginning to form. The facial features continue to mature, and the eyelids are now more developed. The ears are continuing to form externally and internally. The baby is about one inch long and is the size of a bean. The placenta is formed, allowing oxygen and nutrients from the mother's blood to be diffused into the baby's blood, while carbon dioxide and other wastes pass from the baby's blood into the mother's blood. What the mother takes into her system is taken into the baby's delicate system as well.

An Inch of Wonder

Though but an inch of wonder, Mom,
My heart beats rapidly.
And pretty soon my ears will hear
When Daddy Sings to Me.

This tiny thumb has found my mouth,
I know this must be home,
And when you rock me gently, Mom
I don't feel all alone.

It's getting cramped, and when I kick
My daddy laughs with joy,
Is that his hand caressing me?
Is he praying for a boy?

I sense your overwhelming pride,
But know you are afraid,
Our God will guide your every move,
Oh Mommy, it's okay.

Nine months feels like eternity,
I'm eager to be held,
And when they place me on your chest
Your heart will surely melt.

I understand, I am your first!
You fear this great "unknown,"
To me you'll be the greatest Mom

---

2. Thomas Verny and John Kelly, *The Secret Life of the Unborn Child: How You Can Prepare Your Baby for a Happy, Healthy Life* (New York: Dell Publishing), 37.

This world has ever known.

So be assured what waits for you,
As I resume to grow,
Will be the most enormous love,
That you will ever know.

—Karen O'Connor[3]

The preborn grows rapidly now, expanding and perfecting its basic structures and developing more complex interconnections of blood vessels and nerves. Three months after conception, eyes and ears move into proper position and the skeleton is clearly defined. The hands are brought together, and the baby may begin to suck its thumb. The baby's respiratory tract is preparing for his first breaths, and he has developed all the neurons he will ever have. The genitalia have formed themselves into male or female, but they still cannot be seen clearly on an ultrasound. The eyelids close and will not reopen until the twenty-eighth week of pregnancy. The baby can make a fist, and buds for baby teeth appear.

In another month, the baby is five to six inches long. Fingerprints, which differentiate each human being, have now developed on his or her tiny fingers. Meconium is made in the intestinal tract and will build up to be the baby's first bowel movement. Mom may feel flutters in her growing abdomen as the baby begins to move around more. Sweat glands have developed, and the liver and pancreas produce their secretions. He has a fully formed mouth and begins to "breathe" amniotic fluid. This movement exercises his respiratory muscles in preparation for the work of breathing air when he is born. He can now frown, squint, and grimace.

The baby's already learning!

Before birth, the baby's unconscious mind is actively receiving messages from the outside world and has become the repository for life's experiences. These messages come primarily through the sense of hearing, and most have an emotional component. Before birth, the child "records" the sound of Mommy's and Daddy's voices, even the sounds of sibling's voices or those of other significant people in relationship with the mother are stored in the file cabinet of the unborn mind.

What the baby hears is very important. Certain types of music, such as Vivaldi or Mozart, help a baby relax. Rock music or more intense classical music

---

3. Karen O'Connor, "An Inch of Wonder," HomewithGod,
http://www.homewithgod.com/Cards/aninch.shtml. Used by permission.

tends to agitate babies. Even more distressing to the preborn's ears are the loud, angry voices of fighting parents.[4] Talk to the baby in soft, soothing tones. Although he cannot understand the words, he does understand the tone. The mother can help him feel loved and wanted through the emotional tone that is communicated.

One dedicated mother I know sang psalms to her unborn child. I heard her one morning as I was visiting in her home, and it aroused my curiosity. I asked her if she always sang out loud during her personal worship. She explained that she had not until she was pregnant. One day as she was asking God for His blessing upon her Paula, the idea came to her to sing the psalms out loud. God would bless Paula as these thoughts and feelings of trust were communicated to her. So she did. This same mother later felt God was nudging her to read her Bible out loud and to talk to Paula. And so she did.

Another mother I know would gently speak to her unborn boy, Austin, telling him all about God as she understood Him and assuring Austin that he was God's little boy. She prayed out loud that he would feel safe, loved, and welcomed in the womb and that as he grew, he would one day know and trust God for himself.

What do you sense that God is putting on your heart to do for your unborn baby? Test your ideas by the principles of God's Word and the character of Christ. "Whatsoever *he* saith unto you, do it."[5] As we learn to trust God and depend on Him for ideas, strength, and direction, our infant can be bathed in the trustworthiness of God.

During weeks seventeen through twenty, the baby has reached a point where movements are being felt more often by the mother. The eyebrows and eyelashes grow in, and tiny nails have begun to grow on the fingers and toes. He is absorbing his mother's emotions into himself. The emotions that the mother experiences, based on the circumstances of her life and the nature of her relationships, are recorded in the mind of the child.

The baby is beginning to have the look of a newborn infant as the skin becomes less transparent and fat begins to develop during weeks twenty-one through twenty-three. All the components of the eyes are developed. The liver and pancreas are working hard to develop completely.

Weeks twenty-four through twenty-six mark the beginning of the third trimester. If the baby were delivered now, he could survive with the assistance of medical technology. He has developed sleeping and waking cycles, and Mom will begin to notice when each of these takes place. He has a "startle" reflex, and the air sacs in the lungs have begun formation. The brain will be developing rapidly over the next few weeks. The nervous system has developed enough to control some functions. The baby is now about fourteen inches in length and weighs about two and one-fourth pounds.

---

4. Verny and Kelly, *The Secret Life,* 84.
5. John 2:5; emphasis added.

The preborn really fills out over the next six weeks. By the twenty-eighth week, all of the baby's senses are developed, as well as the parts of the brain dedicated to emotional responses and memory. The bones are fully developed but are still soft and pliable. The eyelids open after being closed since the end of the first trimester.

During weeks thirty-three through thirty-six, the fetus will descend into the head-down position, preparing for birth. The fetus is beginning to gain weight more rapidly. At thirty-eight weeks, the fetus is considered full term and will be ready to make its appearance at any time. The mother is supplying the fetus with antibodies that will help protect against disease. All the organs are developed, with the lungs maturing until the day of delivery.

A special time

God wants pregnancy to be one of the happiest times in a couple's life. Together, they have the sacred privilege of bringing a new life into the world and, for the sake of the little one, the mother's physical, emotional, and spiritual needs should be provided for carefully. The mother's health is the foundation for the baby's health and is affected directly by how the mother eats, drinks, dresses, and lives. More than that, the disposition of the mother—how she thinks, feels, and responds to life—is strongly affected for good or otherwise by the state of her health. And the disposition of the mother is a powerful tool for shaping the disposition of the unborn child.

All unhealthy practices produce detrimental effects upon the mother and her dependent child. They are designed by Satan to limit her ability to commune with God, who is her Source of power and strength. When her communion with God is broken, she will follow the dictates of the flesh in one way or another, and that never produces good results. Jesus is the best Friend of mothers and fathers. When parents come to Him and commit themselves to the sacred work of parenting, He will call forth all the power of heaven to aid them in overcoming harmful habits and practices.

The prenatal period is a good time to prepare the house for the new arrival. It's also an excellent time for parents to educate themselves on all the aspects of the work of parenting.[6] This is a task for both parents. Father and Mother are to be a team. Although Mother is the one carrying the baby, Father's influence, help, and disposition are essential for the child's well-being. Parents should share ideas with each other, get each other's input, and seek to understand how they can work together for the good of their child.

An expecting mother needs a wise balance of exercise, sunshine and fresh air, useful occupation (but not excessive labor), plenty of pure water, and rest. It's also important that she dress to protect herself from chilliness and eat a wholesome, nutritious diet.

There are many concepts of what makes a healthy diet—and this is not the

---

6. See the appendix at the end of this book for a list of resources you may find helpful.

place to take up that discussion. However, everything the mother eats affects the unborn child in its developmental stages and will have long-term effects. So a mother should eat wisely and strive to avoid extremes in diet. Some people are so conscientious that they eliminate beneficial items from their diet and still fear almost everything they eat will prove harmful. Others will eat just about anything that their appetite demands regardless of its harmful effects. Ask God to help you to know where the balance is for you in finding a wholesome, nutritious diet that will provide the essential building blocks for your baby.

If you discover that your habits or tastes are contrary to God's will, don't despair. Many of us wrestle with overeating, eating junk food or sugary snacks, eating between meals, and using unclean meats or meat with blood in it, which God forbids.[7] Jesus is our Savior from practices that need to be changed. With Him, we can face our shortcomings and find freedom from them by allowing God to guide and strengthen us. God can change our tastes, our feelings, and even our appetites if we put them under His control.[8]

Caffeine is an addictive substance found in many soft drinks, coffee, tea, and some over-the-counter medications. "Among its many actions, it operates using the same mechanisms that amphetamines, cocaine and heroin use to stimulate the brain. On a spectrum, caffeine's effects are milder than amphetamines, cocaine, or heroin, but it is manipulating the same channels, and that is one of the things that gives caffeine its addictive qualities."[9] It overexcites the nervous system, which is why many people use it. But as it wears off, the exhausted nervous system makes a person feel more tired than if they had never taken the caffeine. To overcome that feeling of depression, many take more caffeine. What caffeine does to a mother, it does to her baby. But the baby is not as well equipped for handling the stress to its system as the mother is. For your own sake, and for the sake of your child, eliminate this stimulant from your lifestyle. Satan is the author of such health-destroying addictions, but Jesus is your Savior and Restorer. Put your confidence in Him. He will help you.

Another danger to consider in relation to soft drinks and caffeinated beverages, as well as abundant candy and sugary sweets, junk foods, strong spices, and overeating, is that they tend to make the mother's system overly acidic. This increases the workload of the various organs of the body and makes the environment of the growing baby unfriendly and stressful.

It is a well-established fact that alcohol is dangerous to the unborn child. Alcohol passes easily through the placenta to the child, and depending on the amount of alcohol and the stage of the child's development, it can maim or even kill the unborn child. The more a woman drinks, the greater her child's chances of being born mentally retarded, hyperactive, with a heart murmur, or

---

7. Leviticus 11; Deuteronomy 12:16, 23.
8. Hebrews 2:8.
9. Marshall Brain, "How Caffeine Works," HowStuffWorks, http://health.howstuffworks.com/caffeine1.htm.

with a facial deformity.[10] Total abstinence is the best choice.

Street drugs are obvious offenders, but I've known a number of pregnant mothers who are so addicted that they are powerless to say "No" to this habit—even out of love for their unborn child. If that is you, know that God is there for you. You can experience God as a tender Father who doesn't give up on you because of your sins. He has all the power you need to be able to say "Yes" to Him and "No" to the bondage of drug addiction. In Him is life.[11] Save your child from this curse, and overcome with Jesus who is able to deliver you![12]

Cigarettes are another major hazard to the unborn. Smoking cuts the supply of oxygen available in maternal blood, and without an adequate flow of oxygen, the baby's growth will slow. Aside from the physical hazards of smoking, there are psychological ramifications as well. In a fascinating study done a number of years ago, Dr. Michael Lieberman showed that an unborn child grows emotionally agitated (as measured by the quickening of his heartbeat) each time his mother *thinks* of having a cigarette. She doesn't even have to put it to her lips or light a match; just her *idea* of having a cigarette is enough to upset her unborn child. Of course, the baby has no way of knowing his mother is smoking, but he knows enough to associate the experience of her smoking with the unpleasant sensation the drop in his oxygen supply produces in him. This thrusts him into a chronic state of uncertainty and fear. He never knows when that unpleasant sensation will reoccur or how painful it will be when it does, only that it will reoccur. And by this means, he is conditioned for a deep-seated anxiety that will affect his outlook on life far beyond the womb.[13]

The child's first window on life

The womb is the child's first world. How he experiences it—friendly or hostile—establishes his expectations of life. If he finds the emotional environment within his mother to be warm and loving, he will be predisposed toward trust, openness, extroversion, and self-confidence. If he experiences that environment as hostile, he will be predisposed toward suspicion, anxiety, distrust, and introversion.

Some children find their world in the womb openly hostile. Their mother doesn't want them. Their father doesn't want them. The parents would get an abortion if they could. The mother may even try various measures to induce a spontaneous abortion. The parents fight or the father is abusive or absent. The mother refuses to make any allowances for the new life within her. She eats and drinks and does whatever she wants regardless of the effects on her unborn child. Studies show that these mothers, as a group, have the most devastating medical problems during pregnancy and produce the highest rate of premature, low weight, and emotionally disturbed infants.

10. Verny and Kelly, *The Secret Life,* 92.
11. John 1:4, 11, 12.
12. Jeremiah 42:11.
13. Verny and Kelly, *The Secret Life,* 20, 21; emphasis added.

One doctor was concerned when his newborn patient repeatedly turned away from her own mother's breast. Little Kristina would eagerly guzzle from the bottle in the nursery but would have nothing to do with her mother. He decided to experiment and asked another mother to try breast-feeding Kristina. Kristina eagerly latched on and began sucking enthusiastically. The doctor approached Kristina's mother and shared with her what had happened. "Why do you think Kristina is reacting this way?" he inquired.

"I don't know," the mother replied.

"Was there an illness during your pregnancy?"

"No," she responded.

The doctor then asked, point-blank, "Well, did you want to get pregnant?" The mother looked at him and stated, "No, I didn't. I wanted an abortion. The only reason I didn't get one is because my husband wanted the child."

This had been no secret to Kristina. The womb had been to her a place of unwelcoming hostility. She refused to bond with her mother after birth, because her mother had refused to bond with her before it. The hostile environment of the womb set her up for distrust, suspicion, and withdrawal.

Some mothers have mixed feelings about their pregnancies. They are ambivalent. As a result, their children receive mixed messages, and an unusually large number of these babies are born with behavioral and gastrointestinal problems.[14] Outwardly, these mothers may seem quite happy about their pregnancies, but inwardly or subconsciously, they aren't sure. Perhaps the pregnancy is a surprise and interrupts school, a career, or some other cherished plan. Maybe there are severe financial difficulties or they just don't feel ready yet for motherhood. On some level, their babies pick up on this and it confuses them.

Little Lisa was conceived at a most inconvenient time for her parents. Both parents were in school, and her mother wanted to complete her education before beginning motherhood. Her family pressured her to quit school, but she determined to finish the one full school year that remained in order to graduate with her degree. Her husband supported her in her decision, and she threw herself into her studies. Once she had accepted the reality of the pregnancy, she deeply loved and wanted her child, but the hectic pace of her school program demanded much of her thought, time, and attention. The mixed messages were clearly understood by Lisa. "You want me, but I'm an inconvenience to you. You love me, but your studies are more important to you." Lisa was born in the midst of that school year, and her mother missed very few classes. She pushed herself past the point of exhaustion to reach her goal. At the same time, she was determined to give Lisa the benefit of breast-feeding. She would nurse Lisa while attempting to study, sleep, or drive the car to the babysitter. Lisa continued to hear the same mixed messages.

Years later, Lisa wondered why she felt like an intrusion. Why did she feel guilty for taking up space on the earth? The mixed messages accepted subconsciously in

---

14. Ibid., 48, 49.

her formative years had molded her view of the world and herself. She learned to believe a lie that her mother never intended for her to believe—that her existence was a mistake.

The good news for Kristina and Lisa and all the others who have experienced less than ideal beginnings (which, by the way, includes most of us) is that with God, it's never too late for a happy childhood. He invites us to be born again into His kingdom where we are wanted, welcomed, and loved unconditionally. He is never hostile and never ambivalent. " 'Can a woman forget her nursing child, And not have compassion on the son of her womb? Surely they may forget, Yet I will not forget you. See, I have inscribed you on the palms of My hands; Your walls are continually before Me.' "[15] "God demonstrates His own love toward us, in that while we were still sinners, Christ died for us."[16]

As a woman opens her thoughts and feelings to the reality of God's love for her, she is prepared to truly love her child. "We love Him because He first loved us."[17] She is prepared to be a welcoming mother. Her attitude sends a clear message to her child that he is loved and wanted, and she looks forward to having a family. Children of accepting mothers tend to be healthier, emotionally and physically, at birth and afterward, than the offspring of rejecting mothers.[18]

Parenting is happening now

You see, a mother's thoughts and feelings are her most powerful tools for molding the personality and character of her child. What the mother experiences emotionally, her unborn child also experiences. What she feels and thinks, so too, does the child. With God, a mother can learn how to keep her emotions, feelings, tastes, appetites, and even her habits at peace and in agreement with Him. Thus, the unborn child is at peace. By the same token, if mother is anxious, stressed, fearful, angry, guilt-laden, or in turmoil, her unborn child feels the same. His stress hormones respond just as do his mother's.

There is no more important calling than for mothers to come to know Jesus personally and to learn how to keep their emotions under the control of reason based on the Word of God. The higher powers of reason, intellect, and conscience are to rule over the lower powers of feelings, emotions, inclinations, habits, passions, and appetites. We can learn to follow Christ rather than negative feelings and emotions. When we do this, Christ can give us the power to say "No" to our wrong emotions, and as we do this, He subdues them.

Margaret recognized her own tendency to get easily agitated over conflict. Understanding the effect this would have on her unborn baby, she chose to place tense situations in God's hands and not enter into them whenever possible.

One day, she was talking with her husband, and a topic came up on which they disagreed. Margaret could feel her pulse quickening and the muscles in her

15. Isaiah 49:15, 16, NKJV.
16. Romans 5:8, NKJV.
17. 1 John 4:19, NKJV.
18. Verny and Kelly, *The Secret Life,* 18.

neck and shoulders tightening. Realizing that the situation was making her anxious, she excused herself and went for a walk to talk with God. As she yielded her emotions to God, He calmed them, and she was able to rest her conflict with her husband in God's hands.

That evening, as she sat in her rocking chair knitting a pair of baby booties, she noticed that her baby was kicking in an unusually agitated manner. "Lord," she prayed, "is my baby easily agitated like I am? If so, please calm the emotions of my little one."

The kicking continued. "Lord, is there anything I can do to help my child?"

The thought registered in her mind to sing to her child. Stepping over to the piano, she began to play and sing, "What a Friend We Have in Jesus." Soon the baby settled down. She repeated this frequently throughout her pregnancy, and it often helped to soothe her unborn baby.

After birth, the baby continued the pattern of becoming agitated as her mother did. Margaret sang as she had done while her child was in the womb. Wonder of wonders, her baby calmed right down! What the baby learned in the womb, she remembered after her birth. Wow! Prenatal influences can be wonderful and work for the right and good. We need God for wisdom to know the difference between normal movement in the womb and negative habit patterns that need intervention.

What difference does Dad make?

Research indicates that in determining the emotional and physical health of her baby, the quality of a woman's relationship to her husband is second only to her own attitude. One study of more than thirteen hundred children and their families revealed that "a woman locked in a *stormy marriage* runs a 237 percent greater risk of bearing a psychologically or physically damaged child than a woman in a secure, nurturing relationship." Even such widely recognized dangers as physical illness, smoking, and the performance of backbreaking labor during pregnancy pose less of a risk to the unborn child than does a nonsupportive or antagonistic father.[19]

Sadly, I've known men who use manipulation, anger, and undue control to manage their home lives. Some go to the extent of physically abusing or threatening the lives of their wives—during their pregnancy. The father's tirades abuse two. The unborn infant experiences the strong negative emotions as his own, without any filter of reason to sort out reality. He hears the father's hatred and rejection. The mother's stress hormones and the infant's stress hormones are felt alike and carry their damage to a lifelong degree. I've personally seen this happening in a number of families, and the spiritual mortality rate is very high.

---

19. Ibid., 49; emphasis added.

When a father so grossly misrepresents the child's heavenly Father, it is very hard for these children to trust God, whom they perceive to be like their earthly father. Satan is the being behind this type of behavior, and children pay a high price because they take in messages of rejection as if they are reality. They tend to be high-strung, fearful, and grow up emotionally unstable. These tendencies stay with them through life, unless they enter the process of allowing Christ to re-parent them.

Instead of becoming Satan's agent to harm the unborn child, a father can be God's means to build a strong, stable home. He is to be the priest, the protector, and the provider. As he learns the difference between the clamors of his fleshly nature and the call of God's Spirit to his heart, he can deny the one and follow the other. God will lead him to minister unselfishly to the needs of his wife and child in many ways. Here are a few ideas.

- Have a genuine walk with God—not out of form, ceremony, or pride.
- Restrain anger and irritation by finding a personal God to help.
- Simply be present physically and emotionally on a regular basis.
- Relieve his wife of heavy burdens and excessive work.
- Be sensitive to her needs and wishes and show that he cherishes her.
- Speak cheerful, affirming words to her and the baby.
- Rub her aching back even when he doesn't feel like it.
- Hold her in his strong, loving arms.
- Pray and worship with her.
- Talk with her about child-raising issues.
- Find solutions rather than leaving conflicts unresolved.

The husband's emotional support is a key element for a happy environment for mother and child. When a mother feels important and loved, her baby will too. When her husband denies himself for the sake of his wife and child, she loves him all the more, and those positive feelings build a healthy environment for the baby. What a truly spiritual husband can do is astounding. He builds strong bonds of trust and confidence that provide a strong foundation for his child's emotional security!

The unborn infant feels the warm greetings between a loving husband and wife. It makes his environment one of peace and safety and tends to a wholesome character and calm disposition. Yes, the father plays a very important role, a key role, in the home environment during this time of life.

The key to success

Parenting is a high calling for both the mother and the father. Who is sufficient for the task? None of us are, of ourselves. That's why the privilege of communion with God is so vital. God is able to supply all that we need to provide a healthy, spiritual environment in which our babe can safely grow. He is willing and able to help us make positive changes in our thoughts, feelings, emotions, inclinations, desires, appetites, and passions. As we learn to give God our negative emotions and cooperate with Him doing the right, we can find freedom to live above the pull of the flesh. In this way, we can keep receiving God's right thoughts and emotions and can share them with our child.

More than that, our communion with God allows the Holy Spirit access to our child. I think of Elizabeth and John the Baptist. The scriptures say that Elizabeth was righteous before the Lord.[20] In other words, she had a very close relationship with God, communing with Him and following His will. And her son shared in her spiritual experience. We are told, "when Elisabeth heard the salutation of Mary, the babe leaped in her womb; and Elisabeth was filled with the Holy Ghost."[21] The babe in her womb shared in the emotions and the spiritual experience of his mother. He responded to the Holy Spirit in the womb. Do you realize what this implies? Wouldn't you want your babe to learn to respond positively to the Holy Spirit before he is even born? What an advantage he would have!

We can give only what we possess. We can share with our unborn child only the spiritual experience that we ourselves enjoy. If you realize that you are not recognizing the Holy Spirit's work in your own life, don't despair. Whether you can sense Him near you or not, He is knocking at the door of your heart[22]—the core of who you are. He promises that when you let Him in and give Him access to all of your thoughts, feelings, and motivations, He will bring light out of your darkness and fill you with His joy. Won't you let Him in?[23]

THE LONE EMBRACE
A SPECIAL WORD OF ENCOURAGEMENT FOR SINGLE PARENTS

Are you a single parent and pregnant? There's no denying the fact that you are facing a difficult challenge. But God has made provision for you too. He wants to become your Husband.[24] He will be your Priest, your Provider, and your Protector. If you have made mistakes in your past, He doesn't despise you for them. Instead, He is opening His arms wide to you, and you can safely throw yourself into them, confessing all you have done wrong. He will forgive you and wash you clean and will see you as a lovely, pure bride.

As you continue to lean on Him, you will experience that He is trustworthy. God is not like your earthly father, who perhaps wasn't there for you. He's not like the husband who abused you or abandoned you. He is kind, tender, and

---

20. Luke 1:6.
21. Luke 1:41.
22. Revelation 3:20.
23. For further help in your Christian walk, I've listed some resources in the appendix.
24. Isaiah 54:5.

always present. His eyes are upon you with love, and His ears are open to your every cry. He will open to your mind the lies through which Satan has enslaved you and help you to replace them with true thoughts. And the truth shall set you free—free to be loved by God and to love Him in return and to shower your little one with the trust and security that you find in God.

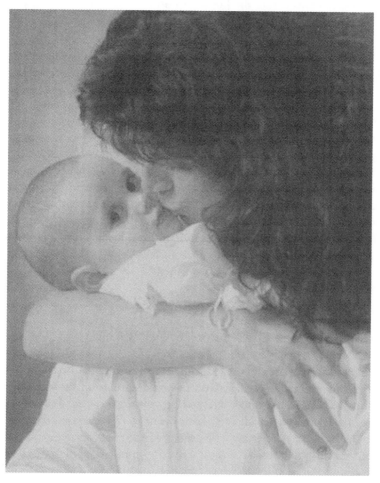

Fearfully and wonderfully made.

Chapter 2

The Parenting Pyramid

The LORD shall guide thee continually.
—Isaiah 58:11

Two-year-old Sam was doing something nearly all little boys enjoy—throwing stones into a lake. His mother sat beside him on a large boulder, tossing pebbles into the water and enjoying Sam's fun. After a time, Sam began to tire of the activity and looked around for something else to do. A nearby boat caught his eye, and walking over to it, he began trying to push it into the lake as he had seen other people do.

"Sam, that's not our boat. Leave it alone," Mother instructed. "Come here! Let's throw some more stones into the lake."

Self-led Sam paused for a moment, frowning. Then he grabbed the boat again.

"Sam, you need to come to Mother now." Sam reluctantly let go of the boat and ambled back toward his mother. Just then, something else caught his fancy. His father had laid out a wet map to dry in the sun and had anchored it with a few stones. All of a sudden, those particular rocks holding down the map took on an appeal that no other rock could hold. Sam just had to play with those rocks! He started over toward them.

"Sam, come here," Mother called patiently. Sam headed straight for the rocks. "Sam, don't pick up those rocks," she said more firmly.

Mother tried again, "Sam, you may not have those rocks; they are holding down the map to dry. Come here. You can throw these other rocks."

Ignoring his mother, Self-led Sam picked one of the forbidden rocks and threw it into the lake. He sent a sullen look in his mother's direction and picked up a second forbidden rock. His mother came running and intercepted his little hand in the act of throwing it.

Firmly, but kindly, she repeated her instruction. "No, Sam, you may not throw these rocks. Come with Mommy." He tried to pull away, so she picked him up and carried him back to the spot on the beach where there were lots of rocks he could throw. He squirmed and fussed, and as soon as she put him down, off he went to the rocks on the map.

Mother carried him back again and said more firmly, "You may not play with those rocks. You can throw these rocks." Sam, still self-led, whined and frowned, but stayed near Mommy this time.

"Okay, Sam, let's make things clear here. Do you see this split in the big rock?" Sam nodded. "You may not go past this crack in the rock. Stay on this side. If you cross it, you will have to take a time-out. Do you understand Mommy?"

"Yes," he replied.

About fifteen seconds elapsed before Self-led Sam was over the crack, heading for the prohibited rocks again. His desire was focused and directed. There was a shoreline full of rocks he could throw, but he wanted the only ones he couldn't have. Mother imposed a time-out, repeated her instructions, and Sam returned to the forbidden rocks the moment his time-out was over.

"Sam, you may not have those rocks. You'll have to take another time-out."

As soon as the second time-out was over, Self-led Sam headed back to the rocks on the map again! Mother continued to work with him. She was patient, yet firm; consistent, while reasonable; kind, but clear with her instructions. She followed through on time-outs and spankings without becoming harsh or angry. She didn't have a moment of rest to enjoy the sunshine and lake, but she did not give in to irritation toward Sam. Still, nothing would deter Sam from going after those forbidden rocks. Finally, Mother picked him up and carried him away—fussing, screaming, and kicking.

We have all been in a similar scenario with our children, haven't we? Conscientious parents try so hard to be kind, consistent, and to teach obedience to their toddlers. Why did all this hard effort fail to bring about willing obedience? Is there a solution that works?

Yes, there is! It has everything to do with discovering the difference between parenting *in self* and parenting *in Christ*. Parenting *in self* produces children who are "mother managed." Parenting *in Christ* allows a child to experience the joy and freedom of becoming "God governed" and "God empowered." Let's look at some of the differences.

In self

This conscientious mother was valiant in her warfare against sin and self. She did all the right things, said all the right words, and had such a good spirit. She was patient and kind—most of the time. She was straightforward, gave clear and simple instructions, allowed time for Sam to make his choice, yet consistently gave consequences for disobedience, and brought him back again and again to make a right decision. But she still didn't gain the obedience she desired. The "I want my way" disposition in her son was stronger than the "I want to please Mother" desire. Her approach failed to win her son's heart to obey her completely. It was as if he lacked the power to obey.

When we do not want to yield, we find ourselves warring against principalities and powers of darkness.[1] Satan rules the heart of the child, and he does not intend to let his captive go free. The authority of mother or father alone is not sufficient to wrestle children free from this influence.

The missing ingredient in this situation with Sam was God. God was present, wanting to help, but He doesn't force Himself on us. Mother forgot to call upon God. She didn't ask for His wisdom and guidance. She didn't ask God to

---

1. Ephesians 6:12.

soften and subdue Sam's heart during their conflict. She knew what was right and thought that was all there was to it! But there is more to parenting than *knowing* what is right—at times it's *warfare* against Satan and his host. In this battle, we need a vital connection to God's wisdom!

Sam needed more than instruction and consequences. He needed a new heart, and only God can create that. Without empowerment from God there is not enough human willpower to say "No" to self and Satan or "Yes" to God and right. Even though Sam tried several times to obey, his wrong feelings and unsubdued inward desires kept driving him to disobey. He listened to and obeyed self and Satan. God wasn't an option in his mind.

Mother was the one in charge of the situation—not God. She didn't recognize that she was calling the shots, making the decisions, and doing what was right in her own eyes and in her own power. Apart from God, there is no power over self's way and will. Every effort of self to subdue self will eventually fail because *self cannot reform self. It can only serve itself.*

Self-led Sam was also trying to be in charge. Although it was an undesirable experience and he didn't get his way, he still chose to obey his thoughts and feelings of "I want what I want when I want it!" Without giving up those wrong desires, there is no surrender of heart. Without a surrender of heart, there is no connection to Christ, no power to truly obey. Thus, Sam didn't yield to do his mother's will instead of his own—and the conflict raged.

There is nothing more futile and frustrating than trying to do right in the power of the flesh. Thanks be to God, there is another option!

In Christ

"There is therefore now no condemnation to those who are *in Christ* Jesus, who do not walk according to the flesh, but according to the Spirit."[2] We are living either "according to the flesh" or "according to the Spirit." There is no neutral option. If we neglect to live according to the Spirit we are—by default—living according to our flesh. In order to find the power that changes our thoughts, feelings, and responses, we need to be *in Christ*.

To be *in Christ* means I turn over to God the position of being in charge. He's the Pilot, and I'm His copilot. He's the Physician, and I'm His patient. He's the Principal, and I'm the teacher. He calls the shots, and I implement His instructions. I choose to be wholly His, to be pliable in His hands, to filter all I say and do through Him before I do it. He asks me to choose to think, say, and do what's right and true, and empowers my choices for the right.[3] I exercise my trust in Him by acting on His promises. " 'With God all things are possible.' "[4] "Now unto him that is able to keep you from falling."[5] "I can do all things

---

2. Romans 8:1, NKJV; emphasis added.
3. Matthew 9:29.
4. Matthew 19:26, NKJV.
5. Jude 24.

through Christ who strengthens me."[6] In Him I find true freedom from the tyranny of self. In Him, I find the power to subdue within me all that is evil, wrong, or yucky.[7] In Him, I find the power for *true* self-control. In Him, I find solutions I never could have thought of on my own.

God is always sending messages to those who listen for His voice. God says, "And thine ears shall hear a word behind thee, saying, This is the way, walk ye in it, when ye turn to the right hand, and when ye turn to the left."[8] He is interested in every detail of our lives. He will direct our steps when we ask Him to.[9] We must learn to recognize His voice to our mind and our Bible-educated conscience. God's voice is not an audible voice, but rather a still, small Voice.[10] The Holy Spirit is the vital Presence of God, leading our reason, intellect, and conscience in using Scriptures and common sense. Often God leads our reason by suggesting thoughts to our minds. When we call out to God, and we get this good idea and we try it and it works, we can know it was from God, for everything good comes from God. If it is fleshly, goes awry, and doesn't work, it's likely not from God.[11]

The solution, then, to parenting difficulties is to bring Christ into our parenting practices. He needs to be the One in charge—not us. He knows how to get the heart of our children. When we are connected with Him as the branch to the Vine,[12] His empowering love can flow through us to our children and work for a change of heart and disposition. He becomes our General in the battle against self and the power of sin. He knows just what it will take to get Self-led Sam to yield up his will and way to Mother and God. As we look to Him for wisdom, He will direct us, step by step, in the process of winning our children's hearts. When God has our children's hearts—their thoughts, feelings, and choices—the dispositions and behaviors of our children will be right.

When a conflict with my child begins, I may not see the whole process God is going to lead me through, but by faith I do know that He is big enough to transform my child's thoughts, feelings, and emotions to serve Him.[13] I do know that as soon as Self-led Sam chooses to serve God and asks God to empower his choices to obey, heart changes and obedience are possible. God waits for him to make that human effort to cooperate. When he cooperates, miracles happen! Inward desires are transformed! Satan is evicted! Self is subdued by Christ's presence, and grace creates in Sam a new heart! Sam becomes a God-governed child rather than a parent-managed child.

---

6. Philippians 4:13, NKJV.

7. Hebrews 2:8.

8. Isaiah 30:21.

9. Proverbs 3:5, 6.

10. 1 Kings 19:12.

11. For more about how to know God's voice, read chapter 4 of both my books, *Parenting by the Spirit* and *Parenting Your Child by the Spirit*.

12. John 15:1–5.

13. 2 Corinthians 10:5.

How does this happen? "Ask, and it shall be given you."[14] Sam needs to be *led in prayer* to ask God to do for him what he cannot do for himself. Prayer connects us with the only One who can change us from the inside out. It opens the channels of communication between God and us.

The parenting pyramid

I like to describe this as a pyramid. The *J* at the top of the pyramid represents *Jesus* or *God*. The *C* represents the child, and the *P* represents the parent. Christ is always seeking to communicate to both parent and child. This is good to know.

If we're *in Christ* and seeking His direction in the moment, He will impress us with an idea, a concept, a scripture, or a bit of common sense that will help us know what course to pursue. This is communion from God to the parent. We evaluate these thoughts to see if they fit God's Spirit, His character, and truth—and conclude, "This idea is likely from God," and so we implement it. There is no sonic boom, no flashing light, and no neon sign—nothing through our senses to distinguish that this idea is from God. We follow His inaudible voice by faith and reason, and gain experience. As we repeat this process, our confidence in Him builds. Christ becomes the Head, the One in charge—not the parent. If we stray with a wrong approach or spirit, God will make us aware of how to correct our course.

When God gives us an instruction, we are to go to our children and tell them what He wants them to do. This is the parents' pathway of communication on the bottom of the triangle. Our voice needs to be the same as God's voice and spirit. In this way, our child hears God's directives in an audible way. Our discipline and instruction may be identical to what Self-led Sam's mother did, but God is in the equation now. When Divinity works with human effort, the outcome will be very different.

As you follow what you sense God is asking you to do, God will communicate the same message to the child that He directed you to say. *"Sam, you don't want to throw these forbidden stones. You can choose to be content to throw all these other stones, and you will be happy. I'll help you! Trust Me."* This is God communicating to the child in the pyramid communication system.

Then, we direct our child to God. In a gentle spirit, tell him of God's power and how His ways are best. Remind him that Jesus promises that He will never leave us or forsake us and that He stands ready to help us.[15] God will help us see when the toddler's heart is soft and ready to make a decision for God and right. We step through this open door with Christ's leading, and call our child to the decision to obey God. God is calling to His heart at the same time.

Don't you want God working on your behalf this way? Sure you do! And He will work for you. Sometimes it will be obvious He is working in this way, and other times it won't be obvious. We can trust that God will influence our *Self*-led Sam to yield up his selfish nature and become *God*-led Sam.

When Sam surrenders to the influence of the pyramid communication system, then a very special thing happens. As he makes a choice to obey, his communication goes up that pyramid to God. It is his heart cry of "I want to obey." This freewill choice is expressed by his outward cooperation of coming to Mother. At this time, God comes into his heart and cleanses all the selfish desires that ruled over him formerly. His emotions may remain negative for a while, but trust and lean on God! In time, feelings always follow faith. You will see the self-led disposition melt from his countenance.

Truly, our children can experience that new heart described in Ezekiel 36:26, 27. The new heart is Christ's dwelling. When Christ comes into Sam's heart, He evicts Satan. He is a jealous God and will not share a divided heart. Satan cannot say "No" when Jesus says he must leave.[16] Jesus is bigger and stronger than Satan and all his imps.

As a result, Sam walks away from the forbidden rocks and willingly throws stones with Mother. This obedience is the outward evidence of an inward reality— a clean heart. Sam no longer longs for the forbidden rocks. When our little ones yield to the influence of the Holy Spirit upon their minds and hearts, they become empowered to obey God, mother, and right. The parent sees this transformation, and is amazed at its completeness.

Do you see how *in Christ* versus *in self* is very different? *In self* is a powerless religion that attempts to wrestle and subdue the flesh by human willpower alone. It fails to change the heart. It can be a relentless uphill climb against a set will. We may get outward compliance for a time, but no inward change occurs. *In Christ,* the child is not left alone in self's willpower but is empowered by Divinity to obey. God directs each step and supplies the power of grace to take that step. Being *under God* is the greatest place for parent or child to be.

Don't try to fight the devil without Christ as your Head in this pyramid of communication. God will teach you how to develop these patterns of seeking Him to be your General, of taking His hand, and of walking through parenting issues with Him. You will find the keys for success that work with the strongest-willed child humanity can produce—for God is stronger. We need Him first and last and all along the way!

15. Hebrews 13:5, 6.
16. James 4:7.

Possessing the land of character

The book of Deuteronomy illustrates this concept. Moses was like a parent to the children of Israel. What God communicated to him, he communicated to the people. God worked on the hearts of the people, and when they yielded to obey God, they enjoyed true happiness. God wants the parents of today to be like Moses—listening to Him and then implementing with their little ones the directions He gives them.

God is a communicating God. He directed all the travels and activities of His people. He set the Promised Land of Canaan before them saying, "*Go up and possess the land.* Don't be afraid of the giants. I will deliver them into your hand. Slay them and possess the land in their stead."[17] But the children of Israel did not believe God. They were not willing to face their fear of the giants. Therefore, God gave them a consequence. They would have to wander in the wilderness for forty years until all of the generation that refused to go in had died. The children of Israel didn't like that direction either, so they decided to attack the giants on their own. They were self-led. They presumptuously went to war without God and were slain in battle. Do you see the parallels to our parenting today? Do we call our child to obedience without God directing the battle? Is it any wonder we experience failure so often?[18] Character building is the battle for who will be in charge—God or self? We need Christ as our General.

God wants us and our children to possess the land that flows with milk and honey—the sweetness and satisfaction of *truly* walking with Him. In order to gain this experience, we must face the giants that dwell in the land of our characters. The giant, Self, and his relatives named Selfishness, Stubbornness, Disobedience, Sassiness, and Uncooperativeness, among others, seem like a giant nation, and we, like Israel, hesitate or fear to challenge them. Truly, they are stronger than we are by ourselves.

But God will teach us how to wield the sword of the Spirit, and in His power, strength, and wisdom we can *slay every giant* in this land. We are to evict, starve, and utterly destroy all the wrong ways in the land of our character. We are to have no pity on destructive habits and responses. We are not to fear them but to dispossess these nations stronger than ourselves *in Christ*. God will lead us in battle, and He will deliver the enemy into our hands as we wield our sword.

God requires us to diligently teach our infants, toddlers, children, and youth of this God. We are to inspire the exercise of their faith to reach out to God, to connect to Him, to be empowered, and then see to it that they do the right. We must teach implicit obedience of the human will to the Divine will. We are to be God's instruments to teach them how to choose and keep the Ten Commandments *in Christ* their Savior and constant Companion.

---

17. Deuteronomy 1:21–23, author paraphrase of KJV.
18. Ephesians 6:12.

Throwing himself back

Eighteen-month-old Willful Willy was about to grab a figurine from the end table when I picked him up and said, "You may not touch the figurine!" Instantly, his little body stiffened, and he threw himself back so hard I almost dropped him on the floor. I felt his anger and displeasure. I was just learning to cry out to God for help, and I did just that. "Lord, what would You have me to do?"[19]

"Sally, this is just a temper tantrum," God assured me. *"It's just the giant Self showing he is master and ruler. Don't let this happen even once, for if you do, Willy, led of Satan, will gain his desired object next time by crying and throwing himself more vehemently until you surrender to his will. Don't fear! I'm here with you."* The Lord directed my thoughts in a way that seemed like my thoughts. God's inaudible voice is difficult to discern until we look at a situation in hindsight and the outcome is known. Looking back, I know that these were God's thoughts and not just mine, but I wasn't sure at this stage of the scenario.

"Okay, Lord," I said timidly. "Let me think. First, You taught me that I must put the child's will, heart, and mind into Your hands. He's Yours, Lord. Then I must call forth his will to surrender to You, and You will perform the miracle of changing his disposition through Your grace."

"Willy, you may not behave this way! This way only hurts you. *I love you too much to let you disobey.* You are all right." I restrained him close to me. "We are going to Jesus to save you from being so upset. Jesus will put happiness into your heart when you choose to obey. Now let's pray."

Willy pulled away from me, unwilling to pray. "Lord, what should I do now?"

"Take him for a grizzly run to get the 'grizzlies' out of him. I'll attend your efforts," Jesus assured me.

"A grizzly run!" I exclaimed. "Then, I'll have to run with him because he is too young to go alone. I don't want to do that!"

Tenderly, God encouraged, *"Sally, you must surrender your heart, your wrong thoughts and negative feelings, and I'll deliver you first! Trust Me. This is the best and fastest way for a* true surrender *of this child's heart and will."*

I struggled for a few moments with "I don't want to" thoughts. Then I chose to yield to God's will and way and gave my feelings to God to change in His time.

"Willy, you need to run with me because you didn't obey me." We ran around the house one time, and Willy began to cry and sat down. I asked him again to pray with me, but he refused. So we ran around the tree twice. By this time, God had subdued my "I don't want to" thoughts and feelings. Again I told Willy to give his ill feelings to God and God would take them away. He looked liked he would cooperate. But when we knelt, he wouldn't fold his hands or pray. His countenance still displayed stubbornness and uncooperativeness.

"Lord, what do I do now?" I asked forlornly.

---

19. Acts 9:6.

"Don't lose courage, Sally. This is an important work. Trust Me—not what you see or feel. Give Me your hopeless feelings. I'll subdue them. Do you think his will and disposition will yield with a spanking or another grizzly run?" God was leading, but it seemed like He wanted to make me think and choose rather than tell me what to do.

"Okay, Lord. Again I give You my wrong feelings. You take them from me." I looked at Willful Willy to label his disposition. He was staring down at the grass, with his face scrunched up in a pout.

"Lord, he's either in despair or passion. Perhaps a spanking is all he needs right now. Lord, attend my ways. My only motivation is to win his heart to You—not to punish him. I'm willing to do whatever it takes, Lord."

This education was given without harshness or anger. I hugged and assured the little fellow that he must choose to do right and he would be happy. He stopped crying. "Give your yucky feelings to God, and He'll take them away," I encouraged. This time, he knelt willingly and repeated a simple prayer after me. Then I tipped his head gently up to me and smiled sweetly at him. He smiled the sweetest smile back. You could see his freedom from the inside out. Jesus had come in, and therefore Satan had to leave. What a joy to see Jesus enthroned in our little one's heart! In Christ, our children can obey. Feelings are changed!

Carrying Willy back to the figurine on the table, I placed him right where he could grab it and said, "Do not touch, Willy."

"No touch," repeated Willy, and he looked up to me with a smile.

"Good boy," I assured him. "Let's play with these toys on the blanket." And we had a good time doing so.

The next time I had to deny him an object he wanted, he looked to me first. I said, "Do not touch, Willy." He began to throw a tantrum, but then he stopped. He looked at me and repeated, "No touch," as he shook his head back and forth. Then he smiled and turned his attention to his toys. He yielded to the fact that I was the one in charge—not him. He was learning that it is pleasant to obey. Was God communicating to Willy from the head of the pyramid? Sure, He was! And good habits are being built by this repetition. Jesus is the key to successful character building from the earliest beginnings. It is only with Him that the giants are slain.

I want Mommy!

Wyatt was led by self—just like Self-led Sam was—but his issue was demanding Mommy to do whatever he wanted her to do. Like many other two-year-olds, he was very clingy to mother. Oh, he would interact with others when he was in the mood, but when he wanted Mommy, no one else would do. When someone else tried to help him, he would scream or even hit them—much to his mother's embarrassment. His mother was conscientious, but all her best efforts to change Wyatt's behavior had not worked, and she was frustrated, as you can well imagine.

One day on a camping trip, Mother and Wyatt were having a lovely time in nature. Wyatt loved it. He had Mother's full attention and time, and he was a very happy boy. After several hours, Mother gave Wyatt some fun things to play with, and she lay down to rest in the hammock. Wyatt didn't like that. He wanted Mommy to play with him. He began to whine and fuss. When that failed to get the desired results, he screamed and curled his fists in anger.

"You may not do that, Son!" Mother corrected. She leaned over in the hammock. "Here. Why don't you bury these pinecones?"

But no, Whining Wyatt didn't want to do that. "Mommy do," he told her.

Twenty minutes went by, and the situation only escalated. Mother made valiant and patient attempts to divert him, to instruct him in right and wrong ways, to nurture him to choose the right, and to discipline him. As she imposed a disciplinary time-out, he still held on to his angry spirit. He would not yield his will to her will. He was determined that she was going to obey him.

Whining Wyatt threw himself on the food packs and begged to eat, although it was not mealtime. Mommy said No, and then he screamed angrily again. He was trying everything and anything to get her to obey him. Satan was his master, but Mother didn't yet see that she was warring against Satan—not her son.

Frustrated and irritated, Mother finally went into the tent and zipped herself in. "Wyatt, you may not have Mommy until you can be happy and speak kindly."

Five minutes went by with Wyatt crying louder and getting angrier. He threw himself on the tent, tried to unzip it, and said naughty things. His mother continued to tell him he must stop his bad behavior—but to no avail. Periodically, she would come out to make him sit down, hoping he'd calm down. Nothing worked.

Tanya was a friend who was camping with them. As she came back from a walk, she saw what was going on. She was familiar with the parenting pyramid and sensed God was placing on her mind and heart the vital missing ingredient of her friend's discipline practices. She held back her thoughts for fear of offending, but felt that God was prompting her to at least offer her help. She finally gathered up her courage and went over to the tent.

"Um, would you like any input with what you're dealing with? I have nothing to urge," she began.

"Sure, go ahead." Wyatt's poor mother was at a loss for what else to do.

Tanya then explained the triangle of communication and the difference of giving the right disciplines *in self* and *in Christ*. She shared the need for prayer to connect the child to God so he could have power over his desire to be in control of his mother, that he could yield his heart and mind to God, and that God could redeem him from these wrong thoughts and feelings by offering better ways to think and respond. Even Wyatt listened.

Wyatt's mother was quiet for a moment as she contemplated these ideas. Satan kept reminding her of her attempts to pray with Wyatt during previous battles and how she'd end up with two conflicts instead of one—one to get him to pray and another to correct the initial disobedience. In spite of this, she concluded to try prayer. Both she and Tanya expected that it would take a protracted process to calm this wound-up child enough to lead him in a prayer of surrender. But they were in for a surprise.

Mother zipped opened the tent and instructed firmly, "Son, you need to calm down." Wyatt flung himself into mother's lap. "No, you need to sit here where Mother put you." And she sat him down outside the tent. Wyatt put his head down and pouted. Mother continued, "You need to talk to Jesus to help you. Wyatt, look at Mommy." He raised his eyes, and his disposition melted somewhat as he looked at his mother's soft eyes. Then she said tenderly, "Son, we need to pray to Jesus to help us." Wyatt folded his hands and repeated Mommy's prayer: "Jesus, help Wyatt to obey Mommy. Help him to let Jesus into his heart to take away those hurtful feelings and to obey Mommy. Amen."

Two-year-old Wyatt sat there a moment still with his hands folded. Then he said, "I want Mommy."

"No, you may not have Mommy right now. You sit there while Mommy tidies the tent, and then you can have Mommy. Mommy decides when." She completed organizing the tent while Wyatt sat there patiently for five minutes. Then Mother came out.

Wyatt asked, "Mommy came back?"

"That's a good boy to wait for Mommy so patiently. That was much better."

God will work with you, too, in the management of your children. The main question to ask in such conflicts is, Who is in charge? Is it Christ or Satan, parent or child, self-control or anger, surrender or stubbornness? Bring your child to Christ, who will subdue the child's evil passions and tempers and make them mild and gentle by His Holy Spirit. *In Christ* brings success in discipline. Why would we ever discipline without Christ?

Not all attempts at prayer work the first time. Often it takes multiple prayers as you teach the process of what is expected before the child surrenders. At whatever moment the child surrenders, Christ comes in and does the work that only He can do—transforms the disposition to serve God and right instead of the giant Self.

This parenting pyramid is the essence of parenting by the Spirit and provides the foundation for every other topic we will address in this book and in the entire series. Let's see how it provides the framework for building character, instilling trust, and training obedience.

THE LONE EMBRACE
A SPECIAL WORD OF ENCOURAGEMENT FOR SINGLE PARENTS

The parenting pyramid is especially helpful to the single parent. You are not alone! God promises, " 'I will never leave you nor forsake you.' "[20] Believe Him. Put away the doubts that Satan presses on your mind. Reach out to God in spite of your feelings and emotions. Trust His Word to you, for He cannot lie. As you experience His working in your behalf, your faith will grow.

As you learn to commune with God, your baby or toddler will benefit in many ways. First of all, he will feel love from you rather than anger. The atmosphere about you will be filled with peace instead of anxiety. Your confidence in God will give him a feeling of security and contentment. As you experience surrendering to God and finding freedom from your negative thoughts and feelings, you will be able to lead your little one to the same joy of knowing God as Redeemer and Re-creator.

Angela and Nathan.
God wants us to teach our little ones
of God's voice to their hearts.

---

20. Hebrews 13:5, NKJV.

Nathan Hohnberger.
Our infant's and toddler's minds
and hearts are like sponges.

The Parenting Pyramid in Action

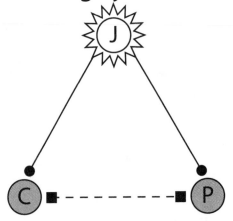

Both parent and child are listening to and obeying their flesh.
Neither are crying out to God.
Communication between them is confusing and frustrating.
God is trying to get their attention, but they are not responding.
True obedience is not possible.
There will be no lasting change for the better.

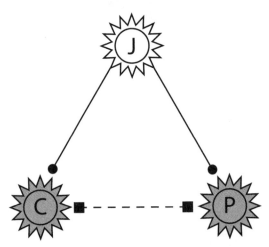

Parent attempts to do right in the power of the flesh.
Neither parent nor child are crying out to God.
Communication between them remains confusing and frustrating.
God is trying to get their attention but they are not responding.
The best the parent can hope for is outward compliance.

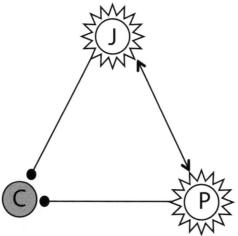

The parent cries out to God and listens to Him.
Two-way communication is established between parent and God.
The heart of the parent is cleansed and made sweet.
The parent begins to send the same clear message to the child
that God is sending the child.

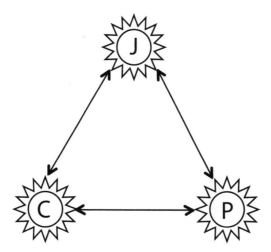

God and parent continue to communicate clearly with the child.
The child listens to the parent and to God.
The child cooperates on the outside while God cleanses him or
her on the inside.
Communication is free and open in all directions.
Genuine obedience is the result.

Chapter 3

Me—A Parent?

Lo, children are an heritage of the Lord: and the fruit of the womb is his reward.
—Psalm 127:3

Nine-month-old Disgruntled Danny wanted down. His mother was carrying him into the store, and he threw himself back so hard that she nearly dropped him.

"Danny!" she exclaimed. "Don't do that! I almost dropped you!"

Danny let out a bloodcurdling cry and twisted his little body in contortions. His mother, struggling to hang on to him, glanced around wondering who was watching. This was embarrassing. Danny's outbursts were so unpredictable and uncontrollable. The only thing that seemed to calm him down was giving him whatever it was that he wanted—food, a toy, to get down, to be picked up. He was insistent. It was bad enough to endure his fits at home, but in public it was almost more than she could bear. She was starting to dread coming to the store.

Motherhood was turning out to be quite different than she had expected! She had breezed through her nine months of pregnancy, anticipating the joy her baby would bring her. She had looked forward to cuddling him, breast-feeding him, bathing and dressing him, and playing with him. In return, she had anticipated his smiles, his cooing, and his trusting little eyes gazing up into her own. Danny was everything she had hoped for—at first.

But the older he got, the more difficult he became. She hated to admit it, but her little blessing was growing into what *felt like* a curse, or at least a major disappointment! Her frustration was growing too. What could she do about it? Did it have to be this way?

On-the-job training

When our firstborn son, Matthew, was placed in our arms, what joy filled our hearts. The discomfort of pregnancy and the pains of childbirth were all worth it. We counted his fingers and toes and gazed into his tiny face. To see the incarnation of our love conjured up a gamut of feelings: happiness, relief, affection, responsibility, concern, and a longing desire for his future.

Thus began our on-the-job training of *what parenting is*—and *what it isn't*! We learned much through life's experiences, study, and experimentation—and so will you.

I thought I knew what parenting was all about. After all, hadn't I been the resident neighborhood babysitter throughout my teen years? Even after I started nurse's training, the children would come knock at my door, begging me to come out and play. Those children loved and respected me, and I them. And so I thought I was prepared for motherhood. I originally operated on the idea that parenting is basically a long-term babysitting project. But God challenged that idea as I read the Scriptures and other biblical books.

Proverbs said to "train up a child in the way he should go."[1] That's an entirely different process than just allowing a child to come up in whatever way self or circumstances dictate. Galatians 5 presents a very marked contrast between fleshly habits and Spirit-led instilled habits—the latter leads to a fulfilling life while the former produces misery. Our thoughts, feelings, and conduct reveal whether God or self is leading. The book of Deuteronomy gave me a very practical view of what it means to walk in the statutes and judgments of God in our day-to-day life. I began to see that a noble character does not come by accident. Rather, it is developed through determined, continual choices to yield one's wrong thoughts, feelings, and emotions to God.

As I read, the Holy Spirit first challenged my misconception that parenting was just physically managing my infant and toddler's life. Next, He showed me that spiritual training consisted of teaching and training the mind (thoughts), heart (emotions), and will to follow God rather than selfishness. I had never seen this before. My work as a parent seemed practical now. I was to deal with my child's thoughts, feelings, and responses. Gradually, I began to see that there is a *big* difference between playing with children and managing and providing physical care for them, and molding their characters to produce well-balanced men and women who love and follow God with all their hearts.

That meant that when my boys were uncooperative, angry, sassy, or unyielding to do the right, they were serving sin and self. I was supposed to pull the weeds of sin and self by instruction, restraint, and consequences. I was also to cultivate the goodly plants of right doing. Through a vital connection with God, they could be kind, learn to share their toys, say "Please" and "Thank you," and obey Mother and Father consistently. My view of parenting was not just corrected. It was enlarged!

Prayer as a form

God also *challenged my misconception* of a false form of prayer. I began teaching my boys to pray when they were very young. I read about a "naughty heart—clean heart" prayer, and I taught them to repeat this prayer after me. They prayed very earnestly that God would take their naughty heart and give them His clean heart. But it didn't seem to change them in heart or disposition. In time, I began to realize that I was actually trusting in the form and the words—not in God. I didn't see or understand the roles of surrender, faith, or cooperation as yet. Let me explain.

When my youngest son, Andrew, was four years old, my mother and I planned our weekly shopping trips together. Part of our routine included my

---

1. Proverbs 22:6.

mother buying gum for my boys as we went through the checkout line, and Matthew and Andrew always looked forward to this little treat. One fateful week, Jim and I decided that chewing gum was not a habit we wanted to cultivate in our boys, and we explained that to them. But I forgot to tell my mother.

On our next shopping trip, Matthew stayed with me in the store while Andrew rode in Grandma's cart. We went different directions, and my mother got to the checkout line before me. When I came along, I saw Andrew with a big smile holding up a piece of bubblegum for Matthew. He had forgotten our family decision and had had such fun poring over the selection of gum at the counter. He had picked out one for himself and one for Matthew and was waiting to start chewing his until Matthew arrived.

Andrew was demonstrating such sweet qualities, and now I had to break the news to my mother and my boys—no gum! "Oh Mother, I'm so sorry I forgot to tell you ahead of time. We have decided to allow no more bubblegum. Andrew will have to put the bubblegum back. We told Jesus we wouldn't chew it anymore, and we must keep our word, so Andrew, put the gum back."

My mother didn't understand our decision. She felt it was unnecessarily severe and told me so. She tried to convince me to relent, but I stood my ground feeling a bit timid, yet determined to follow through on our decision. My mother was distraught, and the boys hung their heads sadly. Andrew put the gum back as a few tears slid silently down his chubby cheeks.

As we drove to the next store, Andrew slipped out of his car seat, dropped to his knees, and sobbed earnestly, "Dear Jesus, I want bubblegum, but Mother says, 'No bubblegum.' Please help me not want bubblegum. Take my naughty heart. Give me Your clean heart. I want bubblegum. Help me not want bubblegum!" My mother began to cry. I began to cry. It was so heartwrenching to listen to his earnest wrestling, which brought him no resolution.

"Andrew, you need to stop crying and get back into your car seat," I instructed. He obeyed but continued to cry on and off for over an hour. The pain of his disappointment didn't go away. His feelings and emotions did not change. He still longed for that gum and had to battle Satan taunting him in his mind and heart.

I look back now and easily see my misconception about prayer, but at the time, I didn't. Andrew endured his loss in his human strength alone, because I didn't understand how to teach him differently. I taught him that *he* must obey in self's willpower! We trusted in the prayer itself to change our hearts rather than in the God we prayed to. It may seem like a fine distinction, but it makes a world of difference. In self, it cannot work! In God, all things are possible. God had to let us have this hard experience to motivate us to see our wrong ways and to seek for a better understanding.

Parents, we can teach only what we ourselves know. I could not lead Andrew into a better Christian experience than I myself was having. We both struggled often to hold down self and do the right, unaided by God. It was a very frustrating experience. Many people who struggle like I did give up on

God and religion rather than recognize their misconception. It took time for me to learn the reality that we cannot change our heart's emotions anymore than the leopard can change his spots. When we pray trusting in our prayers, our repetition of words, or our good deeds to change us, we are trusting in self and not in God. This is a powerless religion—a form of humanism. It is trying to do all that God says apart from Him. In self, Andrew said No to his desire for gum, but self cannot dethrone self. Self is not strong enough to make Satan leave.

In contrast with praying *in self*, praying *in Christ* yields an empowered life. In Him is hope of true change. As we reach out to God in prayer, we make a vital connection with Christ—much as a branch is grafted into a vine. Then the redeeming power of Christ can flow into us to give life to our right choices and acts of obedience. As we choose to connect and commune with Him, He prompts us to think truth-filled thoughts in place of our lying thoughts. As we cooperate with Him, He changes our emotions and desires.

Andrew was caught up in the thoughts of *I want gum. I need gum. I can't be happy without gum.* Those self-led thoughts produced misery in Andrew's emotions. God wanted Andrew to cooperate with Him in thinking God-led thoughts, such as *I don't need that gum. I can be happy in Jesus!* Had Andrew reached out to connect with God's re-creative power to change his heart's feelings, and then cooperated to think God-led thoughts, God would have worked inside of Andrew to remove the desire for gum and replace it with contentment. Right responses would have been the natural by-product of this connection. Andrew would have been freed from the wrong and empowered to obey the right from the inside out. We need to connect to a power outside of ourselves. This is being a Christian *in Christ*—not in self and not in humanism.

Soft and sweet turns sour

God challenged *other misconceptions*. For example, I tended to be too soft in my discipline. I allowed my child to lead and decide what he would and would not do. If he fussed about my wishes, I let him have his way until he pushed me too far and I swung to harshness and anger. I nurtured selfishness instead of training him to surrender properly to God and right,which is a vital step in the Christian life. I missed many opportunities to train my infant to follow God instead of self. I didn't know how important this was—much less how to accomplish it! God had to take me through hard times and allow me to feel and see the consequences of fostering self-will, much like Danny's poor mother did.

My two-year-old Matthew was an energetic, strong-willed child. He often acted as though he was the parent and I was the child and I was supposed to obey his will rather than he obey my will. This was the result of my being too soft. God wanted to balance my softness with a little firmness, but I wasn't yet open to that. At this point in my experience, I saw God's correction as negative and harsh.

My newborn, Andrew, was colicky and cried perpetually for his first month. The combination of managing an energetic two-year-old and caring night and day for an unhappy newborn took its toll on me. One particular day, I was exhausted. For survival, I planned to take a nap that afternoon during Andrew's and Matthew's nap time. I set my tiredness on hold and endured my day. Nap time and relief were in sight. I put Andrew down, and he went through his crying routine while I attempted to put Matthew down for a nap. But in this instance, it seemed that Satan inspired Matthew with the idea that he was not going to take a nap. He became extremely uncooperative. He was following self-led thoughts. In my tired state, he seemed so strong. I reasoned with him for fifteen minutes without success. I tried to outwit him, but it did no good. I read to him without effect.

One hour later, I could not restrain my tiredness, anger, and frustration any longer. In harshness and anger, I tried to force Matthew to surrender to me, and World War III broke out. I spanked him several times to no avail. I shut the bedroom door. He would open it and appear before me downstairs, telling me, "No, Mommy." I locked him in his bedroom, and he kicked against the door until I thought I would go crazy. I didn't know a God who could change me at the level of my feelings, so all this was done in self's willpower, unaided by God. Oh, I prayed and called out, but I did not understand the process of surrender or cooperation with God's leadings in this process.

After three hours of this, I said to Matthew, "Okay, I will not make you nap. I will never make you nap again. You win. You are in control here." And I collapsed on the couch, letting Matthew stay up to play, but no sleep came.

Being too soft, performing parenting *in self*, does not work a heart change either in my toddler or myself. I had much to learn. When Matthew turned six and we moved to the mountains of Montana, we finally sought new concepts from God, and *in Him* we dealt with this issue of going to bed when we told him to go to bed. It took six months, under God, in Christ, and with firm disciplines by both Father and Mother before this bad habit was corrected. How much easier it would have been had I learned to bring my two-year-old toddler to Christ for a divine heart change.

Where's the balance?

Many parents fall for the other extreme and mistakenly think they can raise godly children by using force, domination, control, and punishment. The best they can hope to gain by this approach is outward compliance while the heart of the child is left either smoldering in rebellion or lost in confusion and despair. Being either too soft or too firm will allow Satan's thoughts, feelings, and responses to rule in them because *in self* is without God. To find the genuine balance, we must have a teachable spirit and spend time with God to allow Him to challenge and correct our misconceptions.

When we allow our infants to develop selfish habits by not instilling better habits under God's direction, we reap the consequences. Infants generally follow their feelings, and their feelings usually lead them to selfish, unkind responses. By repetition, selfish habits of "I want" and "I will get" become stronger. And parents get increasingly frustrated with managing a selfish babe.

My son was selfish instead of submissive. He was irritable instead of content. He was driven by habits of getting his will instead of yielding to Mother and God's will. But this need not be if we understand the big picture of having power in Christ.

Both God and Satan are working to set up their kingdoms in the mind and heart of the infant, and we are cooperating with either one or the other. Child care encompasses far more than mere physical care. It includes guiding our children to serve one master or the other. There is no middle ground. If we neglect connecting our child with God, Satan takes over. This is the cause for the selfishness we deal with.

For me, the consequences of daily facing the growing selfish nature in my child made me open to changing my concepts—and this was very healthy. I began looking and praying for a new direction. God loves to help us in the management of our babes in arms—to *redirect* their feelings and responses. He awaits our coming to Him in study and prayer to find new ideas and concepts, and to plan with Him how to handle the situation better next time. He watches for our willingness to let Him challenge our misconceptions and to replace them with His better ways.

Re-evaluate and test my concepts

As I recognized that my ideas of motherhood were not producing a happy, contented infant or toddler, I became willing to *re-evaluate my concepts.* I realized I didn't need to fear this process, for truth can stand investigation and testing. If a concept was not true, I wanted to abandon it. I wanted to operate on tried-and-true concepts. So I set aside my preconceived opinions about parenting and turned to God's Word as my sure source of solid principles. I asked the Holy Spirit to be my Teacher both through the lessons of Scripture and in the lessons of day-to-day life.

God began to open His principles to my mind while I was physically *weeding* my garden. Wherever I pulled weeds, my garden was pleasant and productive. Where I neglected to pull weeds, it was unattractive and less productive. I saw the connection. *Selfishness* was an unsightly *weed* that was growing in the garden of my infant's character. Allowing it to grow unhindered would only make his character more and more unpleasant.

"But, Lord," I argued, "Andrew is just an infant. He's too young to train. I've got to wait until he is old enough to reason with."

"Are you sure, Sally?" God reasoned with my mind. *"Selfishness is like a dandelion root. The longer you leave it alone, the deeper and stronger its root grows."*

"But how do I pull this weed from the character of an infant who can't talk to me, Lord?" God seemed silent of a tangible answer right then.

During my study time, I came across Romans 12:21—"Be not overcome of evil, but overcome evil with good." Somehow, I sensed this was an important key to answer my question. I sat back in my chair and asked the Holy Spirit to help me understand what I was reading. A new concept began to grow. "Well, I need to restrain the evil, the selfish responses, and replace them with better ways of responding, by connecting my child to God and by showing him better ways until he yields to do them." It was simple, yet profound.

As I learned to cry out to God for help, I began to see that I could pull unsightly weeds from my son's character by simply and kindly denying his selfish behavior both as an infant and a toddler. I started saying, "No, you need not be afraid." "You need not be selfish." "You can wait patiently." I could restrain the waving arms, interrupt the selfish outburst, or redirect the attention from "I want" to something appropriate.

The Bible says when we clean wrong from the house of the mind, we must not leave it empty.[2] We must replace the wrong with something better—the right, the truth! Cooperating with God to suggest right thoughts to your infant is like filling your garden with desirable seedlings. When the soil of the heart is preoccupied with good plants, there is less room for weeds. Prayerfully I asked God for direction. Then I told my infant what to do instead of the wrong he was doing. For example, "Mommy is here. God is here. You need not fear." "It's Okay. You can be happy!" "You don't need to eat just yet—you are all right."

It worked well! When I began to cooperate with God, correcting my misconceptions, habits, and approaches, I changed. As Matthew and Andrew yielded to the influence of the Holy Spirit working through me, their feelings and dispositions were changed, too, by Christ dwelling in them.

Beyond telling them what was right—teaching the mind—I learned that I needed to follow through and see that they did what was right—which is training the will. We can train our infants to be content by working with them consistently to see that they do it. When my hand is in God's hand, He helps the infant understand my directions. We discussed this in detail in the previous chapter. I call it the *parenting pyramid*. With God directing my mind on how to deal with my babe, I'm on the road to successfully changing his disposition and behavior. Whatever behavior I want to change, modify, or replace, I need to go to God first and make a plan of what I will do. Reading what others have done is also helpful for problems such as potty training or weaning the child from thumb sucking or pacifiers. Having a plan makes for success. Then, by taking our infant or toddler to Christ, we allow God to re-create his disposition into His image. As the infant yields to obey, then Jesus' divinity empowers his human effort. As God causes the springtime buds to blossom, so He also brings to life in my infant the first buds of right feelings and responses.

Motivated by my son's undesirable behavior, I put forth time and effort to prayerfully search out Heaven's concepts. As I experimented with this new con-

---

2. Luke 11:24–26.

cept, I found it worked better. Inside of me grew a desire to restrain and pull up selfish and ungodly habits in infancy and to cultivate God's pure, wholesome habits in their place; because through a viable connection with Christ it works.

A good foundation

As I continued to experiment with these principles, it proved to be a solid foundation upon which to build a Christlike character, which is simply behaving like Christ. It's having my thoughts and feelings subject to God rather than to self. It is learning good responses to life's trials. This training begun in infancy lays a strong foundation in God for the childhood, teen, and adult years of life.

As Solomon's temple was being built, a strong cornerstone was needed for the foundation. It needed to be one that could withstand extremes of both temperature and pressure. Stone after stone was tested only to crack. Finally, someone called attention to one odd-shaped boulder that had been neglected and often passed by. It had already passed the test of weather. Would it bear the test of pressure? It did, and when the builders moved it into place, it was found to be an exact fit. Bible writers referred to this story from Jewish tradition as an illustration of Christ.[3] He is the long-neglected Cornerstone of our characters. He has borne every test. He is fully able to direct us and to establish our concepts of parenting upon His Word, His commandments, His truth, His example, and His Spirit. This sure foundation is *parenting our infant by the Spirit.*

We would do well to test our concepts of parenting in the way the builders tested the cornerstones before incorporating them into the building. Truth based in Jesus will bear our evaluation, experimentation, and testing. Misconceptions that do not bear the test need to be discarded. We need not fear this process. God loves to help mothers and fathers get started on the right foot. He wants to establish us in the principles of His Word—rather than mere human theory—and to direct us in the application of those principles. When God is directing the change, it will only be for the better.

No schooling in spiritual training

Many of us go into parenting *without understanding the big picture* of Satan striving for the mastery of the mind and character of our infant against Christ. Few of us are educated on how to train the infant mind to be sensitive to the right and want to do it. We think infancy is too early to train, and thus Satan gains the advantage. We don't see the danger, and so we allow self to do its will and way. Our Disgruntled Danny cries, grimaces, twists, and contorts—and we strengthen these negative attributes by either allowing the selfish demands or losing our own self-control. And thus Satan's character traits and habit responses grow and strengthen.

---

3. Psalm 118:22, 23; 1 Peter 2:4–6.

The first three years of life—before the age of reason—are when the child is most susceptible to the influences that surround him—for either good or evil. It is paramount to form correct habits now. How can we do this? How can we take the heart of our infant out of Satan's hands and place it in the hands of Christ? How can we lay a foundation for our child's character in which Christ is the Cornerstone? How can we prevent Satan from getting a foothold by imprinting his character in the child first?

Most of us will learn how to do this through on-the-job training with our own children. If you are reading this book before becoming a parent, you have a great advantage. You can begin to cultivate your heart experience and gain the knowledge that will prepare you to be a successful parent under God. If you are in the position of Disgruntled Danny's mother, take heart. God is willing and able to teach you ways that will work and change character!

In this book I want to show you how wrong habits form a barrier against God and how under God's direction we can change that. We will look practically at the rudimentary beginnings of character development. Most importantly, I pray that you will enter the school of Christ, sit at His feet, and recognize His voice through the Scriptures and your conscience. As we engage our minds with God, He'll help us set up an active training program that will inspire our infants to respond in better ways than what comes naturally. We can give our infants a legacy and love for God that will go with them for life.

One of the most important keys to successful parenting is a teachable spirit— one that admits its need to learn and actively searches for answers to questions. To help you in that process, I have supplied at the end of this book a list of good resources. Some of those sources will help you to understand the child's physical and mental development. Others will give you ideas about setting up an effective feeding schedule and other helpful information. I've also included materials that will help you understand the spiritual side of training and developing a Christlike character.

I would encourage you to explore these materials as diligently as the Bereans responded to Paul. They tested all of his sermons by the Word and Spirit of God. And we must do the same with our parenting practices. There is much valuable experience that others can share that will help us in our work, but we must pass all human ideas through God first. It is not the method that changes our child's habits or disposition, but *Christ directing the method* that works transformation. We should make use of the good tools that can aid us in developing our personal walk with God so that Satan doesn't daunt us so easily.

May God bless you as you educate yourself with these materials. Let Him be your All-wise Guide and Teacher in training the spiritual life of your infant after Him.

THE LONE EMBRACE
A SPECIAL WORD OF ENCOURAGEMENT FOR SINGLE PARENTS

Do you have a Disgruntled Danny? This can change if you are willing to explore new concepts with God. You want to find freedom for him, so don't fear evaluating alternatives to your present approaches.

As you take God into your confidence and tell Him all your troubles in caring for and raising this infant as a single parent, He will direct His Holy Spirit to comfort you and to bring you into all truth. He'll want to pose questions in your mind to help you reason from cause to effect: Where and why is my Danny self-centered? What could I do instead of what I am doing? What would Jesus do to hinder self and inculcate contentedness? What story in the Bible do I know of that has mothers bringing their children to Jesus to find help? Can I do what they did?

If you do this, God will direct you aright—and in most cases, without your outward awareness of His divine direction. He will challenge your concepts and propose new thoughts and directions as you seek for answers through prayer and study. Glean what you can from His Word. Read good books on the subject and experiment with new concepts that come up. The truth doesn't fear testing, for it will only be proven true. But falsehoods don't like the testing process, for they will crumble under the test.

Let Christ become your Chief Cornerstone. Learn to know His voice to your mind, heart, reason, and soul. Let Christ become your best Friend and Savior to guide you in all you think, say, and do. Base what you believe on the Word of God instead of on your feelings. When the concepts you hold conflict with God's Word, take His Word above your concepts and prayerfully experiment to change them.

Jim and Sally.
Matthew and Andrew.

Our life strongly influences our children's legacy of knowing or not knowing God.

Chapter 4
Help With Habits

Put on the new man, which is renewed in knowledge
after the image of him that created him.
—Colossians 3:10

"Daddy, will you tie my shoes?" asked four-year-old Tommy as he slipped his feet into his play shoes.

"I'd be happy to tie your shoes, Tommy, but I think you're old enough to learn how to tie them yourself. Wouldn't that be fun?"

Tommy's eyes widened, and he nodded his head. Father and son sat down together. "This is the way you tie your shoelaces." Tommy's father demonstrated slowly. He showed Tommy several times. Notice that *teaching* first deals with the *mind*.

"Now you try, Tommy."

Tommy picked up the laces and twisted them awkwardly.

"Should Daddy help you?"

"Yes," Tommy replied.

Daddy lifted Tommy onto his lap and, putting Tommy's hands in his, father and son twisted the knot and tied the bow together. "Now you do it, Tommy. Let's learn to twist the knot first." Again he demonstrated, with Tommy's hands in his.

Tommy focused so intently on what he was doing that he bit his tongue. *Training* involves the honest *effort* of *trying*. Teaching deals with the mind while training deals with the action of the will. After a number of tries, Tommy successfully twisted the laces into a knot.

"Daddy, I did it," he said with a broad smile.

"Good job! I knew you could do it. Now you can learn to make the bow."

Tommy tried and tried, but his unpracticed fingers just couldn't coordinate wrapping and pulling the bow through. His face got red, and he started grunting in frustration. Finally, he threw up his hands. "I can't do it, Daddy! You do it!"

"Tommy, I know this is new and frustrating to you. But getting angry and giving up won't help you learn to tie your shoes. Let's go to God and give your frustration to Him and ask Him to help you try again until you get it. You will learn. You don't have to obey anger. Jesus can take away the wrong feelings that Satan tries to push on you. Trying and failing and trying again is learning. Don't give up. I'm here, and Jesus is here to help you."

They knelt down and prayed; Tommy repeating after Daddy. Tommy let go of his anger but still felt sad. He was sure he could never learn to tie his shoes by himself.

"Tommy," Daddy instructed, "Satan doesn't want you to be successful so he lies to you to make you think you should get angry at me or that you can't tie the laces. He is a liar, and we don't have to believe him. In prayer, we chose to believe God instead of our feelings—didn't we?" Tommy nodded his head. "God is trustworthy, where Satan is not. Let's try again. You will learn. Now trust me."

"Yes, Daddy!" After a number of tries, Tommy did it—all by himself! The bow was a bit lopsided—but that was Okay. "That's wonderful! You did it!" Father praised his son. And Tommy beamed!

As Tommy tied his shoelaces day after day, it got easier and easier. After one month of practice, he could tie his shoes as well as his father could. It had become a *habit*. A habit is a way of thinking, feeling, or reacting that is learned by repetition.

Any act repeated becomes a habit, and your habits—together with the thoughts and feelings that accompany them—make up your character for either good or bad. You must come to see that your character determines your destiny. How you think, feel, and react to life's trials is your *character*. God is working to save you from the habits that make up a bad character. He is able and willing to work out a Christlike character in your life. At the same time, your enemy, Satan, is seeking to make you like him. Who will you follow? Either Satan is in charge or God is! You can't be neutral.

The master you consult with becomes your Lord. If you think and rehearse your wrong emotions, then Satan is your lord. If you seek to do God's will, then God is your Lord. You can form the habit of surrendering to your wrong emotions, such as "I want" or "I'm angry," or you can learn to surrender to do God's will and say "I can" or "I'll try with Jesus. I can trust Him." If you form the habit of doing Satan's will, Satan becomes your lord. If you habitually do God's will, Jesus becomes your Lord. The choice is yours.

Tommy learned more than how to tie his shoes, didn't he? Tying shoes isn't a moral issue. But how his father handled the situation had moral implications for Tommy. Approached differently, learning to tie his shoes could have spawned the habit of giving way to passion, yielding to despair, and quitting when things get hard. Instead, Tommy's father used the opportunity to instill some proper habits: to recognize Satan's voice speaking through negative emotions, to go to God to empower choices, and to trust God and find the strength to act on principle rather than on emotion.

Established habits are hard to break. Just imagine changing the way you tie your shoelaces. Even if you discover a better way, you will find yourself resisting the change, because established habits war against the new. Bear these things in mind as you retrain the habits of your little ones.

The stream of habits

Picture a placid stream flowing through a mountain valley, following the channel laid out for it by God. Then, in the midst of a storm, a large boulder bounces down the nearby mountain and lands right in the middle of the brook. Or perhaps, a tree gives way to heavy gales and crashes into the water, and a section of the hillside slides down into the stream. The stream is diverted to a greater or lesser degree from its original channel.

In the beginning, God laid out a channel of thinking, feeling, and relating—one in which He intended the stream of our characters to flow. The storm of sin has caused boulders, logs, and landslides to divert our habits from the original channel. The work of parents is to identify those diversions in their own characters, cooperate with God in removing them, and then help their children in the same way.

As Tommy was tying his shoes, Satan tumbled the boulder of "I can't. This is too hard!" into the stream of Tommy's thoughts. His father recognized the diversion and helped Tommy remove it before the streambed of his character was deformed by the deviation.

Unfortunately, no child is born with the original streambed of character intact. Our heredity and history create landslides that need to be identified and removed. If we fail to recognize this and allow the stream of our thoughts to meander on their own accord in the direction of least resistance, we will not find the original course God intended for us or for our children in our thoughts, dispositions, and deeds. The earlier in life we engage in this work of identifying and removing the obstructions of selfishness, fear, giving up, or irritability, the easier it can be. Allowing landslide to pile up on top of landslide, repeating any wrong response, makes the task much more difficult.

Unfortunately, many parents believe their infants and toddlers are too young to learn to remove these obstructions from the stream of their characters, and the wrong dominates over the right. God wants parents to manage their children's character streams under His guidance—not under the guidance of Satan and circumstances.

The right stream

Jesus wants to be our God, and we are to be His people.[1] He wants to give us His life and wisdom now. He wants to cleanse us and free us from the self-directed life. Connecting with God is like partaking of the "pure river of water of life, clear as crystal, proceeding from the throne of God."[2] He is the fountain of life, and we are the channels through which His life flows.[3] He says, " 'Whoever drinks of the water that I shall give him will never thirst. But the water that I shall give him will become in him a fountain of water springing up into everlasting life.' "[4]

The water that Christ referred to is His gracious presence as revealed in His

---

1. Jeremiah 24:7; 31:33; 32:38; Ezekiel 11:20; 37:23; 2 Corinthians 6:16.
2. Revelation 22:1, NKJV.
3. Psalm 36:9.
4. John 4:14, NKJV.

Word.[5] He is ever speaking to the soul, offering Himself as a well of Living Water to refresh our thirsting hearts. It is our privilege to have a living, abiding Savior. He is the Source of spiritual power implanted within us, and His influence will flow forth in words and actions, refreshing all we come in contact with.

How do we get this Living Water? How do we connect our dry streambed with the Fountain of life? Ask and you shall receive![6] By faith in Jesus—believing He can change me inside at the level of my wrong thoughts and feelings—and by giving Him permission to change me here, this connection is made. Then, drop by drop, choice by choice, and rivulet by rivulet, cooperating by doing God's will and not our own, we strengthen this connection. We unite our weakness to His strength and find the power to do His will. As we do this, God re-creates us into His image.

We need to make this vital connection at the beginning of each day and maintain it throughout the day by continual communion with God. Getting constant direction from Him is our lifeline. As we enter into union and communion with our Savior, He directs our decisions and keeps us in the path of godliness. When we neglect to seek direction from God, we leave ourselves vulnerable for Satan to work through our flesh to lead us in the wrong direction.

To avoid overflowing the banks, the statutes and judgments, of God's intended course in the stream of life, we must learn to be ever filtering our actions through God—"What shall I say or do here? How shall I direct this little infant of mine to You so he will be vitally connected to You? I want my infant to be divinely empowered to know and do the right instead of the wrong. I want this little infant to know the real God from his earliest beginning. Teach me. Direct me. Guide me. Instruct me. Feed me from Your wisdom. Give me this Living Water that I may truly be Yours and bring my child to You to be blessed and empowered, so he can serve You as well. I want my little one to know You as John the Baptist did."[7]

Roll over, Rollo!

It was exercise time for four-month-old Rollo. His mother put him down on his tummy on a blanket in the living room and set some large soft toys near him—just within his reach. She watched him as she went about her work. This was his semi-alone time. Rollo kicked his legs and waved his arms. His eyes were focused on the teddy bear in front of him. He wanted to grab it, but his hands could not coordinate well enough.

It had been so much fun to watch Rollo over the past few months. His random, erratic movements were beginning to be purposeful. He was gaining the ability to control his limbs; his depth perception was developing, and his hand-eye coordination was improving. Useful habits were forming. He reached

5. 1 Corinthians 10:4.
6. Matthew 7:7.
7. Luke 1:41–44.

for teddy again—and this time he got him! It was miraculous!

Another day, his mother again lay Rollo on his stomach to exercise, and another miracle happened. As Rollo pushed one leg against the floor and reached back with his hand and shoulder, he suddenly found himself on his back. He had rolled over. At first he looked startled. Then he smiled gleefully and waved his arms and legs in delight. Were these movements random or purposeful? The mother came over to share his excitement. He wanted to do it again! Mother put him back on his tummy, and this time with fewer erratic movements, over he went again.

"Yeah!" his mother clapped and cheered. "You got it!" Rollo smiled and giggled, waving his arms and kicking his legs excitedly.

Routine is good for all infants—a time to sleep, to eat, to be cuddled, to be bathed, and to exercise. It is not good for infants to be held continuously or carried in a backpack or even sling-carried all the time. They need to learn to coordinate their limbs by exercise and to learn to be content alone. Put safe objects around or above them that they can try to reach. At five months, Rollo could pick up a book, a soft toy, or a teething ring. He became very skilled at turning from tummy to back, and then he learned to turn from his back to his tummy. These movements take entirely different muscles and coordination. This is the standard way to develop habits that become automatic.

If Rollo's nervous system has developed sufficiently to coordinate this complicated movement of rolling over, isn't it reasonable to conclude that God can also work with his mind to teach him how to exercise self-control over negative emotions? Can't he learn how to "roll over" into upright thoughts, feelings, and emotions? Yes, I think so! God's design is to establish both physical and spiritual coordination at this age. Let's get into the Creator's plan and help our little ones trust and obey God by trusting and obeying their mother or father. They can learn to roll over from the experience of fear and irritation to an experience of trusting their father and being comforted by their mother. As they experience this over and over again, it becomes a habit, and that good habit leads to a character prepared to walk with God through life. The experience doesn't have to be tedious—just a consistent walk with God.

Habits start so easily

Thumb sucking is an excellent illustration of how *easily* habits form and how strong they become by repetition. There are many different patterns of thumb sucking.

Timid Tilda, less than one month old, was very hungry. As she waved her little hands around, her hand bumped her cheek. Instinctively, she turned her head toward her hand, opened her mouth, and began sucking her thumb knuckle. Her hunger feelings weren't so bad when she sucked her thumb knuckle—at least for a little while. The next time, she got her baby finger in her mouth in a very awkward position, but this, too, brought temporary pleasure. Her thumb knuckle was the digit that most frequently happened into her mouth, and sucking it became a habit. In time, she sucked her thumb knuckle *deliberately* rather than by chance. Since her parents didn't give her a pacifier, Tilda habitually sucked her thumb knuckle and repeatedly enjoyed the contentment it afforded her. Her parents saw this as a good thing and allowed her to continue; they actually encouraged her to comfort herself by sucking her thumb during fussy times. This is how simply and circumstantially many habits begin.

Amiable Andrew accidentally got his thumb in his mouth a few times, but more often, he put his first and second fingers together in his mouth. Thus, repetition molded his preferred habit pattern of sucking two fingers.

Tom Thumb developed the traditional thumb-sucking pattern. But there are all kinds of combinations—the third and fourth finger or four fingers all at once. You've probably seen older infants and toddlers comforting themselves with a soft blanket on their nose and face while the other hand twists a strand of hair.

What can we deduce from these various comforting habits? Circumstances combined with an inner drive lead to the formation of habit by simple repetition without deliberation or judgment of right or wrong—unless a wise parent under Christ redirects the habit. If habits begin this easily, couldn't we purposefully implant some good habits to aid our infants through life? That's one of the joys of parenthood—showing our children positive ways to look at and respond to life's trials, to see Jesus in everything, and to learn to trust in God from the beginning. We can do this with Christ.

A time for change

The sucking reflex serves a purpose related to eating for nourishment at the beginning stage of life. Also, when a baby feels hungry or insecure, sucking his thumb or pacifier offers a measure of comfort—thus the baby is calm and unstressed. But as the child grows, he needs to be taught new ways to handle the discomforts and insecure moments of life. What would you think if the president of the United States sucked his thumb when he felt anxious?

Most toddlers don't give up this habit of thumb sucking without help. Some find it a very difficult battle. I had a friend who still sucked her thumb when she was twelve years old. Since her toddler years, she had comforted herself by curling up in a chair to look at a book and suck her thumb. When she learned to read, the thumb-sucking habit continued. By the time I met her, her habit had deformed the roof of her mouth, pushed her teeth forward, and maladjusted her bite.

Even worse, in my opinion, was the mental bondage she was under due to this habit. She would withdraw from social interaction into her own little world of shame. "I can't stop sucking my thumb. I'm a retard. I get ridiculed a lot, but I can't stop it." Her habit reinforced the situation that brought her discomfort, so she indulged her habit to comfort herself. It was a vicious cycle from which God wanted to set her free. Some don't find freedom even at this age. I know adults in their twenties and thirties who wrestle with this habit. What begins as a harmless—even helpful—habit can turn into lifelong bondage if not addressed at the proper time and in a constructive manner.

Parents differ in their views of finger sucking versus a pacifier as a means to calm or quiet a child. It's true that each method has its drawbacks, but the advantage of the pacifier is that it can later be taken away, whereas the fingers can only be covered up or made distasteful. However, some parents have encouraged the habit of using a pacifier, planning to take it away when their child is two or three years old, only to find they were starting World War III when they tried to do so. I've known young children to be deceitful and hide their pacifiers, lie about having them, or throw temper tantrums so that they don't have to give up the habit. Whatever method you use, know that, with God, these habits can be replaced with right thoughts, feelings, and new habits, as you make an educated plan with God to change while your child is still young.

This demonstrates the *strength* of habit very well. Physical habits parallel spiritual habits, and both make up our infants' characters. Which habits would God want you to inculcate in the mind (thoughts) and heart (emotions) of your infant that will form the streambed of their life's character? Which habits are boulders that will divert the stream from God's planned course? Wouldn't you want to redirect those habits early in life to help your infant be inclined to follow Jesus rather than to give way to selfishness and Satan?

What misconceptions do you carry? If you're not sure, ask yourself some questions: "Is my child selfish or self-controlled?" Or, "Is he or she agitated or calm, fearful or trusting, fussy or contented, defiant or yielding, demanding or submissive?" God wants our infants to experience the better qualities, and Jesus will gladly teach us how to instill these habits under His guidance. Give Him permission to reveal to you those misguided ideas that keep you from giving your infant or toddler the very best. Don't fear the change that might be required. The most loving thing you can do for your child is to effectively hinder Satan's influence during these important formative years. Keep the stream of thoughts, feelings, and emotions following God's course and under His guidance.

Removing the boulders

As we understand how habits are formed, Christ can guide us to instill good habits and replace poor ones.[8] The earlier we begin this process, the better. Habits established early in life tend to be strong ones—and wouldn't it be good to see that the strongest habits are the best ones? Teaching our infants to respond to God's call to their hearts is the best preparation for the potentially "terrible twos" or the "trying threes."

The key to real change is God's *replacement principle*. Many well-meaning parents focus on what they want their children to stop doing. A better approach

---

8. Psalm 55:19; Romans 12:21.

is to instruct the infant in a Christlike spirit, never with harshness and anger, *what to do instead* of obeying the wrong feelings and emotions that Satan tempts them to follow. Keep your ears open to God for wisdom to work with the child until he yields to do the right.[9] Keep taking him through this process of decision and surrender over and over. In time, Christ's new thoughts, feelings, and resultant responses and habits will replace the old, wrong ways, as we work under Christ.

God is your Teacher in this process.[10] As you consult with Him at the beginning of each day and at every potential conflict throughout the day, you can find His wisdom to direct and instill right habits in your infant or toddler. Satan will try to discourage you by insinuating doubt that God is not there for you. It's simply not true.[11] God is with you as you seek to remove the boulders and logs that Satan tries to lodge in the thought channels of your child.[12] God has adopted us and is working to redeem us from serving sin.[13] Christ is the Creator. He has power over all principalities and powers.[14] He will direct our steps.[15] He will transform us inwardly.[16] God wants His mind to be in us[17] to restore in us His image.[18] He desires to do the same for us at the very beginnings of life as He did with John the Baptist and Samuel, who were raised to serve God and to do what is right from the very beginning. God instructed Elizabeth and Hannah how to accomplish this, and He is willing to instruct you and me as well!

Ivy Infant

Two-month-old infant Ivy was crying. It was time to eat, and she was hungry, but Mother was not available. Grandmother picked her up to comfort her. Ivy calmed down momentarily but soon began to fuss and cry again. Grandmother was wise and prayed for this little one to be patient. "Lord, help Ivy wait for Mommy. Help her to be content. Don't let Satan stir up her emotions. Bring Your angels close to comfort her. What would You have me to do, Lord?"[19]

"Distract her," came to her mind. So she decided to try it and test if this was God leading.

"Ivy, you are all right. Mother will come soon," Grandmother soothed as she cuddled Ivy. Ivy stopped crying.

---

9. Romans 6:12, 13.
10. John 6:45.
11. John 8:44.
12. Matthew 28:20.
13. Matthew 1:21.
14. Hebrews 2:8.
15. Psalm 32:8.
16. Ephesians 3:16, 17.
17. Philippians 2:5.
18. Genesis 1:26.
19. Acts 9:6.

A colorful picture on the wall caught Grandmother's eye. Walking over to it, she held Ivy right in front of it. Ivy studied it intently, enjoying it for a few moments. Grandma watched carefully, and when she saw the pouting look coming back into Ivy's eyes, she went to a different object of interest to distract her mind. In this way, she helped Ivy wait patiently for fifteen minutes until Mother could come and feed her.

This experience gave Ivy a little taste of learning about God and exchanging a negative way of responding for a positive one. She was learning to exercise self-control—even though it was mealtime and she had reason to be hungry. Self-control is cultivated in a child's thoughts and feelings by the grace of God and flows into his or her learned responses to life's trials. In this way, we can establish the foundation of some very important habits of yielding to parents, God, and right.[20] The character stream is kept directed in its appropriate course.

Fun in the tub

"Nathan, it's bath time!" Mother announced cheerfully to her six-month-old firstborn. Bathing Nathan had seemed so awkward at first, but she felt confident now. Nathan had learned to enjoy his bath time too. He loved to splash in the water, play with the soap bubbles, and squeak his yellow rubber ducky. Mother had inculcated this joy in him. She had a new idea for bath time today and sensed it was from God.

Nathan didn't like to get water on his face, and Mother wanted him to overcome an irrational fear of water before he got older. So partway through his bath, she sprinkled a few drops of water on his face. At first he acted startled and looked at her with alarm. "It's all right, Nathan. It's just water." She smiled reassuringly. He relaxed and smiled back at her.

Over the next few baths, Nathan became accustomed to having water sprinkled on his face. So Mother used a very wet washcloth to wash his face. It wasn't long before this didn't bother him either. A habit of being comfortable with water on his face was forming.

One day when Nathan was seven months old, Mother took the good habit further. She tipped his head back to rinse his hair. As she brought his head up, she told him, "Here comes the water, don't breathe," and poured a small glass of water over his head and down his face.

Nathan sputtered a little and looked at Mommy questioningly. She smiled at him. "You are all right. It's just water. It's fun to have water on your face!" Soon this, too, became an enjoyable part of bath time as he learned to hold his breath.

Teaching deals with the mind and tells the child what to do. Training deals with repetitious acts consistently done to train the child in habits of what to think and how to respond.

---

20. Ephesians 6:1.

I'm scared!

Nine-month-old Nelly was fearful of loud noises—any loud noise, whether it was good, bad, or indifferent. One day, guests were visiting, and the men broke into loud laughter. Fear filled Nelly's heart, and her screams filled the air. Mother tried to console her, but she continued to cry. As Mother pondered the situation later, she turned to God.

A still, small, inaudible Voice impressed these thoughts upon her reasoning: *"Mother, this is the beginning of a habit. Loud noises trigger Nelly's fear response. Look into her eyes. Bring her to Me through prayer for a change in heart. She cannot change her feelings and emotions, but I can. Show her what to do instead of yielding to fear."*

Mother wondered, "What can I tell Nelly to do that would be the opposite of fear? Hmm. The opposite of fear is . . . trust. Okay, I'll show her she can trust." She prayed for Nelly that night and asked God to help Nelly understand her mother's directions and to change her feelings of fear into trust.

During the following days, Mother watched for opportunities to help Nelly overcome her fear of loud noises. She chose to challenge Nelly during a good time in her day—not when she was tired or hungry. First, praying silently for Nelly, she turned the stereo up very loud while holding her and speaking softly in her ear, "That's all right. It's just a loud noise, trust Mommy." She smiled reassuringly and turned down the stereo. She set off the fire alarm in a similar way and made it a point to vacuum during Nelly's waking hours.

Nelly chose each day—again and again—to believe and trust her mother. And in a week or two, Nelly had learned to trust Mommy rather than give way to fear. Loud noises became a normal part of life. Mother proved trustworthy. As your infant learns to love and trust Mother, he or she will learn to love and trust Jesus, the Friend of Mother. Every child develops habits of coping or not coping under such stressors. If we do not like the habits our children are portraying, let's show them a better way in—and with—Jesus.

Toddling on to victory

One-year-old Walking Wanda was finally pulling herself up to a standing position using the couch and chairs. Mother was excited for this step of growth. She asked God to help Wanda enjoy walking.

Mother regretfully remembered a day when Wanda was nine months old. Wanda had become very comfortable with rolling wherever she wanted to go. Mother felt it was time for her to learn to crawl and had resorted to using angry words and trying to force Wanda to crawl. Wanda had responded in a similar spirit, and a war of wills began that ended with a passionate spanking. Wanda was confused. She thought that Mother wasn't safe to listen to and became fearful and uncooperative.

Mother recognized that she had lost the confidence of her infant and would need to regain it before she tried to help Wanda crawl again. She asked God for help, recognizing the need to yield herself to God and allow Him to direct her and subdue her anger. Soon after that, Wanda began screaming because she couldn't have the toy she wanted. Instead of losing patience with her, Mother held her comfortingly, prayed with her, and assured her that she was all right. As Wanda experienced repeatedly that Mother was trustworthy, Wanda trusted again.

"Wanda, come to Mother," her mother encouraged cheerfully from across the living room. Wanda stopped playing with her stuffed dog, looked toward Mother, and then rolled over and over in Mother's direction. Mother smiled warmly, tickled her playfully, and picked her up for an affectionate hug. Wanda liked this! They made it into a fun game and played it again and again.

Then one day, Mother sensed that God was telling her, *"It's time to teach her to face her fears by encouraging her to crawl again. I'm with you."*

At first, Mother felt apprehensive. She did not want to repeat that former negative experience. Then she yielded her fears to God and decided that she would trust Him in the same way she was teaching her infant to trust Mommy. She started playing peekaboo with Wanda. Wanda squealed and giggled. She loved this game. Then Mother picked up Wanda and set her on the floor on her hands and knees. With a big smile on her face, Mother got down on her hands and knees in front of Wanda. She wanted to make a fun game out of this new position, for Jesus was with her this time.

Wanda looked fearful and was about to cry. Then she looked into Mommy's eyes, and trust won over fear. She smiled. Mother sweetly encouraged, "Let's crawl, Wanda!" And Mommy crawled in front of her to show her. Wanda rocked back and forth on her hands and knees but didn't move. Mother reached over to help her move her knees, but Wanda burst into tears. Mother stopped right away and picked up Wanda comfortingly. Wanda was still unlearning the fear-filled lessons of the previous experience, as well as learning to crawl.

"Lord, what would You have me to do?" Mother inquired.[21]

"Don't give up on yourself, and don't give up on this process,"[22] came the encouraging reply.

Mother listened to God, and in less than a week Wanda was crawling on her own with excellent coordination and fearless freedom. The fear of this position was gone!

Now Mother called Walking Wanda to her with a big smile on her face and her arms outstretched, while she prayed silently with hope in her heart. Wanda turned to look to her mother, hesitated a moment, and then took her first step. Mother cheered and encouraged her. Then Wanda's little legs wobbled, and she sat down. But she wanted to try again. Day by day, her muscles gained control and her steps got more confident. And there were no signs of the old experience bringing fear to Wanda's thoughts or feelings.

Isn't it great to have God there to help us unlearn and relearn on the job? God can re-parent every one of us. And as we learn better ways to respond to

---

21. Acts 9:6.
22. Galatians 6:9.

situations, we can teach good responses to our infants too. Encouraging the right is the best way to cooperate with God to push out the wrong. This is the *replacement principle*. It works with one-month-olds, one-year-olds, or one-hundred-year-olds.

A big boy and his "bink"

Landon was two and a half years old. His mother was sensing God encouraging her to eliminate the pacifier habit. She wrestled within herself. "But it's going so well right now. Landon loves his bedtime routine with his 'bink' and Cuddles [his pacifier and stuffed animal]. He sleeps so well. I don't want to disturb this. His baby brother has just started sleeping through the night, so this just isn't a good time. But Lord, is this You?"

God affirmed to her that it was. *"I'll be with you, and yes, this is a good time."*

So Landon's mother—against her inclinations, feelings, and emotions—followed God. She had been thinking for some time about how she was going to make this transition. She planned not to remove the pacifier by arbitrary force, but to enlist Landon's will in the change.

Many mothers find a tough war of the wills when dealing with the pacifier habit. Sometimes this is caused by a forceful, compelling, and dominating approach. Such an approach is not of Christ and will fail in gaining the child's heart. It trains only *outward* compliance. Remember that you are warring against Satan, not your child. On the other hand, if your approach is too soft, you will get a similar response for the same reasons. Success is found in a balance of mercy and justice, led by God. Landon's mother was seeking for the right balance.

First, she asked God to be with her and to give her wisdom and tact. She read of others' experiences and made a plan with God. After worship and breakfast, she sat down with Landon to begin the process of change by planting new ideas.

"Landon, you are a big boy now. You are two and a half years old. Big boys pray to Jesus and throw away their bink because they don't need it any more. They can sleep all on their own without their bink."

"Okay, Mommy," Landon replied at first.

"Would you like to throw your bink away now?"

Landon thought for a moment and then shook his head and said, "No."

"That's all right, Landon. You can think about it some more." Mother had only wanted to plant the idea in his mind.

"Lord, what next?" Mother prayed. She remembered reading that poking a hole at the end of the nipple would make it less satisfying to suck, so she did that.

At nap time and bedtime, Mother repeated the idea to Landon that big boys throw their bink away. He took his bink and Cuddles and went right off to sleep both times. He didn't like the bink as well with the hole in it, but his habit was stronger than a little loss of enjoyment.

Seeking her General, Jesus, that evening and in the morning, Mother decided to try one last thing before telling him he had to give his bink up now. She wanted him to make his own decision. So while Landon wasn't looking, Mother snipped the tip off the bink to lessen its appeal even more.

At naptime, Landon looked closely at his bink and exclaimed, "Mommy, look at bink!"

"Bink is getting old and needs to be thrown away," she suggested. "After all, you are a big boy now. Are you ready to throw it away?"

"Not today Mommy, I will throw it away tomorrow maybe." And with this reply Landon put the bink in his mouth, snuggled Cuddles, and went off to sleep.

That evening, Mother consulted again with her Redeemer about what step to take next. When morning came, she called Landon to a decision to throw away his bink. But she added a motivation, "If you choose to be a big boy and throw bink away, Daddy will buy you a sandbox for big boys." Then she prayed with him. Landon wanted a big boy sandbox and time with Daddy, but he also wanted to put off making this decision just one more day. Knowing he needed to make a decision now, Mother asked him, "Does Mommy need to throw it away for you, or will you do it?"

"No, Mommy, I'll do it." The call to a decision was just what he needed. And with Mother's hand in his, they walked to the wastebasket together, and he threw the bink there, saying, "I'm a big boy now. I need to throw bink away." Mother praised God for His leading and directing, and she praised Landon for choosing to be a big boy. They knelt in prayer for God to bless his decision. Mother encouraged him in his choice by speaking of the benefits of being a big boy.

Going to sleep without the bink seemed hard. Father reasoned with him and reassured him that tomorrow he'd have a sandbox because he chose to be a big boy and throw his bink away. "You can sleep without bink. Jesus will help you. Think about playing with Daddy in the sandbox." Landon cried a little but chose to trust Daddy, and God helped Landon fall asleep.

Playing in the sandbox the next morning was a big hit with Landon. It was loads of fun being a big boy with Father in the sandbox! With joy he declared, "Big boys throw their binks away."

Landon was so excited with his success and with the sandbox that he called his grandmother to tell her all about it. Then he had to tell Grandpa—and others. With each repetition, the joy of being a big boy grew. No longer did the old habit rule him, for he had chosen to be a big boy and look at all its benefits. Saying "Yes" to Mommy, Daddy, and Jesus made it possible to say "No" to his past habit, because God helped him see so much good in its place.

With God, you, too, can have this kind of success. God will teach you how to meet the core needs of your infant and toddler in new and better ways and show him or her how to replace new ways for old ones. He will show you how to clear away obstructions so that the stream of character stays in the channel of submission to God.[23]

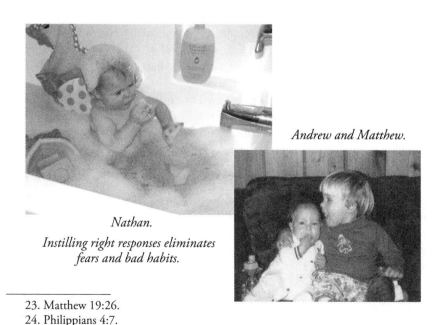

THE LONE EMBRACE
A SPECIAL WORD OF ENCOURAGEMENT FOR SINGLE PARENTS

Are you feeling overwhelmed by the faulty habits you see in your own life? Does it seem to you like the landslides of life have diverted the channel of your character and created bad habits? Perhaps your upbringing was poor or downright bad. Perhaps you struggle with rejection issues, and you feel everyone is against you. Being alone drives feelings of isolation, yet relationships bring so much pain. Fears well up within you, and you wonder if you will go crazy.

Take courage! God is in the business of re-parenting all of us from the wrong habits learned in our infancy, childhood, and youth—even our present trials of life. We cannot change our thoughts and feelings but God, the Creator, can! Come to Him. Accept His adoption. Be His child. We can rest safely in His arms. Learn to recognize His voice and to trust Him. In this way, God will unlock you from the prison in which you find yourself and give you the peace that passes understanding![24] Our habits can strengthen or weaken our connections with God, and in Christ we can choose the habits we will have.

Andrew and Matthew.

Nathan.
Instilling right responses eliminates fears and bad habits.

23. Matthew 19:26.
24. Philippians 4:7.

Chapter 5
Thoughts—Feelings—Emotions

Keep thy heart with all diligence; for out of it are the issues of life.
—Proverbs 4:23

Six-month-old Tired Tara squirmed in her swing. Her mother didn't notice at first, so Tara started to fuss. Mother was talking on the phone to Aunt Sue about Uncle Bill's recent heart attack, and she didn't realize that it was past Tara's nap time. She reached over from where she was working at the kitchen counter and wound up the swing, smiling at little Tara. Tired Tara settled down for a moment, but then her body clock reminded her that it was time to sleep. She began to fuss again, and this time Mother picked her up while still intent on her telephone conversation. Tara quieted down for a few minutes and then began to wiggle, squirm, and fuss louder.

Mother was irritated. "This is an important conversation," she thought. "Why can't Tara be still just for a few minutes?"

"Mother, have you noticed what time it is?" Mother recognized the still, small voice of her conscience, and she glanced at the clock.

"No wonder Tara is fussy," she thought. "It's almost half an hour past her nap time. Lord, You can have my irritation. I'll tend to my little girl." This mother had wisely designed a daily routine to meet the needs of her infant, as well as those of the rest of her family. This schedule made life predictable for everyone in the home and provided Mother direction in understanding what Tara needed right then.

"Aunt Sue," she interrupted, "I just realized that it is past time for Tara's nap. Can I call you back in fifteen minutes?"

Speaking reassuringly, Mother carried Tara to her room, changed her diaper, snuggled her in the rocking chair, and sang her favorite lullabies. Five minutes later, she laid Tara in her bed, and Tara went right to sleep. That was what Tara needed. It was time to sleep.

Tara's only way of getting Mother's attention was to whine and fuss. She was uncomfortable. She had a need. Mother needed to figure out what that need was—a diaper change, a meal, a burp, a nap, help with gas removal, or directions in self-control. Because Mother had a consistent schedule, there were some good habits established already. This consistency allowed Tara's body to know when it was time to eat, time to play, or time to sleep. At six months, this made managing Tara easier. It also contributed to one of the foundations of parenting an infant—what Proverbs 4:23 calls keeping the heart. "Above all else, guard your heart, for it affects everything you do."[1]

---

1. Proverbs 4:23, NLT.

The heart of the infant will determine his course for life. God wants us not only to guard our own hearts diligently, but also to guard our baby's heart. But what is this heart that God is referring to?

The heart represents many things. It is the core of our affections, our feelings, our passions, our appetites, our inclinations, our desires, our habits, our thoughts, and more. It is the sum of all our thoughts, feelings, and emotions. God knows that if our thoughts, feelings, and emotions are kept pure and holy, we will have wholesome, healthy habits and responses to life. On the other hand, if they are allowed to run in whatever direction the flesh may prompt, we will be miserable and make others unhappy. Our thoughts and feelings, combined with the habits they produce, make up our character—which is either in allegiance to God or to Satan. There is no middle ground.

God wants to help parents prepare their infants for a life of purpose and fulfillment. Therefore, He asks us to take hold of His strength to subdue all selfishness and evil passion in ourselves and in our infants, and cultivate in their place the pure joys and innocent pleasures of obedience to His ways. This is guarding the heart with all diligence.

Under God's guidance, we parents have the privilege of developing our infants' characters to follow God rather than Satan from their little beginnings. If we neglect their hearts—their thoughts, feelings, and emotions—selfish habits will automatically be established and become their character. Unaided by God, they can only behave selfishly and become unpleasant to be with. However, by properly steering their thoughts and feelings, we can establish good thoughts, good responses, and thus good behavior. Led by parents who themselves are led of God, our infants can cultivate and learn self-control.

Remember how Tara responded so nicely to Mother's rocking and singing routine before sleep? She quickly yielded to routine and settled down before going to bed. Good responses were becoming healthy habits. Mother's consistency was building a healthy trust in Tara, and this unusual, delayed nap time did not have any long-lasting effects on Tara.

The negative version

But let's consider a different scenario. Suppose Tara's mother did not believe in having a predictable routine and allowed circumstances to dictate how she spent her days. What kinds of thoughts, feelings, and emotions would this instill in Tara? Let's look.

Tara wiggled, squirmed, and then started crying. As usual, her mother was on the phone with a friend. She reached over from the kitchen sink to wind up Tara's swing. Tara settled down momentarily but then began to fuss again. Mother felt irritated; putting her hand over the ear not occupied with the phone, she stepped into the other room. Tara burst into tears, her wails getting louder and louder.

Finally, Mother got off the phone, impatiently jerked Tara out of her swing, and proceeded to feed her. She didn't stop to think that Tara had eaten just two hours earlier and didn't need food again so soon. Without the discipline and regularity of a schedule, Tara didn't know what to expect, and her mother was never sure what was bothering her daughter. Was she hungry, sleepy, or needing some activity? Mother wasn't sure.

Irritation began to build in Mother, while insecurity was taking root in Tara. Mother didn't know what to do with her fussy baby, so she either ignored her or smothered her with the wrong kind of attention at the wrong time. It became a vicious cycle in which Tara lost trust in her mother, because Mother wasn't there to meet her needs. Little valuable training was done. Life was chaotic, and anxiety was the norm. It seemed that Tara could not be comforted or satisfied. Often she was fed when she needed to sleep. She was exercised when she needed to eat. Her emotions were confused. She sensed that she couldn't trust her mother and that "Mommy doesn't really love me." But she was incapable of reasoning why. She simply responded to the insecure emotions with tears and fussiness. These kinds of responses became habitual—and through repetition, her character will be formed.

Character is generally not formed by solitary actions. It is the repetition of positive or negative thoughts and feelings that prepare the way for behavior of the same nature. By a repetition of responses and actions, habits are formed and character is confirmed for good or evil. Do you see it? The infant's life has everything to do with the feelings and emotions that we present to him, and these responses become his habits of life.

The underlying Spirit

The newborn infant senses the atmosphere of the home without the filter of reason to interpret what she feels. Is the environment calm or anxious? Does the mother or father handle her roughly or tenderly, confidently or timidly? Is she truly welcomed into the home, or is she viewed an inconvenience? Do Father and Mother treat each other with love and respect, or do they demean each other? It is not our words so much as our attitude and spirit that communicate to the infant whether home is safe or unsafe.

The atmosphere of our home sets the stage for the feelings and emotions that the infant will accept as normal. Are we giving him or her an environment that builds contentment or anxiety, trust or fear, belonging or insecurity, happiness or sadness? An outwardly correct home cannot cover up for the infant the stronger stimulus of the emotional atmosphere.

Newborn Nikki came home from the hospital to a very unsettled situation. Father had lost his job, and the family was preparing to move to another state. Father and Mother's relationship was strained at best. Father would launch verbal tirades against Mother and sometimes become physically violent with her or with household items. Mother responded with tearful despair. This mother desperately wanted to protect her newborn from these negative emotions and to provide a sense of stability and safety in the home. She planned a reasonable schedule for feeding and sleeping and cuddled her infant, singing hymns and speaking softly to her. When she put Nikki down in her bed, she would play a lullaby tape that had been given to her. She hoped in these ways to compensate for the negative emotions that so overpowered the atmosphere of the home.

Years went by. Nikki grew into childhood and early adolescence. The lullaby tape had been stored away for years. One day, as Mother was cleaning out a storage area, she discovered the tape and put it into the tape player. Nikki heard the music from another room. After a few lullabies, she came to Mother with a very troubled heart. "Mother, what is that tape you are playing? I don't ever remember hearing it before, but it makes me feel just awful."

The powerful negative emotions that characterized Newborn Nikki's home had become a part of the emotional memory that made up who Nikki is today. Although she can't remember what happened back then, she is still affected by it. The music that Mother used to mask the home atmosphere was simply associated with the negative feelings that predominated there.

If you realize that the atmosphere of your home is not what it should be, don't despair. "With men this is impossible; but with God all things are possible."[2] Pray with David, "Create in me a clean heart, O God; and renew a right spirit within me."[3] God will answer, "A new heart also will I give you, and a new spirit will I put within you: and I will take away the stony heart out of your flesh, and I will give you an heart of flesh. And I will put my spirit within you, and cause you to walk in my statutes, and ye shall keep my judgments, and do them."[4] Then cooperate with God to replace bitterness with forgiveness, harshness with kindness, sour looks with cheerful smiles, and despair with hope. This is the work of heart keeping, and it begins with each of us as parents. When we are keeping our own hearts diligently, we will be enabled to provide a heavenly atmosphere for our infants and in so doing, guard their hearts.

Our newborns' feelings and emotions are like the trigger that drives the bullet from a gun. These feelings, combined with the infant's thoughts, drive his responses. In other words, our infants' behaviors are by-products of their thoughts and feelings, which are often driven by our own feelings and thoughts. To a great extent, we are responsible for our children's behaviors.

For example, if there is fear and anxiety in the home life, it drives a fearful, or at least a fretful, response in the child. On the other hand, a vital connection with God can give us parents freedom from *our* wrong thoughts and feelings and thus bring a heavenly atmosphere into our hearts and homes, and eliminate this cause of the infant's fear response.

In addition, even when we are providing the right atmosphere, Satan can push emotional buttons in our children's hearts and cause negative responses. These negative emotions can be corrected by teaching our infants a better response. We

---

2. Matthew 19:26.
3. Psalm 51:10.
4. Ezekiel 36:26, 27.

may bring our babes to Jesus for His blessing, just as did the women of Galilee. He will free them from the wrong spirit that is troubling them.

God says to keep our heart with all diligence. With care and persistence, we are to keep our thoughts, feelings, and emotions—as well as those of our infant—within the boundaries of God's ways. When we recognize that our child is straying into self's way, we can cry out to God for help and cooperate with Him to bring our child back.

Fearful Fabian

Fabian was an energetic fourteen-month-old. One day, he climbed onto one of the dining room chairs, stood near the back of it, and leaned way over. Mother saw him from the kitchen and gave quick, firm instructions. "Sit down, Fabian, or you'll fall." Just then, down he went—head first onto the corner of a nearby table.

He let out a bloodcurdling scream. His mother picked him up and tried to comfort him, but he screamed all the more. She carried him to the kitchen and began to apply an ice pack to the bump on his head, but Fabian pushed it away.

"Fabian, you are all right," Mother calmly soothed him. "This hurt will go away. Trust me. Let's pray to Jesus to make it all better."

Fearful Fabian settled down a bit and folded his hands. Prayer was familiar to him. Mother asked Jesus to take away Fabian's fear and help the hurt to stop. Mother kissed the bump to make it better and saw a bruise forming. So she started to apply the ice and pressure again. This time Fabian cooperated and let his mother do what was best. After ten minutes, he was ready to get down from mother's lap and resume playing.

These are important habits to learn. During the first few years of life, children are rapidly expanding their mobility skills and learning much about the world around them. Inevitably, there are going to be bumps and bruises in the process. Loud noises startle them, dogs jump on them, cats scratch them, siblings drop them, and they fall and skin their knees. How you respond to those little hurts can instill either fear or trust.

Responding calmly and prayerfully can instill trust and courage in your child. He learns that these little hurts get better and he doesn't have to lose control of himself to get through it. Seeing to it that your child gets the treatment he needs—not necessarily what he wants—is an important factor in developing the trust necessary between parent and child. And this is where you build his trust in God too—through you. If your child can trust you, he can trust your God. If he cannot trust you, he cannot or will not, trust your God.

This is where the parenting pyramid makes such a big difference. We cannot change the child's feelings, but God can.[5] Leading a child to connect with God through prayer gives God access to the child's heart where real change can oc-

---

5. 2 Corinthians 10:5.

cur. The results are seen in the behavior. Fabian's fear was replaced with trust. Whatever is repeated becomes habit, and habits form character. So what is your home instilling—fear or trust?

Frustrated Florence

It was suppertime, and the family was sitting around the table enjoying the lovely meal that Mother had prepared. Eighteen-month-old Florence was eating with the family. She babbled and pointed at the table. Neither her mother or father, her brother or sister, could understand what she wanted. "Do you want potatoes, beans, dressing, bread, butter?"

"No, no, no!" Florence again repeated her babbling.

"I'm so sorry. I just don't understand you," Mother responded. Florence's little face screwed up in annoyance. She banged her little fist on the high chair and kicked her feet in frustration. Then she withdrew into despairing silence.

"Lord, how can I help Frustrated Florence? She gets so upset. She is not being naughty. She just can't talk well enough yet to say what she wants. But her frustration is a poor response to the situation, and I don't want that to become a habit. Can I somehow help her communicate better? Can we cultivate patience instead of all this frustration? How, Lord, how?"

God didn't seem to give Mother any ideas for several days. He seemed to be so silent. Mother knew that God is a communicating God and waited for Him to direct her in His way and in His time. She began to study various resources to see if she could find any ideas that would help.

One day, a friend, who was unaware of Mother's prayers, gave her a book about sign language. As Mother scanned the book, a lightbulb went on in her mind. "Lord, are You suggesting that I teach Florence some sign language to help us over these frustrating situations?" Mother went to the book and found a few simple signs: FINISHED, MORE, and PLEASE.

Just then, Florence toddled over to see what Mother was doing, and the lessons began. Florence caught on quickly. At supper that night, Mother asked her to say "please" for something she wanted. Florence understood. A smile spread across her face, and she swiped her hand across her cheek. She started to get frustrated again when Mother wanted her to eat more—and kept turning away. The response of irritation was automatic.

"Lord, help," Mother prayed silently. Then looking in Florence's eyes, she asked, "Are you finished eating?" and made the sign for "finished." Florence imitated it. "Okay, that means you are all done now. No more eating. Are you sure you are done?" Florence gave the sign cheerfully again, and Mother washed her face and hands and put her down from the table.

What a difference these alternate communications made! Repetition confirmed new ways of responding instead of getting irritated and frustrated. Mother continued to seek God for more ideas and proceeded to work with Florence to help her enunciate her words better. When Florence was capable of speaking more clearly, Mother would not accept baby talk. When a keyword was too hard for Florence, Mother suggested a synonym that was easier to pronounce. It was time well spent. Florence learned healthy responses in place of her thoughts and feelings of frustration.

God wants to help us establish good habits in those early years, because character is formed to a great extent in the first three years. This is a most important time to build the foundation of our infants' characters—managing their thoughts and feelings—to train them to trust God, to try new and better ways to resolve issues, and to come to Jesus instead of pulling away.

Before they reach the age of reason, we must teach our children to obey us over their feelings and emotions. We must teach our infants to follow habits of self-control and to come to God. What happens if we neglect this work?

Ted and the fireplace

Three-year-old Trying Ted walked into the living room with an air of authority that told he was used to being in charge. He stood at the entrance of the room surveying the situation. Jim and I, Ted's parents, and one other couple were guests in this home. We had all been visiting pleasantly with the homeowners, but Ted's demeanor caught everyone's attention. He had a look that said, "Adults don't intimidate me in the least—nor are they worthy of being consulted or obeyed!" We sensed that trouble had arrived.

Ted noticed the decorative fireplace that was set in the wall and decided he was going to check it out. We could all read his intent. Striding over to it, he began to pull noisily on the fireplace knobs, twisting, turning, and jerking them. His parents saw what he was doing but did nothing. In shock, we all waited for the parents to do something. The homeowner gained his wits first. He realized that the parents were not responding, so he stood up. Stepping quickly over to Trying Ted, he stated firmly, "Ted, this is too dangerous for you to play with. You need to leave the fireplace alone." Ted looked up at the man and twisted the knobs yet more vigorously. "Ted, you may not play with my fireplace. Now come away." But Ted didn't obey.

He had been trained by default that his wishes and desires were his number one consideration. What he wanted, he got—with little restraint or redirection. His mother tried to smooth the situation over by excusing Ted's behavior. "It's tough to be a parent today and be patient with our little ones. Poor Ted fell asleep just before we arrived here, so he didn't get the sleep he needed. Poor Ted! Be patient with him."

Does God want us to be patient with selfishness in its infancy? God says, "Train up a child in the way he should go: and when he is old, he will not depart from it."[6] Is it love to confirm selfish thoughts and feelings in a child? Do we really believe that he will just grow out of it when he gets older? Or is it more likely that little selfish thoughts grow into big selfish thoughts just like little weeds grow into big weeds?

---

6. Proverbs 22:6.

Trying Ted grabbed both sides of the little fireplace and shook it with great vigor. I thought the fireplace would surely come off the wall! The homeowner exclaimed vehemently, "No, stop that!" but feared to touch the boy. Ted didn't appear even to hear him. He took the stance of a sumo wrestler and attempted to lift this fireplace out of the wall again.

His mother called sweetly, "Oh, Ted, come here. Let's find something fun to play with in your toy bag." Trying Ted shook the fireplace all the harder.

"Because sentence against an evil work [selfishness] is not executed speedily, therefore the heart of the sons of men is fully set in them to do evil."[7]

Mother finally stood up, walked calmly over to Ted, and showed him a coloring book. Trying Ted gave his mother a look of disgust. Mother touched him gently on the shoulder. He defiantly pulled away from her, insisting, "Leave me alone!" And she left him alone! Ted continued doing what he wanted to do.

Who is controlling Trying Ted? Is it God or Satan? It's one or the other.[8] There is no middle ground. The Bible says, "By their fruits ye shall know them."[9] The countenances, the responses, and the behaviors of our children give us a window into their thoughts and feelings and tell us whom they are obeying and listening to. Whose character is Ted portraying? Satan's! Then we can deduce that Satan is leading him, and Ted is obeying him. This parent is allowing Satan to be her son's lord, leading him in habits of selfishness without restraint! "A child left to himself bringeth his mother to shame."[10]

Mother spoke up to the adults again, "Oh, it is so hard to be a Christian and always be kind and sweet to our little ones. I can hardly wait until he gets older and I can reason with him so life won't be so hard!" Her shoulders drooped with exhaustion. This poor mother was held in bondage by a terrible misconception. She was sincere in her misconception but suffered the consequences nonetheless. God wanted to free her!

Up to this point, Ted's father had stayed out of the way, but his narrowed eyes and set jaw told the rest of us that his toleration was reaching its limit. With thinly veiled frustration, he commanded, "Ted, come here." Ted acted as though he didn't hear his father. Father called again and again, his irritation increasing. Ted looked at his mother, then to his father, and grinned. What clue does this give you about Ted's thoughts and feelings?

Father got up and marched over to Ted, picked him up, and carried him back to his seat. Ted fought and kicked, yelling in his baby lisp, "Let me go!" Father wrapped his arms around the boy like a straitjacket and hung on.

Mother scooted next to Father and nervously began to excuse Ted's behavior. "Honey, don't expect so much of him. He didn't get his nap. He's only a little boy and doesn't understand what you're doing to him. He needs to go

7. Ecclesiastes 8:11.
8. Galatians 5:16–24.
9. Matthew 7:20.
10. Proverbs 29:15.

outside and work off some of his energy." With this encouragement, Ted wrestled harder to get free from his father's restraint, but Father held on all the tighter. Mother lost her temper. "You are so strict. You expect too much. You're not even kind! You've got to love him if you ever expect him to obey you!" Trying Ted squirmed and screamed, but Father would not let him go. To stop the arguing, he carried Ted out of the living room and into the kitchen.

Poor Trying Ted was caught in a tug-of-war between two ditches—the militant domination of his father and the overindulgence of his mother. Both extremes fostered wrong thoughts and feelings that expressed themselves in selfish behavior. Must Ted wait until the age of reason before he can be free from this bondage? Must Satan rule until then? No, no, no! A thousand times, no! Ted can be free now if his father or mother will enter the parenting pyramid and put God in charge. God will lead them to find the proper blend of justice and mercy.

After thirty minutes alone in the kitchen, Ted's father still had not brought Trying Ted to surrender. He screamed the entire time against Father's "injustice." The parents left for home, carrying with them the greatest thorn in their life—their son under the control of Satan.

What will Trying Ted be like as a teenager if this program continues? Do you see how self gets stronger and bolder when it is not properly restrained? How is Ted going to learn self-control? Obviously, this is acceptable conduct in his home. Can you see how his thoughts and feelings should have been dealt with long before now, so he wouldn't be so obnoxious at the tender age of three? Children are what their parents make them by their instruction, discipline, and example. Ted's defective character published his parents' unfaithfulness to seek and follow God. Unless they seek God to redeem them from their misconceptions, Ted is on the pathway of being ruined by indulgence.

True love is seeking to correct our imbalances. True love will lead us to go to Jesus to learn for ourselves how to surrender our hearts and minds to God so that we can show our infants and toddlers how to surrender their hearts and minds to serve God. True love is bringing our infants and toddlers to Christ to find freedom from selfishness while this trait is still small. This work is best done *before* the age of reason.

God will be your personal Teacher as you endeavor to learn from Him how to instill unselfishness in your little ones.[11]

"Mine" Micah

Two-year-old Micah was beginning to understand ownership. "This is Daddy's hat; that is Mother's kettle; and this is Micah's toy." His mother wanted him to learn the joy of sharing with others, so she invited two-year-old Ulysses and his mother for an hour of playtime one morning. Before their friends arrived, Mother sat Micah on her lap and explained, "Micah, Jesus has blessed you with

---

11. John 6:45.

THOUGHTS—FEELINGS—EMOTIONS

some very nice toys, and He is happy that you take good care of them. You enjoy your toys, don't you?" Micah nodded, and Mother continued. "In just a little while, your friend Ulysses and his mommy are coming over, and you are going to get to share your toys for a little while."

The two boys sat on the living room floor with Micah's toy basket. Unruly Ulysses reached over to Micah's basket, picked up the toy avocado, and began to cut it with the play knife. Indignation arose in Micah's eyes. He leaned over and grabbed the toy back from Ulysses' hand saying, "Mine!"

Ulysses looked hurt and was about to grab the toy back when his mother intervened. "Ulysses, let's ask Micah for permission to play with his toys before you pick one up." Then turning to Micah, she asked politely, "Micah, may Ulysses play with your toys with you?"

"Mine," Micah replied. "No! Mine!" and placed his little body squarely between Ulysses and his toy basket.

Micah's mother sat down beside him. "Micah, we want to share our toys with our friends." Then she was stumped. She cried out to God for what else to say and was quiet for a moment. One thought came to her mind that seemed Christlike. "It's fun to share your toy with Ulysses so he has something to play with. Remember how Daddy shares his ruler, his drill, and his hammer with you and how happy this makes you to work with Daddy?"

Micah remained in indecision. Not to decide for God is to decide for selfishness. It was obvious he didn't want to share. Mother cried out again to God, "What shall I do, Lord?"[12] Not getting any obvious idea from God, she followed her reason based on God's Word. "I need to bring Micah to a decision to obey what is right over his feelings," she said to herself.

"Micah, come with me and we'll pray to Jesus to help you decide to share." Micah needed power to obey. Kneeling in prayer, he repeated after Mommy, "Jesus, help me choose to share. Help me learn to share. Amen!"

"Now, Micah, which of your toys would you like to share with Ulysses?"

Micah walked back over to his toy basket. His little heart struggled with the decision. "It's fun to share, Micah," encouraged Mother. Micah handed the toy avocado back to Ulysses, but still looked at it longingly.

"Micah, let's get out your farm set and animals and see how much fun it is to play together." And so they did. Micah's mother showed Micah how to be the farmer and care for his animals and give an animal to his friend. In turn, Unruly Ulysses' mother showed Ulysses how to share one of his animals with Micah.

And so they played and began the process of denying wrong thoughts and feelings, and replacing them with godly ones. By repeatedly cooperating with right thoughts and feelings, the right habits get stronger. Selfishness is starved. Prayer brings Christ into the equation, and He becomes the child's personal Savior from wrong thoughts and feelings. As the child cooperates to think right

---

12. Acts 9:6.

thoughts, it is God that creates right feelings inside him, and these together create a Christlike character in the child.

"This is the covenant that I will make with them after those days, saith the Lord, I will put my laws into their hearts, and in their minds will I write them." "How much more shall the blood of Christ, who through the eternal Spirit offered Himself without spot to God, purge your conscience from dead works to serve the living God?"[13]

What would have happened if Micah and Ulysses had played together unsupervised while the two mothers visited? They would have fussed and grabbed and not learned proper ownership, which includes sharing from a cheerful heart. Selfishness would have been left to grow up like a dandelion weed in the heart of the stronger child, while despair would have taken root in the heart of the more sensitive child. As they are in childhood, so they remain as adults—unless they find Jesus and deliverance from the character formed in these young years.

As these two mothers modeled right attitudes and responses for their children, they incorporated a powerful tool that works for good or evil in the life of every child. Let's look further at the principle of "monkey see, monkey do!"

THE LONE EMBRACE
A SPECIAL WORD OF ENCOURAGEMENT FOR SINGLE PARENTS

If you want to prepare your infant or toddler for life here and heaven to come, then the first lesson to teach him is self-control as it is in Jesus. No undisciplined, headstrong person can hope for success in this world or reward in the next. Each of us will need to enter the school of Christ that He may personally lead our reasoning after His way of thinking. He'll do this through His Word, through the aid of His Holy Spirit, and through experience regarding the role of our thoughts, feelings, and emotions in our character development.

God wants us to keep our heart—our thoughts and feelings—with all diligence. And as we learn how God keeps us, we can bring up our infants in the same way with Christ. As we learn how to give our fears, anxieties, and character weaknesses to God and exchange them for His thoughts, we can share that with our little ones. God is there for you!

---

13. Hebrews 10:16; 9:14.

Landon and Nathan, sharing their toys under Andrew's supervision, reflect the thoughts their parents instilled.

Chapter 6

Monkey See, Monkey Do!

Beloved, now are we the sons of God . . . we shall be like him;
for we shall see him as he is.
—1 John 3:2

Have you ever gone to the zoo and watched the monkeys? They are such fun. They stare at you with great big eyes, very interested in whatever you might do, and often they imitate you! If you move up and down and wave your arms, they are soon doing the same. If you smile real big, they smile real big. If you act like you're angry, they get angry. If you shout, they go wild. When you calm down, they do, too. If you are eating, they want to eat too. They hold out their hand to share whatever you have. They watch you very closely and do what you do. They are so cute.

Monkeys don't just imitate people. They imitate each other. When a young monkey sees his mother grooming a sibling, picking through its fur, he copies what he sees. Through imitation he learns how to rummage for food, learning what to eat and what not to eat. He learns the family pecking order, the group pecking order, when to be dominant, when to be submissive, and the roles of male and female. What a monkey sees, a monkey does!

Monkeys aren't the only imitators. I've watched toddlers at the zoo, imitating the monkeys. When a monkey jumps up and down, waves his arms, and calls *"ooh, ooh, ooh, ooh,"* Tommy Toddler watches with great big eyes and does the same. Tanya Toddler watches Tommy Toddler and is soon copying him.

Of greater concern than imitating monkeys is the fact that our infants and toddlers imitate us! They watch our responses to circumstances—both good and evil—and follow the principle of "monkey see, monkey do!" They become like us in many respects. Although this can be a tremendous influence for good, too often it tells for evil. How important it is for us to give our children something worth imitating!

Monkey behavior is fine for monkeys—but I don't want my infant or toddler to constantly behold the impulsiveness of monkeys and imitate that, do you? A wild bull is fine for the rodeo—but all too often I've seen mothers or fathers behaving like a wild bull at home, reacting in anger whenever their will is crossed and crushing anyone who gets in her or his way. Do we want our toddlers to watch and imitate that kind of modeling? The sloth is a marvelous animal and well adapted for its habitat, but some parents imitate their slow lifestyle and make slothfulness a virtue. Because of this, many homes flounder for the basic necessities of life. Some mislabel this as faith, but the truth is that such individuals lack the push to acquire skills, become industrious, and work consistently. Where did these parents learn these imbalances? And more importantly, how can they remedy them so that the next generation follows a different pattern?

Let's look at the law of "monkey see, monkey do!"

The window of greatest opportunity

Sally was only a few months old and was sitting in her infant seat while her mother folded the laundry. She had been watching her mother contentedly at first, but then started fussing. Mother studied Sally for a moment. She had been learning about the principle of imitation. She felt a pull in her emotions to get irritated at Sally for fussing and interrupting her work. "Lord," she prayed silently, "I don't want to model irritation for my daughter. Please help me to offer her something better. Please subdue my heart." She picked up Sally and cuddled her for a moment. Then, looking into Sally's eyes, she thought, "Sally can learn to smile instead of frown and wail. That would be God's will and my will for her."[1] So Mother smiled very sweetly at Sally, but Sally wasn't looking. She was all caught up in her emotions and didn't notice what Mother was doing.

Mother soothed, "Sally, you don't need to cry. Mommy is here. God is here. Everything is all right. Look at Mommy."

Sally continued to fuss, but now she looked at Mommy. God was working in Sally's heart and mind also to tell her to obey her mommy. Sally's response was just like those monkeys in the cage at the zoo. She looked at Mommy's big smile, and her fussing started to settle down. Mother continued to smile and talk soothingly to her little daughter, and soon Sally began to smile. Then her fussy feelings took over. Crying out to God again, Mother continued to smile and tickled Sally's ribs with her fingers. Again, Sally returned a lovely big smile. Mother noticed it was getting close to nap time, so she changed Sally's diaper and put her to bed. Sally settled right down and went to sleep.

The principle of "monkey see, monkey do" started a good habit in this instance. In spite of being tired, Sally responded to Mother with a smile. As Mother repeats this kind of positive interaction with Sally, her habits will be established and her character confirmed. If the mother never taught her a better way to respond, the fussy way would become Sally's habitual response and would continue to get stronger as she got older—wouldn't it? Of course, it would!

The character is formed, to a great extent, in the early years, long before the ability to reason is developed. Christian psychologists, Ron and Nancy Rockey, have documented the far-reaching implications of the early years. It is the parents' window of greatest opportunity to positively influence their child for life.

---

1. Romans 12:21.

For the first year or so of life, children do not use spoken language. However, they interpret voice inflections, tone and pitch, facial expressions, and body language, and are very sensitive to emotional upsets. During this time, the brain's neurons are forming pathways that inevitably become habits or modes of thinking, and the mind is most vulnerable, absorbing information through all the senses and through emotions.

During the first year of life, babies learn 50 percent of everything they will ever learn, and in the second year, they learn an additional 25 percent. These early lessons are the foundation, the framework for the formation of the thoughts and feelings of the future adult. What infants learn from their parents, their primary caregivers, becomes the value system upon which future decisions are made.[2]

The habits established during these early years have more influence than any natural endowment in making men and women either giants or dwarfs intellectually and spiritually. The earlier in life one learns *hurtful habits,* the more firmly will they hold their victim in bondage. On the other hand, if correct and *virtuous habits* are formed early, these will go with the child for life. In most cases, those who in later life reverence God and honor the right, have learned those lessons before there was time for the world to stamp its image of selfishness upon the soul.

Is it any wonder that Satan doesn't want us to recognize the far-reaching implications of what we model for the child at this age? He wants to implant his habits in the beginning, knowing they will go with the individual for life. Thus, he wants us to believe that the child needs only physical care and that the intellectual, moral, and spiritual training can be done later—but most of the foundational learning is done by the time a child turns three! And most of that learning results from the principle of "monkey see, monkey do!"

What will we model?

For instance, where do some of our little ones get their fear of dogs? Usually, by the "monkey see, monkey do" principle.

Tiny Tim's mother is terrified of dogs. Every time she finds herself near one, her breathing accelerates, her heart pounds, her body stiffens, and she frantically looks for an escape. Her fearful response to dogs teaches Tiny Tim how to relate to all dogs—both mean and friendly. By the time he is a year and a half old, he screams before his father or mother even see a dog—any dog. He has learned this response of fear well before the age of reason—hasn't he? It has become an automatic response based on imitation, not reason. Over time and with repetition, the fear turns into anxiety which prompts a self-protective

---

2. Ron and Nancy Rockey, *Chosen* (Nampa, Idaho: Pacific Press® Publishing Association, 2001), 117.

fight-or-flight reaction—either attacking the dog aggressively or running away from it, even when there is no real danger.

On the other hand, if Tiny Tim's parents habitually treat dogs with respect and kindness, and if the dogs Tiny Tim meets are friendly and safe, what would be his "monkey see, monkey do" response? Tim would like to get close to the doggy and cuddle and play with him just like his parents do. Instead of screaming in fear when he sees a dog, he would expect a pleasant experience. The same child can learn to obey the emotions of either fear or love, depending on the example of his caregiver. Our children are, to a great degree, what we make them.

It begins with me

What if you are a Tiny Tim who grew up with an irrational fear of dogs and you don't want to pass that on to your child? By ourselves, we cannot change our feelings and emotions any more than the leopard can change his spots.[3] But God says that He can subdue all things.[4] God is a big God, and He can transform our irrational fears. He longs to set the captive free, but He needs our cooperation. We must give our wrong thoughts and feelings to God for Him to cleanse them and return them to us purified.

Our thoughts are what cause us to feel the way we do. Tiny Tim caught on to the same misbelief about dogs that his mother had. Subconsciously, she exaggerated the danger that dogs present. She imagined being attacked by the dog, being bitten in a terrible way, and perhaps dying. She told herself that this was likely to happen and that it would be "just awful," and she couldn't stand it. She may not have recognized these thoughts consciously, but they controlled her nonetheless. Consequently, she did what most people do in situations that trigger anxiety. She tried to avoid dogs. When she avoided dogs, she felt better temporarily—until she met another dog. Then the anxiety ruled again.

But God wants to free her from her anxiety. This requires an unlearning and a relearning. God wants to help us identify exaggerated misbeliefs and replace them with the truth. I call it the *replacement principle*. Tiny Tim's mother can begin to say to herself, "The likelihood of being attacked and killed by this pet dog is very low. I'm in God's care, and He will allow only what's best. I don't need to fear this dog. I can learn to recognize when a dog is friendly or hostile and how to relate wisely to the different temperaments of dogs. I don't need to scream. With Jesus, I can remain calm." There are many texts of scripture she can read and meditate on that reinforce the reality that we are in God's care and need not be controlled by fear.

The next step is to actually face the thing she fears. In consultation with God, she should make a plan to get close to friendly dogs. She might start by practicing yielding her thoughts and emotions to God while staying in the same

---

3. Jeremiah 13:23.
4. Philippians 3:21; Hebrews 2:8.

room with a dog. "I need not fear this friendly little dog! It is not like the angry dog that bit me as a child. I was afraid then, but this dog isn't something to be feared. I'll trust God rather than my fear."

Then she could begin to sit near the dog while rehearsing the truth, "God has not given me a spirit of fear, but of love, and of power, and of a sound mind."[5] When she senses God prompting her, the next step might be to calmly approach the dog and pet it. As she challenges her fears repeatedly, the truth will set her free.[6] The day will come when she feels no fear in the presence of a dog.

This is what it means to take God at His word. We believe God's Word above our feelings, emotions, and history—and we act upon it. When we do so, His perfect love casts out all our fear.[7] As we choose to cooperate with God's leading and believe His Word, God makes it real on the inside to the level of our thoughts and feelings.[8] In following God, we are redeemed from fear's dominion. We discover that God is there for us and that He is still a Redeemer today!

Now the fearful parent is prepared and empowered to model this new way for her child. She can lead him out of his fear response because she understands the battle with the wrong thoughts and feelings. She knows how to cooperate with the grace of Christ that can change the thoughts and emotions to be free to serve God instead of Satan.

Take your infant to Jesus and pray for God to lead you in how to instruct him to lay down his fear of dogs and exercise trust in Jesus instead. Then play "monkey see, monkey do" with him. Smile, pet the dog, and enjoy him. Assure your infant that it is Okay. Take his hand to touch the doggy. As these positive experiences are repeated, the fear subsides. He copies you and soon enjoys dogs. God subdues the fearful emotions inside and places trust in its place each time you do this—until one day, the fear no longer exists. Helping your child to face his fears while he is little is an important step.

Modeling is teaching

How to properly pet a dog needs to be taught to both the fearful and the trusting infant. Almost all infants and toddlers tend to grab a dog's hair and pull, unless a wise parent—one who is under God—teaches them a better way of being friendly. In other words, proper handling of dogs is learned by the repetition of proper instruction.

Model before your one- or two-year-old child how to pet a dog softly and kindly with an open hand. By patient instruction and consistency, they will learn a better way to enjoy the dog, and the dog can enjoy them too. If you have a more aggressive child and they quickly grab and pull a dog's hair and hurt the

---

5. 2 Timothy 1:7.
6. John 8:32.
7. 1 John 4:18.
8. 2 Corinthians 10:5.

dog, do not scold, fret, yell, or spank them in anger. Rather, stop them quickly, kindly, and patiently, and show them how to pet the dog nicely with an open hand. If calm instruction is not adequate for your child, then take him to Jesus, pray for him and try again.[9]

If you yell, scream, and lose your self-control, what will your toddler imitate when you do not do what he wants you to do? Just that! What monkey sees, monkey will do—maybe not immediately but in time. All that the child sees goes into his brain and is accounted for in due time.

If you throw things when you get angry, your child will learn to do the same. If you are morose, withdrawn, and negative, your child will learn to be like that too. If you are bubbly, free, and seek Jesus, your children will mimic this behavior as well. Whatever your nature, that will tend to become your child's nature as well. So, whatever you want your child to do, you must do first. Changing your child's behavior begins with you.[10]

One-year-old Tiny Tim got excited about petting the puppy, but in his inexperience and lack of coordination, he hit the puppy instead of stroking him. Mother calmly corrected him, "That is not the way to pet a puppy. You'll hurt him. This is how you pet the puppy." And Mother opened up Tim's hand and stroked the puppy with him. Tim let Mother hold his hand to stroke the puppy, but as soon as she let go, he grabbed a handful of fur and yanked on it. "No, no, not that way," instructed Mother sweetly. "This is how you pet the puppy. Softly and nicely." This time, Tim concentrated on making his hand stroke puppy the same way his mother's hand did. Tim was beginning to learn by the "monkey see, monkey do" method. When Tim refused to take instructions and was rough with the puppy, his mother would take away the puppy. By repetition, he learned quickly.

Modeling confidence

Life for a toddler is generally full of little mishaps. As they develop their mobility and venture into the world around them, they experience hurts of various degrees. How we respond to those hurts can make a big difference in how they will face life in later years. We can overreact or we can underreact. Of course, by no means should we neglect real injury.

Julie's mother was learning to drive a van with a stick shift. Three-year-old Julie was sitting unrestrained on a box in the very back of the van. As Mother drove up a hill, she came to a stop at an intersection. When Mother attempted to pull out from the stop sign, the vehicle lurched forward. Julie fell backward off the box she was sitting on. When her body hit the doors at the back of the van, they flew open, and Julie fell onto the road. Fortunately, friends who were following the van stopped and picked up Julie. They waved down Julie's mother, who thanked them and asked them to put Julie back in her van. She told Julie that she was just fine and didn't have the child checked for possible serious injuries. As

---

9. Proverbs 15:1.
10. John 17:19.

these types of situations continued to occur in Julie's life, she learned that her legitimate needs didn't matter to her mother. That is one extreme—not taking serious situations seriously.

The opposite extreme is also very common—being overly reactive to every minor hurt. Let God give you input to lead you to find balance. God wants to help us avoid both extremes and help our child respond to all of life's hurts with trust in Him.

One-year-old Falling Fay was learning to walk. One sunny afternoon, as Mother weeded a flower bed, Fay crawled over to a rock wall and pulled herself up to a standing position. Mother cautioned her, "Be careful, Fay. You might fall." Fay let go of the rock wall and took a few steps toward Mother. But her little feet were not accustomed to the uneven gravel pathway. She wobbled, slipped, and sprawled face-first. Mother came running anxiously while Fay lay still for a moment wondering what to do. "Oh dear, are you all right?" Mother asked. She quickly picked up Fay and checked her over. Falling Fay saw her mother's fearful look, felt her mother's nervous touch, and heard her mother's worried voice. She took it all in and began to cry. She learned to equate fear with falling and concluded that falling is a terrible thing.

As these kinds of experiences were repeated, Fay became conditioned to fear harmless hurts and to exaggerate their threat in her mind. Thoughts of fear produce feelings of fear that confirm false thoughts. In this way, a habit is established and becomes an automatic response. The more this response is repeated, the more compelling it becomes. The infant becomes sensitive and peevish to things that actually threaten no real harm. She expects a lot of attention when she experiences little hurts.

A better way for Mother to respond to Fay would be to gently say, "Oh, you took a little tumble! You're all right, Fay. Just get up." She could walk over to Fay with a smile and cheery disposition and calmly help her to get up and go again. Fay would feel safe. She would conclude that everything is all right and that falling is a normal part of learning to walk. Will an infant trained in this way fear falling? No! She will take her little tumbles in stride. She will be free from fear, and trust will be built into her character. Which way will you train your infant?

Modeling joyfulness

Eighteen-month-old Lionel and his golden retriever puppy were visiting his grandma one sunny midwinter day. Grandma dressed Lionel in his snowsuit and took him for a ride on a sled. As she pulled him through the drifts of freshly fallen snow in the front yard, the puppy, who was a big as Lionel, kept jumping back and forth over the sled. She was so excited to be playing with "her boy" in the fluffy snow. Once in a while, she would knock Lionel off the sled, and he would land face-first in the snow. Lionel took it all in stride. He didn't cry in fear or get angry at his puppy. Why? Because his mother had been teaching him that little mishaps are not a big deal, and he was learning well. He had been taught the attitude that this was just a little annoyance that he could easily endure. Lionel lay calmly where he fell and looked to Grandma for directions of what to do next.

Grandma asked, "Are you Okay?"

Lionel replied clearly after a pause, "Yes."

"Can you get up?" Grandma inquired.

"Yes," was his simple reply, and he began to try to push himself up. But the deep fluffy snow gave way, and he floundered in his bulky snowsuit. Grandma helped him to his feet, and he climbed back into the sled for more fun.

Grandma wanted to reinforce the good lessons Lionel was learning. She wanted him to see how much fun sledding could be. She pulled him on a course that curved around the trees in the yard. As she pulled him slowly around the corners, she would say, *"Putt, putt, putt."* When they got to an open area, she would speed up and swing him around fast, saying, *"Vroom, vroom, vroom!"* She laughed and smiled, and so did Lionel. Soon he was saying the sounds with Grandma and joining in and doing the right sounds at the right time. When they would approach the fast area, Grandma instructed, "Hold on tightly!" He would hold on, and most of the time, he stayed on the sled. Once in a while, he would fall out into the soft snow. As Grandma laughed, Lionel did too. After an hour of play, he knew just what to expect. Truly, what our little monkeys see, they do. By imitation, right responses are learned. Lionel learned that sledding is fun.

We want our infants to learn to look for the joy of hearing and heeding adult instructions, and this is a fun way to learn. How much easier it is to inculcate the right thoughts, feelings, impressions, and inclinations at the very beginning of life rather than have to unlearn and relearn simultaneously at a later age.

Other models

As parents, we have both the privilege and the responsibility to model a Christlike character for our infants and toddlers. Then the "monkey see, monkey do" principle will be a positive influence. Through us, our children may learn to associate with Christ, who is their very best Friend and Influence.

In addition to us, our little ones will associate to a greater or lesser degree with their siblings, their grandparents, their cousins, aunts and uncles, and their peers in or out of church. On top of that, the things they view on TV, hear on the radio, or see in town all have their affect on their developing minds. A parent needs to evaluate all of these influences honestly with God—not sentimentally. Consider the effect of these different influences upon the character and habits of your impressible child. Then prayerfully decide how to deter the negative associations or improve the less than ideal ones. Remember that bad habits are more easily learned than good ones and are harder to give up as well.

"Bang Bang" Billy charged through the front door with his six-gun blazing. Three-year-old Timid Tommy watched wide eyed as Billy pointed his toy gun at the dog and yelled *"Bang, bang!* You're dead!" Billy was only visiting for an hour, but he used that hour to shoot everything in sight. Tommy had never seen such a thing before, but monkey see, monkey do. He picked up his hammer and imitated "Bang Bang" Billy with his six-gun.

The next morning at breakfast, Tommy pointed his spoon at his mother exclaiming, *"Bang, bang!"* After breakfast, he played shooting the dog dead, his toys had to fall over, and he became obsessed with shooting his father, mother, or little brother with any object he had in his hands at the time. He'd say, "Shoot you dead," and want the person to fall over.

Mother and Father quickly realized how detrimental and totally consuming this new game had become. Tommy wasn't interested in any other play and seemed fascinated with the idea of violence. They were amazed at how quickly and strongly this habit had taken root. It took weeks of communing with God and applying creative ideas to redirect Tommy's thoughts. A three-year-old mind has a hard time grasping the difference between target practice and ungodly violence. Timid Tommy had to be taken to God many times to find the power to replace his new habit with a positive one.

This experience was a rather startling wake-up call to Tommy's parents to guard his association carefully, while giving him the very best in themselves and Christ. This is the challenge facing all parents today—to give our children the best, while guarding them from all the rest. This raises a logical question in the mind of many parents: what about day care?

THE LONE EMBRACE
A SPECIAL WORD OF ENCOURAGEMENT FOR SINGLE PARENTS

If our infants and toddlers behold violence, they will become violent. If our infants and toddlers are handled roughly, they will become rough. If our infants and children are belittled and learn to cower for survival, they will either learn to do the same to others weaker than they are or they will go through life feeling crushed. What a child beholds molds his character just as surely as an apple falls to the ground. It is just as sure as the law of gravity. By beholding we become changed into that image. If you don't like the negative, un-Christlike behavior in your child, then evaluate what he is seeing in you, in your home, and in the lives of others he spends time with. Come to Jesus and let the changes in your child begin with you.

As your infants and toddlers behold a parent under God's control, they will take in your calmness and self-control as it is in Jesus. They will see love, joy, peace, patience, longsuffering, gentleness, goodness, and a proper faith as well. They will be beholding Christ through you. You cannot do this of yourself, but you can in Him. Then the beholding law can work to change your child into the image of Christ. Isn't this what you want? If you let Him, God can make your choices real through the power in His Holy Spirit working through you.

The "monkey see, monkey do" principle will draw your infant or toddler to Christ, as he or she beholds the true Christ through you.

Landon shows the power of "monkey see, monkey do" to Nathan in play and in life.

Chapter 7
Day Care Destruction

Thus saith the LORD; Cursed be the man that trusteth in man, and maketh flesh his arm, and whose heart departeth from the LORD.
—Jeremiah 17:5

Paula was a young mother on her way to day care to drop off her three-month-old Lily for the first time. Today was the day Paula planned to return to the workforce. She had extended her six weeks of maternity leave, but financial difficulties had come up. Her husband worked hard to pay the bills, but it seemed that there was never quite enough to make ends meet. Paula and her husband had decided it was time for Paula to go back to her nursing job, but what would they do with Lily? They had no family nearby, and none of the members of their church were in a position to babysit Lily. As they considered their options, Paula's friends encouraged her to leave Lily at a small day care center near the hospital. Paula had some reservations, but her friends minimized her worries by reminding her that a lot of parents use the day care option and find it works just fine. "Don't be so overprotective," they chided. "In fact, it will be good for Lily to be with other children. It will help her to socialize properly."

As Paula entered the Crossroads Day Care Center that morning, she paused a moment to observe what was going on. The atmosphere was anything but peaceful. A toddler, who appeared to be about three years old, was screaming in one corner, clinging to his mother's leg. His mother was trying to calm him down so she could leave.

Paula noticed a middle-aged woman in the center of the room, holding a crying eighteen-month-old while a fearful three-year-old clung to the woman's leg, as the mother of the two children explained their specials needs. "That must be the lady I spoke to on the phone; the one who is in charge here," thought Paula. "Her name is Sherry. She looks nice. But how in the world does she keep up with all these kids? She told me that two of her helpers moved away, and she's looking for more qualified help. How does she manage in the meantime?"

The door behind Paula opened, and a little tornado entered. A sassy four-year-old girl shoved her way past Paula, calling back instructions to her mother and two-year-old brother. She wore a grungy pair of pants that clashed with her shirt. "Get over here," she commanded her little brother. When he ignored her, she got his attention by slugging him in the stomach. Her mother left quickly amidst his cries of protest. She appeared relieved to leave her little ones behind.

Just then, a five-year-old boy came out of the bathroom. Paula smiled at him and thought, "He looks like a nice boy!" Her first impression changed when the little guy caught sight of the sassy little girl, screwed up his face in an ugly sneer, and began to hurl insults at her. As he turned, Paula saw he was wearing a T-shirt with a picture of a ferocious cartoon animal—it seemed to fit his character. He ran over to the table where the little girl was coloring and pushed her over. He tried to grab the coloring book and crayons she was using, but she rallied quickly and shoved him back.

There were several choices of coloring books and boxes of crayons, but both children wanted the same set. Sherry was still trying to comfort the clingy three-year-old and ignored the argument. Soon the little boy had the girl pinned to the floor, and she relinquished the coveted items to him. She sullenly retreated from the battle scene, but resentment simmered in her eyes.

Paula was rather disheartened. Was it really a good idea to leave her precious little one here in the midst of all this turmoil? She was about to leave with Lily, when the door behind her opened once again. This time, a mother walked in with three children who seemed different from the rest. They were nicely dressed and well behaved. They said Goodbye sweetly to their mother and settled down to playing quietly by themselves.

Paula brightened. Maybe this day care idea could work after all. Maybe her Lily would grow up like these nice children. She approached Sherry and put her precious Lily into her arms. As she headed for the door, she thought, "Sherry really does seem like a sweet lady. She probably knows how to handle all these children better than their own parents do." And with confidence in the Crossroads Day Care Center, Paula left for work.

What would you do?

What would you do if you were Paula? Would you settle for the most convenient option regardless of the long-term effects on Lily? Would you wish you didn't have to leave Lily there, but fear offending the day care provider and disagreeing with your friends? Or would you consider that God has a thousand solutions for your situation and go to Him to find just one? Would you invest the time needed to determine God's will for you?

Many parents hope against all odds that their child will be the exception to the "monkey see, monkey do" principle and grow up unscathed by the chaos of negative association. Is that you? Is such hope realistic? Is this the influence you want for your child?

The decision Paula was making was not an easy one. Like Paula, many of us make choices based on the expectations of others or our own convenience rather than making the effort and taking the time to know God's will. Many of us don't grasp how much God wants to be involved in our lives and how He is able to save us from a lot of detours and heartaches. God can help us out of the ditch when we go off the road, but how much better to stay on the road in the first place!

Every parent needs to seriously ask himself or herself some honest questions: "What is motivating my decision? Is this God's will or mine? Am I driven by timidity or fear of a conflict? Is the good of my child in the light of eternity my main concern, or am I settling for a short-term solution with long-term problems?" I urge you to make a commitment to seek God and follow Him rather than the dictates of your circumstances, emotions, and the expectations of yourself and others. This is the only safe course of action.

Who will rule?

In the beginning, God created everything. He is the Source of life. He is the Fountain of wisdom. He is the Boss. We were made to depend on Him for all that we need and to submit to His authority. Life works well when we do that. When we don't, we are headed for trouble. Our biggest problem since the Fall is that we have a tendency to usurp God's authority in our own lives and in the lives of others. Instead of letting God be God, we try to become our own gods. Or we let other people take the place in our lives that only God should hold.

When a friend, parent, spouse, pastor, or anyone else gives us advice, we are to take it as just that—advice. We have the privilege of taking that advice to God and seeking His will. Sometimes He uses the good advice of someone else to help us. Other times, He will ask us to go directly against that advice. The final decision of what we do rests between God and us.[1] We must know and do God's will even if it runs directly against our ideas or the ideas of well-meaning people.

But how do you know God's leading? How do you sort out God's direction from the opinions of others?[2] Let me explain.

God has created us with what I call *higher powers* and *lower powers*. He made the *higher powers* of reason, intellect, and conscience to rule over the *lower powers* of our emotions, inclinations, desires, and passions. Satan tries to pervert the higher powers by exciting and misusing the lower powers. God works through our higher powers—our conscience—to keep the lower powers pure and wholesome. Satan works through the lower powers, which are our feelings and emotions, to compel us to obey them. These are calculated to overrule reason. But God's still, small voice appeals to our higher powers and leaves us free to choose whom we will obey. We cooperate with one or the other.

Our reason, intellect, and conscience *in harmony with the Word of God* are the primary avenues through which God guides and directs our lives. He also speaks to us through nature, the impressions of His Spirit, and providential leadings. So, we need to learn the many facets of God's voice, knowing also that not every thought is from God. Some thoughts are our own. Satan plants others in our minds. We must learn to judge our thoughts according to the standard

---

1. Acts 5:29.

2. See chapter 4 in both of my books *Parenting by the Spirit* and *Parenting Your Child by the Spirit* for greater detail in discerning the voice of God.

of the Word of God, the Spirit of God, and the life and character of Christ in order to distinguish the voice of God to our conscience from other voices or thoughts. Our conscience led of God, according to the Word of God is our *higher powers* that leave us free to choose.

When Satan stirs up our *lower powers* of strong emotion, destructive desires, hurtful habits, and lustful passions, we feel compelled and driven to obey them. Often we don't recognize that we have another choice. Our responses to the lower powers are often automatic, and as a result, we find ourselves outside of God's will, wondering how we got there. When Satan is leading us, we are independent of God.

A Christian must learn to follow Christ instead of the lower nature. We must learn to be fully dependent upon God and come to distinguish His inaudible voice through our judgment. Our higher powers, led of God, are to rule over our lower powers.

As Paula stood there at the entrance of the Crossroads Day Care Center, she was disturbed by the behavior of the majority of the children. God was speaking to her through her conscience, which registers right and wrong. She was rightfully uncomfortable with what she saw.

But while God was pointing out real concerns to her, Satan was stirring up emotions calculated to mislead her logic. She feared offending Sherry, disagreeing with her friends, and crossing her husband. She couldn't see any other solution to her financial problems. Her reason was quieted by the appearance of three better-behaved children. She didn't stop to think that this might have been a one-time visit for them.

Paula sensed she should consult with God, but that felt awkward and would take time and effort. She chose to believe what was convenient at the time—not necessarily what was right or best for Lily. She soothed her troubled conscience with the lying thought that Lily would be like those nice children—not the others.

With one tiny positive against great odds of the negative, Paula trusted the day care provider in spite of all she saw. Her lower powers ruled over her higher powers. Against a wealth of evidence that God allowed her to see, she chose to believe that the "monkey see, monkey do" principle would be overruled in the case of Lily.

What Paula didn't understand is that we are either serving God or Satan. There is no middle ground. If we are not consciously consulting with God, studying to know the truth, and searching to know His will, we are, by default, self-managed, and Satan leads us in detours away from God. Satan takes control of every mind that is not decidedly under the control of the spirit of God.

Many of us parents see the destructiveness of the world. We seek refuge in our churches and communities only to discover they are often not much better. So we accept the wrong as Okay, as this mother did. Some mothers accept the world's way out of necessity or frustration. Others simply close their eyes to the obvious results. What will happen to Lily? What will she observe day in and day out at the Crossroads Day Care Center? Will she imitate the quiet girls in the corner or the noisy, angry, outspoken ones?

"Monkey see, monkey do" holds true

For the next year, Lily spent a minimum of nine hours a day, three to five days a week, at the Crossroads Day Care Center. She had few waking hours with her parents at home. The day care center had the greatest influence on Lily's character. Remember, this is the period of her life where she is learning 50 percent of everything she will ever learn. What she learns here will mold her value system for life and her responses to trials. She is like a little sponge—absorbing emotions, voice inflections, attitudes, and impulses—without the filter of reason. What did her eyes see, her ears hear, and her heart feel?

Lily saw, heard, and felt unrestrained displays of anger almost daily. She observed the other children solve their problems through quarreling and violence. She learned to hit and throw temper tantrums to get her way. God says, "Ye have heard that it was said by them of old time, Thou shalt not kill; and whosoever shall kill shall be in danger of the judgment: But I say unto you, That whosoever is angry with his brother without a cause shall be in danger of the judgment."[3] The arguing, combative spirit that predominated in the characters of many of the children Lily associated with day after day brought her great discomfort and instilled in her the need to fend for herself to protect herself from being hurt.

Lily also experienced the other extreme, as she saw the more sensitive children withdrawing like whipped puppies when the stronger children beat them down. She watched the clinging, fearful child struggling with self-destructive thoughts. This response can be as destructive as outward passion. Lily learned that another way to avoid facing problems is to disconnect or withdraw into a turtle shell.

An overworked caregiver took care of Lily. She tried heroically to maintain a semblance of order, but had to let a lot of misbehavior slide by uncorrected simply because she could spread herself only so thin. A pat of butter covers one slice of bread quite nicely, but not five pieces of bread! She was looking for qualified workers to employ, but didn't have sufficient staff at the time. The lack of correction taught Lily that disobedience is acceptable and misbehavior is the norm. Sherry often became frustrated and vainly tried to stifle her irritable disposition. Lily soaked up these lessons as well. They were like seeds planted in the fertile soil of her mind. The continued exposure to these things watered and warmed those little seeds until they began to germinate.

Lily was often left to cry and cry, because the other children's needs were a higher priority to deal with than hers. Diaper changes were delayed. Meals and naps were not regular. A feeling of insecurity began to take root in Lily's heart. She couldn't trust that her legitimate needs were going to be seen as important

---

3. Matthew 5:21, 22.

and cared for promptly. Satan used these circumstances to plant a terrible lie deep into Lily's subconscious mind—that she was not loved and wanted. The lack of spiritual instruction in the center left Lily uneducated in connecting with God and untrained in the power to live above her wrong feelings, emotions, and thoughts. And the repetition of insecure responses in her mind and heart deepened her habits of insecurity.

Over the first six months, Paula noticed changes in Lily's disposition. She seemed more irritable, but Paula didn't see that as significant. Besides, Paula wrestled with an underlying feeling of guilt over the situation, and this led her to pamper Lily's outbursts. She had so little time with Lily that she didn't want to spend it correcting Lily's peevishness and teaching her better ways to respond. The demands of being a working mom left Paula little time to pray, study, and seek God. So, Satan's lying thoughts continued to lead her. Her lower powers controlled the direction of her life. Oh, she prayed for God to protect her little one, but she didn't have the time to work with God to answer her own prayers. As a result, Lily's deeper needs were neglected at home, as well as at the day care center. Her insecurity continued to grow silently.

By Lily's first birthday, she no longer wanted to cuddle with her mother. She pushed away from Paula. She was not interested in playing with Mother on those rare moments Paula was available. The lessons she had learned over the past nine months were now coming out very clearly in her selfish nature. By eighteen months, she was short-tempered, irritable, disobedient, and independent from her parents. The weed seeds, planted so consistently by the influence of the other children, began to sprout above ground now. But Satan continued to feed Paula more lying thoughts. "This is normal behavior. All children go through different stages. She'll outgrow it. I just need to be patient with her." Those character weeds put down deeper roots amid these misconceptions.

Does a garden outgrow its weeds? No! The weeds must be uprooted and replaced with beneficial plants. A character garden will never outgrow selfishness and insecurity. Those weeds must be identified, uprooted, and replaced with love, obedience, and trust. Unless Lily's parents begin to operate on a different program, the direction of Lily's life is set. As she grows, these negative traits will grow with her. She has been trained in the service of Satan and self rather than in the service of God and right. She has been taught to believe that she must obey her feelings and emotions, and Satan leads her onward and forward to bring discord into her home. Satan is all too successful in ruining our homes through the influence of our untrained infants and toddlers.

As doggy sees, doggy does

If you place a mild-mannered puppy in a kennel with vicious dogs, what kind of dog will he grow up to be? At first, he may cower in fear, try to run away, or ignore the other dogs. But eventually, he will have to learn to fight to survive. As doggy sees, doggy does. With time and repetition, he will tussle, fight for his food, bite when others get in his way, and develop a vicious disposition just like the dogs he runs with. By beholding we become changed. If you put that same puppy into a kennel with well-trained dogs with even dispositions, what will he grow up to be like? The answer is obvious. As doggy sees, doggy does.

So too for our infants and toddlers—their environment will mold their ideas of what is normal. Either good or evil can become the normal reference point for the mind of the child. Satan works very diligently to gain the advantage during these important early years because he wants to develop negative character qualities that will go with the child for life. He wants parents to delay dealing with their infants until it seems too late to correct them without arduous efforts. Then he will discourage parents by making it seem that it is too hard and too late to turn the tide. Why even try? So, parents, beware of the environment you trust your infants and toddlers to. Be honest with yourselves about its ramifications and long-term results. We can connect to God and be empowered to change at any age.

Do you want your heritage, your precious child, to be Satan's slave? Of course not! Then see that your child's environment is as godly as you can make it. Allow him to behold no evil that will plant the seeds of insecurity and anger. Make a covenant with God to do all in your power to prevent Satan from having your child!

We have the privilege of giving our offspring the best and guarding them from all the rest so that their characters can be strong for God instead of self and Satan! What environment will you choose for your little ones? Will you choose to drop your child off at Rug Rats Ranch, Wild Kitty Day Care, or Jungle-O-Rama? Or will you seek God's direction regarding the very best alternative for you in your unique situation?

Cowbird parenting

Are you familiar with cowbirds? They have a style of parenting that is unusual among birds but seems to be growing in popularity among people. Cowbirds don't build their own nests because their work of gathering insects for food keeps them on the move too much and tending to a nest full time would be inconvenient for them. So they prefer to presume upon other birds to build a nest and raise their young. They want someone else to do the taxing work of raising and feeding their offspring. They watch another bird's nest, and when the eggs are laid and the parent is gone, the cowbird lays one of its own eggs in it.

However, there are extreme hazards to this parenting style. Robins have been known to be intolerant of cowbird eggs. They recognize their eggs and push them out of the nest. Gray catbirds will peck the egg until it is destroyed. Other species simply build a new nest floor over all the eggs and lay another clutch.

When I found a babysitter for my firstborn and returned to work, I wrestled daily with the idea that someone else was molding the character of my child. The training they gave would not be *my* views and concepts. They would not likely care for Matthew the way I would. I knew his basic physical needs would be met, but few babysitters are equipped or dedicated enough to go beyond that and deal with character training. They have their own life to live. They are usually like hirelings—they don't have the interest that a shepherd has for his sheep. For most people, watching your child is a job, and they will get by with doing the least they can. It took God many months to get my attention and make me aware that He wanted me to come home, simplify my life, and raise my own children.

There's another side to cowbird parenting. Many birds don't reject the cowbird's egg. They incubate it and hatch it along with their own. Over 140 species of birds have been known to raise young cowbirds. Two major problems commonly occur for the foster family. The cowbird's incubation period is often one day shorter than that of the host species, so it hatches first—cowbird advantage number one. Advantage number two is that it is larger than the host chicks. Its mouth is bigger and reaches up higher than its adopted siblings, thus enabling it to get the majority of the food the parents provide for their family. As a result, the host's offspring are poorly nourished and sometimes even die. As the cowbird grows, it physically crowds the smaller birds out of the nest.

Some mothers I know try to stay at home to care for their own children by opening their own day care service or by taking in foster children. They have big hearts and wonderful intentions, but in most cases that I have seen, the needs of so many children make it next to impossible for them to provide the character training their own children need. And often, the children they care for in addition to their own have big needs! The mothers become like the little songbird trying to care for the large cowbird chick, as well as her own. A supermom couldn't handle all that is on her plate. The children may be physically cared for, but their emotional needs and character training are simply crowded out for lack of time or energy. These mothers need God for balance.

Let's not be "cowbird parents." Let's take full responsibility for our young. If we cannot be at-home parents, we are intelligent enough, resourceful enough, and God-led enough to find alternatives in order to raise our child to follow God and not the ways of Satan and the world. God is big enough, and we can turn to Him for help. We must let God be in charge, seek His will for our family, and not follow another's expectations.

A blueprint for parents

The book of Deuteronomy is one I have found to be extremely helpful in the process of parenting by the Spirit. I've pointed out some of its lessons in chapter 2 of this book, but I encourage you to read it for yourself, one chapter at a time, and list the obvious lessons it teaches you. Sit quietly before God. Ask God to help you make practical what it's telling you. You'll be surprised at how much you can learn being God-led. Go over it again and again, and you will learn more each time you do.

You will see God as your Leader, guiding you from the land of bondage to the Land of Canaan. As a parent, you are to be to your children what Moses was to Israel. Like Moses, we must recognize that our children are the property of God and seek Him at every step to know and do His will. Only in this way can we become the faithful, visible leaders God intends us to be for our infants and toddlers. Don't fear this. You will discover that God is there for you to give you a better alternative than "day care destruction." We will discuss some of those possible alternatives later in this chapter, but the main point I want to communicate is that God understands your situation and your needs. Nothing is too hard for Him. The difficulties you find overwhelming don't overwhelm Him. Make it your first concern to put Him in charge and seek to know and do what He directs you to do.

He is a communicating God. Give Him your time and your ear, and He will direct you as He did Israel of old. He wants to be our God, and He wants us to be His people. Israel was instructed not to fear the enemy—the giants in the land. Perhaps you are facing giants of financial trouble, marital discord, or sickness. Maybe tyrants of selfishness, appetite, anger, bitterness, or lust rule in your life. I see a strong parallel to the giants of misbehavior that are in our children's characters through mismanagement, inheritance, the principle of "monkey see, monkey do," and the cultivation of wrong habits. God wants to lead you in battle with all of these giants. The book of Deuteronomy can give you practical ideas for how He does this. It can teach you how to cooperate with His work in your life. Trusting in Him, you can face any giant He asks you to face.

This book also applies the Ten Commandments to daily life. Here is recorded the instructions we are to give to our children regarding what to think, how to serve God, and how to respond to trials.

As parents, we are to teach these Ten Commandments to our children diligently. We are to talk of them when we sit down, when we walk about, when we go to bed in the evening, and when we get up in the morning.[4] In other words, God's principles are to become a part of everything that we do. All day long, we have the privilege of communicating with God. As He instructs us how to serve Him instead of our flesh, we can find solutions that work. We can reflect His character with the proper balance of mercy and justice to our infants and toddlers. In turn, we can help them develop habits of turning to God, seeking His will, and obeying His promptings. Under God, we can teach our infants that they do not have to obey their wrong feelings and emotions. They can trust us in the place of God in these beginning years. This is leading our children into the Land of Canaan—into Christ—that they may learn to walk with Him.

This is God's desire for our children. Is it your desire also? If this sounds like too high of a calling and you would rather find an easier task, you can ask God to bring your desires into agreement with His. Cooperate with Him in spite of your feelings, and in time, you will find your highest satisfaction in desiring what God desires.

---

4. Deuteronomy 6:7.

God is able and willing to implant His desires within you. Satan is at hand to insinuate doubts through the seemingly insurmountable difficulties and challenges that you face. Perhaps you don't have an ideal situation and you don't see how you can possibly be at home to give your child a better experience. We'll examine some different alternatives in the next section, but the most important thing you can do is to trust God and seek to understand and follow His solutions *for your difficulty, today*!

Creative alternatives

Let's replay Paula's story with a different twist.

As Paula stood there at the entrance of the Crossroads Day Care Center, she saw with her eyes, heard with her ears, and felt with her heart the negative influences Lily would be subjected to. A still, small Voice called to her heart, *"Don't leave your precious Lily here. I have other options for you. 'Seek ye first the kingdom of God, and His righteousness; and all these things shall be added unto you.' "*[5] Other voices clamored for her attention. "Don't be such a worrywart. Everyone does it, and it works out just fine. It will be too much trouble any other way. It's just not worth it. Your friends won't understand and neither will your husband."

She paused and then made her decision, "Sherry, I've changed my mind. I won't be leaving Lily here today." She turned around and walked out the door with Lily in her arms. As soon as she got home, she called her supervisor and explained that she needed more time to think through her options and that she wouldn't be coming back to work right away. She expected to lose her job for good, but her supervisor was very understanding. "Just let me know what you decide, Paula."

Paula sat by her phone, wondering what to do next. Smiling at Lily, she announced, "Mama is not sure how we're going to make ends meet, Lily, but I do know that you come first. Let's go for a walk and see if God gives me any ideas."

Bundling up Lily in her stroller, Paula set off for a walk in the park. "God, I don't know where to go from here, but I sensed that You did not want me to leave Lily at the day care center. We might lose our house if we can't make the payments, and You know about the other bills piling up. What can we do?"

As Paula walked and talked with God, ideas began to form in her mind. She saw specific areas where she and her husband could lower their standard of living and still be very comfortable. God gave her a view of the emptiness of pursuing the "American Dream," while neglecting the things in life that really count. She began to feel that nothing could compensate for the opportunity of raising her Lily to know a personal God.

She would be willing to move into a less expensive house, make do with just one car for their family, simplify her food preparation, use less expensive groceries, discontinue their cable and Internet services, and cancel her magazine

---

5. Matthew 6:33.

subscriptions. She could do with fewer new clothes, and they could go tent camping for their vacation instead of taking that trip to Hawaii they had been hoping for. Some of these thoughts left a lump in Paula's throat, but she decided to trust God. He wouldn't ask her to part with anything she really needed to be happy.[6]

Paula and her husband did make many of these changes. They stopped Satan running them ragged on the treadmill of life and made time for the really important things of life—relationships with God, each other, and their children. While they were in the process of simplifying their possessions, Paula had to work part time. She was able to schedule some shifts during time that her husband could be available to take care of Lily. When he was not available, God provided a grandmother across town that would love Lily without spoiling her.

Lily developed from a happy, secure infant into a bubbly, inquisitive toddler. She loved her parents and responded positively to them. As Paula reflected back on the day she almost left Lily to "day care destruction," she thanked God for showing her another way. No amount of money can compare with a child who is growing in God's ways.

Perhaps you *must* work outside the home. Then simplify your life to the irreducible minimum so that you can give your best in the morning and in the evening to your child and family, and let God lead you to the best alternative there is for the daily care and raising of your child.

Ask God to guide you to a godly neighbor, a responsible youth, a grandmother, or a church member, who has your religious ideas, to be with your child and raise them much like you would while you are away making an income. Simplify your life to reduce the number of hours you need to be away working. Put your children at the top of your list of priorities—not at the bottom by default. Give them the very best that you, under God, can give them.

If day care is truly your best option, carefully and prayerfully investigate a number of centers before making your selection. Make sure that your children will not be subjected to physical, or emotional, or spiritual abuse, ridicule, profanity, humiliation, godlessness, uncleanliness, favoritism, or character demoralization. The day care should be cheerful and brightly colored. It should offer a variety of wholesome things to do, such as coloring, finger painting, puzzles, pictures to look at, singing, etc., and it should follow a predictable schedule. Is God respected? Does the staff pray at mealtimes? Does the center have a story time in which Bible stories are regularly read? In addition, the center should be adequately staffed with caring adults who are pleasant, even tempered, and cheerful, and who put the comfort and safety of the children ahead of making a profit.

---

6. To learn more about simple living, see chapter 3, "A Life of Simplicity," in *Escape to God* by Jim Hohnberger. Also see the appendix at the end of this book for resources about money management.

Discuss their philosophy about child rearing, training, and discipline with the child care director(s). Pay attention to the staff—their attitudes and how they act toward the children. Also take note of the facility and the parents of the other children. Make sure there is a balance between learning activities, indoor play, outdoor time (during good weather), and quiet time. Observe the attitudes and activities of the children. Do they seem happy? Do they seem to get along with the other children?

Minimize as much as possible the time your children need to be away from you. Give them as much of yourself as you possibly can during the hours you are not at work—even if it means saying "No" to other good things, such as church work, evangelism, or community service. Work with the hearts of your children under God's direction so that the parenting pyramid stays open in all directions.

May God bless you as you seek to give your children the very best and guard them from all the rest.

THE LONE EMBRACE
A SPECIAL WORD OF ENCOURAGEMENT FOR SINGLE PARENTS

The work of the single parent is often daunting. Trying to be both father and mother while working full time to make ends meet can zap the energies of the hardiest soul. It may seem to you that day care is your only option, but you fear the negative impact on your children. If you seek God and consult with Him for what course you should take, He will direct your steps. He can fill the gap that the lack of a partner has left in your life. He will be a Parent to your children if you will make Him the Principal of your home. You can assume the role of the underteacher so that He can show you how to make the unseen God real and tangible to your children from infancy. Even our infants and toddlers can be under the shadow of the Almighty if we bring them there.

As your heavenly Husband and Father, God can show you alternatives to day care centers that go far beyond the few alternatives I've suggested here. God has many options. Lean on Him and do your part to the best of your ability. Parenting and spiritual education is not a passive work that just happens. It requires planning and prioritizing as well as energy, time, and organization. God will direct you through His Holy Spirit. Learn to talk with Him as with a Friend. You may not be rich in money, but you will be rich in faith, trust, and children who grow up to know and love you and God. There is no greater occupation on this earth than raising our children to follow God. He will enable you to do the right when you let Him lead you!

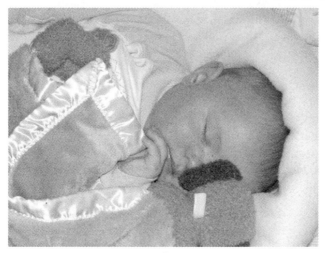

Nathan.
What will we do, led of God, to protect their innocence?

Chapter 8
Not Too Young to Learn

Abide in me, and I in you. As the branch cannot bear fruit of itself,
except it abide in the vine; no more can ye, except ye abide in me.
—John 15:4

Have you decided that you want to connect your infant or toddler to Christ? Do you like the idea of Christ working within the heart of your infant to re-create him so that he obeys from the inside out? Are you searching for more practical ways to connect your child to Christ? In this chapter, we'll focus on how to connect your infant to Jesus, and in the next chapter, we'll talk about the toddler. We'll be building heavily on the concept of the parenting pyramid that was introduced in chapter 2.

I am not promoting sheer behavior modification or a method that will make your child obey you. Mere methodology leaves humanity in charge and will always fail to transform the heart. When we do this, we rely on our own wisdom, judgment, and discernment alone.

The concept that I want to continue to convey to you is that God is very real, very attentive to you, and very available to help you. He can do what you cannot do—change your disposition or your child's disposition from the inside out. When you recognize Him continually as the Source of your life, your direction, your wisdom, and your strength, you will have grasped the essential, fundamental principle of parenting by the Spirit. Walking with God in a practical way prepares you to train your infant and toddler to walk with Him. As parents, we may be taught of God[1] how to connect our infants to Jesus, as the branch is connected to the Vine, so that they can produce the genuine fruits of self-control and self-denial.

The first skill that must be mastered in order to walk with God is accepting that He is in charge—not you. It is learning to know His will in contrast with your own and yielding to do His will in spite of your feelings in another direction. This means learning to filter all your thoughts and purposes through God before acting upon them. This experience will deepen the further you go along the Christian pathway.

As parents gently but firmly establish the fact that they are in charge, rather than their infants, they are establishing a vital foundation. When the infant experiences the parents' authority as safe, nurturing, and positive, he is prepared to willingly accept God's authority as he grows older. As parents train their infants to yield to their instructions and exercise self-control, they are giving their little

---

1. John 6:45.

ones foundational experiences for surrendering to their heavenly Father. As parents teach their children to trust and obey them, they are giving them important lessons in trusting and obeying God.

When God impresses you with a plan of action to take with your little one and you implement it, He will be working with you to change the disposition of your child from the inside out. A discipline given under the instruction of Christ will bring far different results than will the same discipline given independently of Christ. There is no power in the disciplinary method in and of itself. The power is found in Christ who stands behind the method that He is directing you to use. The branch is connected to the Vine, receiving life. The parent is Jesus' instrument, but it is God that creates the changes in disposition.

Swaddling Susanna

Little Susanna, one month old, was fussing. She was Mother's first baby, and Mother still felt a bit awkward about caring for her. Mother checked her diaper and then cuddled her. Susanna had been fed just a little while ago, and it wasn't yet nap time. What did she need? Mother turned to God for a solution. It seemed odd to cry out to God—this was a new idea for her. She was uncertain of His voice, because it is not audible as she wished it were. Still cuddling the fussing Susanna, Mother prayed and waited quietly for God to speak to her conscience, appeal to her reason, guide her with Scripture or an impression from the Holy Spirit, or whatever method He might choose to use. It seemed to her like a long time—perhaps five minutes. An idea entered her mind, and she decided to try it. Why not? She didn't feel any certainty that this was from God. But it seemed to be worth a try.

Laying Susanna down, she wrapped her in the snug swaddling fashion she had seen at the newborn nursery in the hospital. This, too, was awkward, and again she cried out to God for help. She wrapped her daughter the best she knew, and it looked quite nice. Then she rocked her little Susanna while singing some sweet tune, and quickly the infant settled down. Because of the positive outcome, Mother concluded that this was how God was leading her. Everything good comes from God, so she thanked God for His help. Setting Susanna on the couch in the living room, Mother finished folding the laundry. Susanna was happy, alert, and content. "Being snuggly safe must feel good to my Susanna," Mother concluded and used this method again in similar circumstances. It helped for a couple of months.

Some mothers find snug wrapping comforts their infants. Others swaddle them in a backpack or a front pack. All these can be successful. The infant is safe, close, and often happy. God is willing to help you in the management of your infant. He is there for you. Why not cry out to Him and begin to understand His voice to your mind, heart, and soul?

The seeds sown in infancy by the careful, God-fearing mother will become trees of righteousness that will blossom and bear fruit. The seeds of submission, obedience, and self-control are vital lessons to learn in infancy. God is in this process of training, and as it is repeated, the child settles into yielding and trusting Mother more and more. Before the child is old enough to reason, he may be taught to yield submission to Mother.

Few parents begin early enough to teach their children to obey. Many cater to their child's will for the first two or three years; they withhold discipline or instruction, thinking the child too young to be taught obedience. But all this time, self is growing strong in the little being. Every day makes the parents' task of gaining control more difficult.

Little lessons bring big blessings

Barbara's mother knew in theory that she was to start training early, but wondered, "When do I start, and how do I start?" Barbara turned one month old and then two. Her mother knew the value of sticking to a good schedule, but she sensed there was more she could be doing. She asked several friends who were mothers what they thought. They advised, "Don't worry so much. Just relax." "Just wait until she starts eating solids." "When she starts walking, begin to train her." Mother tried to "relax," but in her personal time with God she felt pricked by her conscience that she should be training her daughter now. Still, she didn't know what that meant in practical terms.

When Barbara was three months old, God led Mother to her first opportunity to discipline in a new and different way under His generalship. Barbara had been crying for no apparent reason. Mother knew it wasn't her colic cry or her hunger cry or her tired cry. As she communed with God for wisdom, she had the thought that this cry was unnecessary. So, she blew in Barbara's face gently and then smiled at her saying, "You don't need to cry, Barbara! Mommy is right here. Mommy loves you!" Barbara didn't like being blown on! It made her catch her breath in surprise, and she stopped crying and studied Mother's face.

Momentarily, Mother felt she had done something terrible and thought Barbara wouldn't understand. "Lord, was that Okay?" she asked as she continued smiling and speaking soothingly to Barbara. She sensed that it was all right, and so with the next occurrence of needless crying, she blew in crying Barbara's face again. In a matter of a few days, Mother noticed that Barbara quit crying in this manner. Simple repetition was training Barbara to restrain this unnecessary cry. This was good!

We may not know the thoughts or response mechanisms at work in our little ones, but God does. Often simple little measures in a Christlike spirit can begin to train them in the way of self-control and self-denial. And Jesus is there, directing and teaching the class through the mother, and the results are wonderful. Doesn't it feel good to not be alone, Mother? Isn't it good to have a Helper this near for us? Yes it is! And God loves to bless us with His wisdom and our little ones with power to follow our directions.

Barbara loved her bath time and raised cries of protest when Mother took her out of the tub. As Mother sent up a prayer to heaven,[2] she again thought to

---

2. Acts 9:6.

try blowing in Barbara's face. At times, this would stop her from crying, but it didn't always work—and this time it didn't.

"What now, Lord?" The idea came to give Barbara a gentle flick on her cheek to catch her attention. It worked this time. Barbara restrained her crying, and Mother comforted her, telling her she was all right. This was the beginning of training Barbara through very mild means under God that "No" means No. Barbara quickly learned. Mother was learning how to train her infant to form good habits and accept discipline. Mother was learning and changing too. She had to lay aside her harshness, anger, and all her negative and irritable approaches. God taught her to control her voice in talking to her dear little one. God gave her not only wisdom but also power.

Barbara, at six months or so, had a few tantrums in which she'd just cry and cry for no apparent reason. As Mother was seeking God on a daily basis, she brought this problem before Him; and one day a solution came to mind. The next time Barbara would not settle down, Mother picked her up to cuddle and pray with her. Then she sang some scripture songs. That did the job. Barbara settled down contentedly. Mother repeated this discipline whenever Barbara seemed out of control, and Barbara learned the habit of surrendering her out-of-control spirit to her mother. One day, the crying occurred while they were in the car. "Lord, what shall I do?" Mother thought of playing scripture songs on the CD player and tried it. Barbara stopped fussing and went to sleep. Other times, Mother would sing to her, and that worked as well. As you can see, our methods to restrain our children from selfishness change as they grow. We need God as our continuous Guide. How could God help you with your crying Barbara or Ben? They are not too young to learn.

Waking between sleep cycles

A sleep cycle for an infant typically lasts about forty-five minutes. The infant may wake up between these sleep cycles, but if you leave him alone to cry for a few minutes, he will usually go back for another cycle of sleep. Many parents get the baby up prematurely and then have to contend with the irritability of a tired baby.

One mother experimented with this idea and found that her baby was much happier when she returned to sleep. Mother also prayed with her infant at nap time and for her when she'd stir. In a short time, her infant would wake up after two cycles of sleep and be consistently happy. She would play contentedly in her crib until Mother came to get her. It was such a joy to hear her little talk and giggling noises through the baby monitor. For the most part, she did not complain when it was nap time or bedtime.

Building on this success, God impressed Mother to put a blanket over the baby's car seat when it was nap time as they were driving in the car. This was baby's signal that it was time to sleep. The baby learned quickly to yield to Mother's wishes and to sleep even when on the go. As the baby got older, Mother chose a favorite soft toy that she could hold only at nap time, and this was enough to tell her it was time to sleep. She complied so sweetly. Infants are not too young to learn.

You and God may formulate many different patterns that say it is time for a nap and that can help your infant be willing to nap on time at home or away. These habits lay the foundation of obedience. They may seem like small things, but they are not. Every good habit we instill and train with God's help is a building block of self-control and obedience. Every good or bad habit begins in a small way. God will teach you too!

Comfort for Clarissa

Two-month-old Clarissa was crying. Mother picked her up to comfort her. She checked her diaper, and it was dry. It wasn't mealtime or sleep time. "Hmm," thought Mother. "I wonder what is bothering Clarissa?"

"Lord," she prayed, "what would You have me to do? You are the Revealer of secrets. You know Clarissa's problem; please help me figure this out."

She didn't sense any obvious leading from God, but as she thought about possible causes of Clarissa's distress, gas came to her mind. She had read how exercising an infant's legs in a bicycle fashion, rubbing the tummy, or sometimes burping her could relieve gas pain. Mother began with burping. No results. Then she laid Clarissa on the bed and gently moved her legs back and forth. Intermittently, she would rub Clarissa's tummy and then work her legs again. At first, it didn't seem to help. Then, all of a sudden, Clarissa passed a lot of gas, and her crying began to settle down. Mother studied her little face. She still looked uncomfortable, so Mother continued to rub her tummy and exercise her legs. In a few more moments, Clarissa passed more gas, and then her face relaxed, and her crying turned into sweet cooing. Clarissa was easily comforted, and her trust grew. She experienced that when she cried, her mother would figure out just what she needed and fix it. Isn't that just the way God deals with us? God gave the solution to resolve the gas issue through Mother's reason, and He can do the same for you.

Reading to Riley

God gave Mother the idea to incorporate a daily story time for Riley when he was about six months old. Every day, right after his afternoon nap, Mother would snuggle him in the rocking chair and read him a story. He loved being close to Mother, listening to her voice, looking at the pictures, and "helping" her turn the pages. She started with about ten minutes of reading and gradually increased the time to about thirty minutes. It worked very well until Riley was about ten months old. He still loved the story time, but he tired of sitting still. He would squirm and fuss, wanting to get down to play with his toys.

The family made plans for a long flight, and Mother wanted Riley to learn to sit still so she could handle him on the airplane. She began each day by inviting God into their home during her personal time. She committed herself to train Riley without harshness or anger under God's leading. She brought Riley to God for His blessing and to connect Riley with the Power he needed to learn to submit and obey.

She continued their story times—focusing on connecting Riley to Christ. At first, Riley would wiggle and fuss. Mother patiently and consistently held him and prayed out loud for him. Riley began to learn that screaming and fussing didn't work. He began to yield and settle down. As Mother continued to work with him consistently, he learned to sit quietly with her for longer and longer periods of time. When the family finally took that long flight, Riley was well prepared and was known on the airplane as the "happy baby." In stark contrast to well-trained Riley was a little boy I'll call Rebel.

Rebel, the little rabble-rouser

Jim and I were in the airport waiting to board our plane when we first saw him. He was an eighteen-month-old bundle of self-will. His parents were trying to hold him on their laps, but he would have none of it. He wiggled down first from his mother's lap, then his father's lap. They made a weak attempt to restrain him and then surrendered to his stronger will. It appeared he was used to getting what he wanted. Free of his parents, he stood there sizing up the possibilities for entertainment.

Toddling toward the window, Rebel shoved his hands between two preschool-age girls, pushed them apart, and took his place gazing out the window. His parents watched him from their seats, but did not attempt to intervene. No instruction, no training in a better way, and no restraint of his wrong ways was given.

Soon losing interest at the window, Rebel ambled around the rows of seats filled with people. When he'd find an empty seat, he would climb up in it to look around from the higher vantage point. He had no thought of asking permission of the adult in the next chair or of showing any respect of the other person's space. His parents showed remarkable restraint of themselves until Rebel started to climb into the lap of a stranger. Then they came to pick him up. I think they planned to carry Rebel back to their seats, but he fussed so insistently that they relented, put him down, and allowed him to continue his quest for independence and fun.

What false concepts of happiness was Rebel learning to believe? What habits was he building? What training was being done? Would it result in an obedient and self-controlled individual, or would self-will be strengthened? Any act repeated is training. Rebel was being trained to follow self—"I want"—without restraint. He was doing his own will—not his parents' will. Who was in charge—Rebel or his parents? Shouldn't God be the One in charge, leading the parents who lead the child?

Rebel wandered aimlessly around the waiting area, roaming farther and farther away from his parents. His parents monitored his activities from afar, but avoided interfering for fear of his retaliation. I'm sure they sincerely believed they were doing what was best for Rebel, but they were slaves to their misconceptions. They didn't understand that there is a better way to bring their child happiness.

Then something interesting caught Rebel's eye. He walked up to a man who had a stroller containing a little boy just about Rebel's age. This little boy had a number of toys, and Rebel decided to share. He picked up a plastic truck and started to throw it across the aisle. The stranger father restrained his arm just in time and retrieved the truck. Rebel was not dissuaded. He grabbed a little teddy bear and started to do the same thing. The new father said, "No! You may not throw these toys!" He picked them all up and held them out of Rebel's reach. In retaliation, Rebel started pushing and pulling the stroller in jerky back-and-forth movements. The child in the stroller started to fuss, and the parents' annoyance was plain to see. The father put his foot on the stroller to hold it still. Rebel's parents watched but did nothing. Rebel saw one item the father had left in the stroller—a teething ring. He picked it up, put it in his mouth, and began to chew on it. The owner grabbed it from him, and Rebel turned to his parents, annoyed at the audacity of these people who crossed his wishes. Rebel's father, from about twenty feet away, motioned with his finger for Rebel to come to him. Instead of obeying, Rebel turned and stomped off in the opposite direction. Rebel's father continued to watch from a distance.

I stopped watching this scene, and a few minutes passed. Then my attention was drawn to the parents talking a bit anxiously. I noticed that Rebel was nowhere to be seen. Going in opposite directions, the parents set off to try to find their boy. Ten minutes later, Rebel's father came back with the little rabble-rouser in his arms. Rebel had a large package of candy in his hand. Whether the boy helped himself to the candy in a store nearby, or whether the father rewarded his being found, or whether the father used it to bribe him to come back with him, I'm not sure. But the results are the same in the character training of this boy. Is it love to reward ill behavior? No! Rewarding bad behavior guarantees more bad behavior, more self, more stubbornness, and this eventually wounds everyone involved!

This child was a by-product of the parents' training. What we do—and what we do not do—trains our children's characters to be either godly or selfish. It is not true love to nurture and cultivate disobedience, irritation, and self-will!

One lesson that parents need to repeat again and again is the lesson that the child is not to rule. He is not the master. The parents' wills and wishes are to be supreme. Inculcate this habit in the early years. Teach the child how to exercise self-control *as it is in Jesus*. Give him nothing for which he cries selfishly or unreasonably, even if your tender heart desires ever so much to give in. If the selfish will gains the upper hand even once, the child will expect to do it again. The second time, the battle will be more vehement. Poor Rebel is headed for a hard life, isn't he!

Turn the clock ahead

Let's look at the results under the program of child training Rebel's parents have begun. By the time Rebel reaches the age of four under this program, he will have developed no concept of boundaries. He will not understand or accept any restraint of his will or desire. Everybody's things are his things. There is no distinction of others' ownership. He will not have learned that you cannot touch or use other people's things without permission. His parents will be going crazy watching him every moment to keep him from stealing, using, or breaking other people's things. Any restraint will infuriate him. Both parents are fearful to say "No" to him. He will have a terrible temper and will lash out at anyone—parent or child—who doesn't let him do as he wishes.

Will he be happy? No. He will be miserable. He has been led to believe the falsehood that "My way now is my ticket to happiness." How? Because this is what this parenting style has taught him. His reference point for normal life has been "I get my way!"

His parents have taught and trained him by what they allowed him to do at the ages of one, two, and three. Habits are formulated by every act that is repeated. Habits become fixed into character—his thoughts and feelings—which drive his responses to life. Rebel's habits were formed to be selfish, and Satan had the mastery of his little heart. Lessons of self-denial and self-control were not taught when they needed to be. God was left out of the equation. Without God as the Head, Rebel automatically served another master. There is no middle ground. Had his parents understood how to connect their son to Christ, to take him to prayer and call forth a decision for right, he could have learned self-control, and he would have been much happier. Our babies really are not too young to learn!

During the first two years of life, teach your little ones that there is a God in heaven who loves and cares for them. Help them to experience the happiness that comes when we trust and obey Him, instead of allowing ourselves to be controlled by negative feelings and emotions. As they learn to practice self-denial and self-control in little ways, you will have a Riley story instead of a Rebel story.

Learning with a leaf

Jim and I were conducting a weekend seminar at a distant church, and Jim was the speaker for the worship hour. I entered the sanctuary as the service was beginning and was about to head for my seat, when I noticed Determined Della. She appeared to be about fourteen months old and wasn't the least bit interested in sitting still. Her mother was though, and vainly tried to occupy her little girl while still paying attention to what was happening up front. It didn't seem to be working very well, and she looked quite frustrated. Della was a little wiggle worm!

"Sally, why don't you offer to take care of Determined Della so that this mother can hear the sermon?"

"Lord, is that You?" I moaned. "I really don't feel like doing that. I'd rather hear the sermon myself than engage in a battle of wills with a child I've never met before. But . . . not my will, but Thine be done.”

I slipped up the aisle and tapped the mother on the shoulder. “Would you like me to watch your baby so that you can listen to the sermon?”

She looked rather surprised, checked with her husband, and then handed me Della—gratitude written all over her face. Della didn’t seem so grateful. She tried to cling to her mother and started to cry. I walked quickly out of the sanctuary, and as I entered the foyer, she broke into a very loud and desperate cry. It was a lovely fall day, so I stepped outside and found a bench under a shade tree. Sitting down, I cuddled her and prayed with her for God to comfort her. Committing myself to God’s care again was for me more than for God. I needed the assurance that He was with me to help me with this child. As I comforted her and smiled, Della looked into my eyes and decided that I was all right and soon stopped crying. I interested her in some bushes, trees, and flowers that were outside, and we became friends in five minutes.

I wanted to hear the sermon, so I carried her back into the church. As soon as Determined Della saw her mother through the sanctuary door, she began to cry out for her. Back outside we went to save the people from her hearty cries of “I want.”

“Della, you don’t need to cry. You cannot go to Mother just now. You can be happy with me. It’s all right.” I was quite sure that she understood my words, but she cried louder. I prayed and walked with Della, trying to reassure her, but she didn’t settle down.

“Sally, mild measures are not working. She needs a firmer consequence.”

I’m inclined to be too soft, so I thought that this must be God impressing my mind. Taking her into the bathroom, I prayed with her for God to help her submit to me and be content to be quiet. *“Shhh,”* I whispered to her. She cried more. So I gave her a mild spank on her leg. “Della, look at me. Listen to me.” This worked! I smiled at her, told her she could be happy if she chose. I continued to smile very pleasantly, and she stopped fussing.

I took her out to the foyer where I could hear the sermon, but I closed the sanctuary door so she couldn’t see her mother and sat down holding Determined Della on my lap. She wiggled and squirmed to get down to play. “No, you may not get down. You can sit quietly in my lap.” I looked around for something to amuse her. A leaf that had blown in from outside caught my eye. I picked it up and offered it to Della. She smiled and held out her hand. “You can have this as long as you are quiet and happy. If you get fussy, I’ll have to take it away from you.”

Little did I know that this was God’s training program to be used for the next forty-five minutes that would make good changes in her life.

For a few minutes she was intrigued with the leaf, then she began fussing and reaching for the sanctuary door indicating she wanted Mommy. “You don’t need to fuss. You can have Mother later, not just now. You are all right. Play with your leaf.” To my surprise, she put on a smile to match mine and resumed playing with the leaf. Some time passed, and I was getting into the sermon again, until I was made aware that Determined Della was unhappy again. She threw the leaf to the floor and began to fuss.

"Lord, what would Thou have me to do?[3] Attend my words."

"Della, you can choose to be happy again. You can sit quietly on my lap." She looked into my eyes as though she was trying to read if I meant what I said or if I'd give in to her. She fussed again with her arms toward the door. "Not now, Della. You can have Mommy later." And she broke into a cry. "Lord, what should I do now?"

Back into the bathroom we went. I said firmly but lovingly, "Della, you have been a good girl. Choose to be again. Jesus is here to help you and me, too. You can stop crying." She stopped crying, but just then her mother came into the bathroom, and Della wanted her. Again I said, "No Della, you can stop crying. You can have Mother later. You are all right." And I carried her back to the chair in the foyer. Amazingly, she settled down. She took the leaf once again and began to play with it. As her mother walked past us and back into the church, she waved to her little one, and Della waved back but didn't cry this time. "Amazing," I thought. "Thank You, Lord!"

I was so surprised at Della's understanding and self-control. Yet I shouldn't have been! I had worked with her *in Christ* rather than *in self*. I didn't trust my method—I trusted my Savior. He blessed my efforts and gave Della understanding just as He gave me understanding.

For the remaining fifteen minutes of the service, Della played with the leaf. The lessons in surrender were repeated again and again using various instructions or consequences as I sensed God leading me. Della lost the leaf when she fussed. When she yielded to my directions or smiled, she got the leaf back, and soon she understood this process. Sometimes she yielded quickly; other times, she was stubborn. I was consistent with her and continued praying for her silently or with her.

At one point, Della intentionally began to tear the leaf. I told her, "No, you don't want to tear the leaf." She looked directly at me and tore off another little piece. "No, you may not tear the leaf. Choose to be happy and play nicely with your leaf." Her little eyes were scrutinizing me to see if I meant what I said. She started to tear at the leaf again, so I asked her to give it to me. She did! "You may not have the leaf if you are going to tear it. You may not cry either. Sit still and be quiet, and I'll return the leaf to you." She obeyed, and I picked up another whole leaf for her.

She enjoyed it for a little while and then began to tear it again while looking at me. "No, you may not tear the leaf," I repeated. She stopped tearing it. Repetition and consistency are the training grounds. As I remained *in Christ,* with a gentle demeanor combined with clear expectations and unwavering follow-through, Determined Della became Delightful Della.

The service ended, and Della's mother came to see us. To my delight and

---

3. Acts 9:6.

surprise, Delightful Della had learned well. She was very excited to see her mommy, but instead of crying for her mother to pick her up right away, she looked at me for direction. "Yes, you may have Mother now. You have been a very good girl."

It amazed me what could happen within one hour of teaching and training under God's direction. The branch showed connection to the Vine. What could God do with you and your little ones? You can go to Him for instruction just like I did. Just be open to do what comes to your mind in teaching and training your infants do what is right. Trust that God will work through the method He brings to your mind to change your child.

God loves to help us in the management of our infants. Miracles happen when we connect with God, commune with Him, and follow His lead the best we know how. This requires a surrender to God on our part to do whatever is necessary and not put off the correction for later. This is the method that needs to be learned, experienced, and practiced over and over again.

The first months of life are not too early to train our little ones to respond with trust and submission to life's discomforts and trials. In fact, these years of infancy will influence the child for the rest of his life. Children need far more than mere physical care. They need parents who are connected to God and who are willing to learn how to connect their precious little ones to Him and establish heavenly habits.

THE LONE EMBRACE
A SPECIAL WORD OF ENCOURAGEMENT FOR SINGLE PARENTS

Single parents face many unique trials, and it is so easy to be overwhelmed. You feel that all you can do is just try to survive from day to day. The idea of building a solid foundation of character for your infant may seem unattainable to you. Satan builds up all the negatives of your situation, and he seems so believable. Whether your life's hardships are real or supposed, the solution is the same.

"I am the LORD, the God of all flesh: is there any thing too hard for me?"[4] " 'Come to Me, all you who labor and are heavy laden, and I will give you rest.' "[5] God cares for you. He wants to help you in the management of your children. He knows the emotional and physical turmoil you have been under. He understands how your infant has been wounded emotionally—for whatever reason. Your child feels your anxiety and negativity as though it is his own. He can't reason through these things, but you can.

You have God. He can be your heavenly Husband. He will willingly, kindly counsel with you. He will not manipulate you, compel you, or lay guilt trips on

---

4. Jeremiah 32:27.
5. Matthew 11:28, NKJV.

you. If you are a father, God can be your Counselor, Guide, and a safe place to spill out your heart. God is there for you, period! He is trustworthy. Try Him and learn for yourself.

Once you are abiding in Him, you have His power and wisdom to know what to do. You can find peace amidst your storm and a faithful Companion at your side to give you safe counsel. Turn to Him and then give your infant *you*! In Christ's power, you can change your infant's environment from one of anxiety and despair to one of joy and happiness. You can become a protective shelter for your child—one in which he or she can grow up healthy and happy. Don't delay. Seek and find this peace in Jesus. Then give it to your little one! This can be a reality for you—even in your circumstances.

Landon Hohnberger beginning to walk—the beginning of advancement in character building.

Chapter 9
Toddling On to Victory

And the Lord shall guide thee continually, and satisfy thy soul in drought, and make fat thy bones: and thou shalt be like a watered garden, and like a spring of water, whose waters fail not.
—Isaiah 58:11

As our infants become toddlers, they enter an exciting time of life. Their ability to explore, experiment, and experience the world around them expands. They learn to talk, to walk and run, to begin to care for themselves, and so much more. Their little minds are like fertile gardens just waiting to flourish. God wants to help you to occupy the soil of their hearts with wholesome, fruitful things so that their energy is channeled in useful directions. Satan is always watching for an opportunity to plant noxious weeds in their characters. By staying closely connected to God and tending the garden of the heart, you can reap a lovely harvest in the attitudes and habits of your growing little ones.

In future chapters, we'll discuss more about how to occupy our little ones with good things so that Satan does not have idle, bored children to work with. In this chapter, I'd like to address how we help our toddlers find victory in areas that often trouble them.

Victory is the by-product of connecting with God. Connecting our toddler to Jesus is like grafting the branch onto the Vine. As the sap from the Vine gives life and fruitfulness to the branch, so wholesome, truthful thoughts from God feed the soul of both parent and child and give them life and fruitfulness. Learning to think the thoughts God suggests is the key to changing wrong behaviors and attitudes.

One very effective way to feed your toddler good thoughts is by reading to him or her. Set aside a regular time each day to sit down with your toddler and explore a book. Cuddle him and teach him the value of sitting still. Your child can learn how to treat a book—how to turn the pages without tearing them and how to put it away nicely when you are finished reading.

Choose books that instill godly thoughts and shun those that don't. Stories that exemplify cruelty, violence, critical remarks, unkind words, rudeness, or abusiveness will contribute to a warlike child. Stories that illustrate obedience, kindness, purity, courtesy, and self-control will contribute to a peaceful, respectful child. Some very lovely books have been published about colors, ABCs, animals, and the names of common things. Look for good character-building books and use them to teach the right words and thoughts to your toddler.

Selected Bible stories are very beneficial. *My Bible Friends* is an excellent series that I read to my boys and am now reading to my grandchildren. The children just love the stories—even the one-, two-, and three-year-olds. They listen attentively, and the older ones can often tell you the story themselves.

Pay attention to the artwork in the books you choose for your children. Is it realistic? Is it uplifting? Does it portray colors found in the natural world? Avoid silly, foolish drawings and choose pictures that attract your child's mind to the kind of character you want them to develop. Their minds absorb all these various concepts which then enter into their thought processes as they engage in life. They can learn good responses to life's trials, how God loves us and is always there for us, and Jesus' example of how to treat the people around us.

Music is also a powerful educator and can be used for good in many ways. Seek to bring into your home good quality music that is pure, uplifting, and harmonious. Singing is one of those teaching tools that God may direct you to use to instill wholesome thoughts in your child's mind. Keep in mind that it is not the singing that is the secret to success. It is God attending the new thought and action which the song suggests that empowers the change in the heart of your child.

I can stop jumping

Two-year-old Jack loved to jump. His father had taught him how to jump on the trampoline with him, and it was so much fun! So much fun, in fact, that Jack wanted to jump all the time. Climbing onto his bed, he began to jump up and down. Mother explained that he should not do this and set him down on the floor. He climbed right back up and started jumping again. Mother carried him downstairs and put him down by his toy box. Jack immediately climbed onto the couch and began to jump there. Mother was afraid he would fall off the couch and hit his head on the nearby table. "Jack, you may not jump on the couch. Please get down now." She placed him on the floor. He headed right over to the dog's bed and began jumping there. Jumping was good exercise for Jack, but he needed to learn the proper place and time for jumping.

After an hour of this, Mother was exhausted. "I'm getting nowhere! I tell him kindly what not to do, and nothing changes. It doesn't pay to be nice!"

A new thought interrupted her frustration, *"Would you like some help?"*

"Well, of course, I would. Is this Jesus?" There was no evidence to her senses this was God, just the kind spirit that came with the thought.

"Bring Jack to Me, and I can help him to do the right.[1] *I will instruct thee and teach thee in the way which thou shalt go. I will guide thee with Mine eyes."*[2]

"Well, this impression is not an audible voice, but it is according to the Word of God. I've heard about bringing my child to Christ for His blessing and that God wants to help me in the management of my child. I think I'll give it a try." So Mother brought Jack to his knees with her, and they prayed a simple prayer to Jesus.

---

1. Psalm 119:37.
2. Psalm 32:8.

"Dear Jesus, help Jack to obey Mother and stop jumping on everything. Help him to understand."

The rest of that day went quite well. Jack seemed to lose interest in jumping and settled into throwing his blocks and running to get them. Mother was pleased, but sensed that this was not a permanent change. "Lord, how do we get to the heart of this issue?" she prayed silently as she worked.

The next day, a friend stopped by to visit. She was very excited about a new series of books for children she had received recently called the Ladder of Life.[3] These books featured a variety of songs designed to help parents teach good character qualities to their children. As the mother thumbed through the teacher's book, one song caught her eye. "No jumping on the bed is what my Daddy/ Mother said. . . . When no one is around, I'll think of what they said, And then I'll not be jumping, jumping, jumping on the bed." Jack's mother went to the piano and began to play and sing the song. The tune with the words was quite lively. Jumping Jack came over to the piano to listen, climbed up into her lap, and then started singing the cute little tune with Mommy.

God attended the words of this tune. He used it to help Jack understand that there is a proper place and time for jumping and that there is a time and place to refrain from jumping. As Mother and Jack sang the song over and over again, new thoughts produced better choices which bore the fruit of self-control in Jumping Jack. God used this simple means of implanting right thoughts in Jack's mind to replace the wrong ones. The next time Jack started jumping on the bed, Mother started singing this little song. Jack climbed down off the bed, and singing along with Mother, went to play with his toys.

I can wait!

Two-year-old Impatient Irwin was a chatterbox and didn't like to wait when he wanted something. It had been quite an accomplishment to teach him how to ask for something instead of crying for it. The family was gathered around the table for a delicious breakfast of pancakes and fresh fruit—Irwin's favorite. Irwin was buckled into his high chair, and his mouth watered as he waited for prayer. Just then, the phone rang, and his father excused himself.

Impatient Irwin begged, "Mommy, eat now!"

"No, honey. We'll wait for Daddy to finish his phone call. Then we will eat."

"Mommy, eat now? Pancake!"

"Mommy doesn't want you to ask anymore. We will wait for Daddy. It will just be a little while. We can wait. You must choose."

Impatient Irwin got more insistent.

"Irwin, Mommy has to take you down from your high chair. You need to go play, and Mommy will call you when we are ready to eat." Irwin began to cry. Mother smiled sympathetically at him.

---

3. See the resource list in the appendix.

"Let's ask Jesus to help you wait patiently for Daddy. You don't have to obey your feelings of 'I want.' Jesus will help you and change how you feel inside here." And Mother pointed to his heart.

Irwin didn't want to pray, but Mommy prayed out loud while she held Irwin on her hip. "Dear Jesus, help Irwin choose to come to You to pray that he can be happy to wait a little while. We want to be a happy family and enjoy this good breakfast together.

"Come, Irwin. Let's pray for help from Jesus. He is your best Friend." This time, Irwin knelt beside Mother and folded his chubby hands together.

"Pray after me, Irwin," Mother directed. Irwin nodded. "Dear Jesus . . . come into my heart . . . and help me . . . be willing to wait . . . for Daddy. Help me . . . be patient. Amen."

Irwin cooperated. "Now," Mother instructed, "you can choose to be happy and play with your truck here while waiting for Daddy. As you do this, Jesus will change your feelings to obey Him. You will be able to wait cheerfully."

Irwin wasn't sure he wanted to play. He wanted to go to his high chair and eat. But he chose this time to cooperate by pushing his little truck across the floor. After about one minute, Irwin asked, "Eat now, Mommy?"

Right then, God brought to Mother's mind a little tune from the Ladder of Life book called "Sometimes I Have to Wait." She started singing the song the best she could remember it, adding a few words that fit Irwin's specific situation right then. "Sometimes I have to wait . . . wait . . . wait. When I want pancakes and it's not time, I listen to Mommy and Jesus, and I can wait. Sometimes I have to wait . . . wait . . . wait." Irwin looked up at Mommy and then quietly started pushing his truck again. Whenever Irwin started expressing his impatience, Mother would start singing again, and Irwin waited patiently.

Finally, Irwin's father came, and they all sat down to eat that luscious meal with happy hearts and smiles. Partway through the meal, Irwin wanted more blueberries. Mother was busy with his baby brother, but Irwin wanted the blueberries right away. Mother began to hum the "Wait" tune, and Irwin stopped demanding to be waited on immediately.

If we are consistent, in Christ, our toddlers can develop habits that contribute to a peaceful home. They can learn the art of "sometimes I have to wait," and this surrender can become the norm when Jesus abides in our home. In this way, our children can learn how to connect to Jesus and bear character fruit like His.

Another habit toddlers need to be taught is respect for their own and others' things. They need to be taught about proper ownership—what is mine, what is yours, and what belongs to someone else. They can learn to care for their toys and to share them when it is appropriate. They can be taught to respect others' belongings and ask permission before they touch them. Sometimes, they will be told "No" when they want to play with something that is not theirs. With God, they can learn that "No" is Okay, and they can still be happy.

I can be happy with my toys!

"Samantha, you may not play with my Precious Moments figurine, but you can play with these stuffed animals." Mother turned around from the desk where she was working just in time to see Samantha reaching for the fragile statuette. Samantha, age three, pulled her hand back but started to pout. Mother put her arm around Samantha to draw her in for a hug, but Samantha pulled selfishly away. "That is not the way to respond, Samantha. You don't want to do that." And Mother sent up a prayer to God, who knows just how to win Samantha's heart. "Hmm," thought Mother, "I wonder what I could replace this temptation with . . . I know!"

"Samantha, let's play train with your stuffed animals. That is lots of fun!" Mother lined up several chairs while Samantha watched dubiously. "This first seat is the engine where you and I will sit to drive the train. The other chairs are for passengers to ride with us. Here, you put honey bear up there to ride." Mother recognized that Samantha was wrestling between her stubborn "I want that figurine" attitude and the desire to surrender and play with Mother. She sensed that God was talking with her to bring her daughter to a right decision. But now God put another thought in Mother's head.

"Nudge her with her stuffed bear. Smile to encourage the decision."

To Mother's delight, Samantha smiled back at her, took the bear, and placed him on the second chair. Her enthusiasm grew, and she ran to collect all her animals to ride the train. Then Mother placed Samantha on her lap, and they pretended to drive the train out of the station and through the countryside. They laughed and had lots of fun. Arriving at the next station, each animal had to get off the train while the conductor called for new passengers, and the fun was repeated.

Giving Samantha something good to do in place of what she should not do is a good application of the *replacement principle* and is an excellent tool in character development. The replacement principle nurtures right choices to serve God and right instead of self and wrong. And we have the Creator at our side, changing our irritation or self-will on the inside, which only He can do.[4] Samantha found happiness in obeying her mother and God. Next time, it will be easier. Redirecting the thoughts of your child is an important tool in parenting.

Toddlers can learn to make choices, and it is important for them to do so. The power to make a good decision is an essential skill they will need for life. But at this stage, don't give them a choice to do wrong. Limit their choices within a framework of what is good for them. For example, "Barbara, would you rather have Cheerios or oatmeal this morning?" "Riley, would you like to wear your green shirt or your red shirt with your blue pants?" "Clarissa, would you like Mommy to read you the story about Moses or Chipmunk Willy?"

---

4. Ephesians 3:16.

I can enjoy my vegetables

Matilda liked sweets! Her parents had allowed her to have sugary snacks between meals because she liked them so much. God taught them that this was not good for Matilda. She would be healthier if she ate only at mealtimes and ate a healthy dessert after finishing her other food. It's harder to change a bad habit than to train the right habit to start with, but they were committed to deal with this issue before Matilda got any older.

The family sat down together for lunch. Mother had prepared baked potatoes, lentils, steamed peapods, and a raw vegetable salad—with oatmeal cookies for dessert. Three-year-old Matilda sat in her high chair surveying the table.

"Mommy, cookie."

"Let's eat our meal first, and then Mommy will give you a cookie. Here is your lunch. Would you like to eat your peapods or your salad first?" Mother was helping Matilda to learn to make decisions within acceptable choices.

Matilda pushed her plate away and cried, "Cookie! I want a cookie!"

"No, Matilda, you may not have a cookie. You can choose to be happy with your vegetables. Mommy and Jesus are here to help you."

Matilda's little face screwed up in a pout, and she slumped down in her high chair. Mother prayed silently, then picked Matilda up out of her high chair. "Let's ask Jesus to help you enjoy your lunch, Matilda." Matilda began to cry and repeated a prayer of surrender after her mother; but when Mother started to put her in her high chair, she began begging for a cookie again. Mother picked her back up and carried her away from the table.

"Matilda, you may not eat until you are ready to eat your vegetables. You may play with your toys."

Matilda burst into tears again. "Mommy. Me hungry!"

"I know you're hungry, sweetheart. As soon as you are ready to eat your vegetables, you may come back to the table."

"Me come now, Mommy." Matilda's eyes softened.

Returning Matilda to her high chair, Mother wiped away her tears tenderly. "You need to choose to do what is right, Matilda. Jesus will help you. Here are your peapods, they are so good." Matilda ate her peapods and enjoyed them because Jesus was in the equation, and God changed her heart's desires when she surrendered to do His and Mommy's will.

"Matilda, would you like your potatoes next or some salad?"

"Salad," she answered.

If Mother had relented and given Matilda that cookie because she was crying for it, Matilda would have learned to cry the next time she wanted something and expect to get her way. This would have developed the selfish, controlling side of her character.

As Mother consistently taught Matilda to make right decisions in Christ's spirit and took Matilda to prayer when self got too strong, she was connecting her to Jesus. Jesus empowered their success. This kind of training teaches the toddler that she does not have to obey her negative feelings and emotions. She learns that Jesus is right there to help her as soon as she calls out to Him. Then as she follows God's bidding, her emotions are brought into subjection to Him, and she is happy and free to serve God.

I can care for my body

As the toddler grows, she becomes more aware of her body and more capable of caring for it. One aspect of this growth is potty training. This important lesson can bring good dividends when taught under Christ's direction. It can help our toddlers to build self-respect and self-control.

Two-year-old Landon stood in a peculiar stance in the corner of the living room with a preoccupied look on his face. His mother noticed him and asked, "Landon, are you making a poopy in your diaper?"

"Yes, Mommy," he replied.

Mother thought to herself, "I think Landon is ready for potty training. He's been telling me over the past two weeks when he is urinating and when he needs his dirty diapers changed. He's also talking quite well—that will help a lot!"

The next morning in her personal time with God, Mother reviewed a book she had read earlier that offered some very helpful advice about potty training.[5] "Lord, is this the day to begin?" She sensed that it was. "Please attend Landon and me today, Lord. May this be a positive experience for my little boy."

When Landon got up, Mother dressed him in potty training pants. "Landon, today you are going to learn how to go potty like big people do." She picked up a doll, led Landon into the bathroom, and showed him his new training potty. Kneeling on the floor, she told the dolly all about potty training as Landon watched with big eyes. Turning to Landon, she instructed, "Now it's your turn, honey. You teach the dolly how to potty in the toilet." Landon smiled shyly and then repeated to the dolly the instructions Mother had just given.

During family worship, Landon's father committed Landon to God and prayed that he would be able to understand the new way and have a willing heart to learn. Mother knew that potty training would take a large share of her time that day, so she had planned a lighter work day. She encouraged Landon to drink a lot of water and sometimes offered him diluted juice. She wanted him to have lots of opportunities to go potty successfully. Throughout the day, both parents prayed to confirm God's presence with them.

Before breakfast, Mother put Landon on the potty, but he didn't need to go. Right after breakfast, she put him on the potty again. He seemed a bit nervous, and Mother sent a silent prayer to Jesus. The idea came to her to give Landon a book to look at while he was waiting. Landon relaxed, and in a few minutes, he went! He was so pleased with himself. Mother affirmed him warmly and then showed him a chart she had made for him and let him put a

---

5. The book Mother read was *Potty Training 1-2-3: What Works, How it Works, Why it Works,* by Gary Ezzo and Anne Marie Ezzo.

favorite sticker on it as a positive reward.

She told him that every time he said, "I have to go potty," and then went to sit on the potty, he would get a sticker. When the chart was full, he could have some small reward, such as a dessert or a little toy. Periodically she'd ask him if he was wet or dry, and he was rewarded with a sticker when dry. This helped him to develop an awareness of clean and dry.

At first, Landon was excited and enjoyed all the extra attention. But after a few hours, the excitement wore off, and he got busy playing with his blocks. A new sensation caught his attention—the feeling of warm urine running down his leg. He didn't like that and complained to Mother. As she helped him put on dry clothes, she talked to him about learning to sense when you have to go and then going to the potty right away. She picked up the dolly and told him that there is a muscle that lets you go pee and that this same muscle can hold the pee. She had him open and close his hand to understand muscle control. It worked well. Landon followed Mother's example and gave dolly the same instructions. "You can stop going pee when you squeeze that muscle like you can squeeze your hand. You don't have to have accidents when you learn to do this."

The second day went better until noon. Landon put enough stickers on his chart to win a dessert for lunch. This was a good motivation for staying clean and dry—Landon loved desserts! But he tired of the effort after lunch and had more accidents. He was very unhappy with himself. Mother comforted by saying, "It's Okay. You will learn. Keep trying." That evening, something clicked. He recognized the sensation that told him to go potty, squeezed that little muscle, and didn't wet his pants. His understanding grew.

The third day went very well. The main training was basically complete, although it was time consuming. By the fourth day, Landon was ready to advance to the potty seat on the toilet instead of his little chair version. Mother kept a step stool in front of the potty so he could climb up easily. He was learning to control that little muscle and liked staying clean and dry in his big boy underwear.

To eliminate bed-wetting, Mother restricted Landon's fluid intake in the evening, and she and Father took turns getting up in the middle of the night to take Landon to go potty. It worked very well. Within a few weeks, he was consistently dry in the morning, and they could eliminate getting him up at night. His new habit of sensing and controlling his body was strengthening.

About two weeks later, unexpected company came. Mother was less attentive and Landon was distracted. Accidents happened. Mother resolved to keep potty training a top priority for the next two weeks regardless of guests, phone calls, or other intrusions. Within a few weeks, potty training was completed.

It took longer for me to train my boys than it did this mother, because I didn't read other resources, had few ideas to work with, and didn't know Jesus the way I do today. I encourage you to explore all the various ways of teaching your child that God might lead you to. When God is leading the instruction, right thoughts and ideas will be implanted in the minds of our children.

Jesus said, "According to your faith [belief] be it unto you."[6] What our children believe about themselves affects what they do or don't do. Andrew didn't believe that he could climb a mountain. Let me share how God helped him learn the truth.

I can climb a mountain!

My Andrew was four years old when we left Wisconsin and moved to Montana to find a real God that could empower us to change our wrong ways. God had begun His training school with me as a parent four years earlier, but I seemed to be a slow learner. Some of my training worked well, but other areas still needed to change.

One of those areas was Andrew's lack of endurance in walking or hiking. Now I must admit, I had trained him to be weak in this area. I coddled him, did things for him when they got hard, and didn't expect him to have to walk very far. We would start out on a walk, and after a hundred yards or so, Andrew would plead, "Carry me, Mommy. I'm tired." And without a thought, I'd pick him up.

Until we moved to Montana, Jim had very little to do with child rearing, and I really wanted him to be more involved. I almost changed my mind the day we decided to go for a walk up a little mountain near our home. We started up the lovely path and enjoyed the awe-inspiring view of the Rocky Mountains. We had walked for about five minutes when Andrew begged, "Mommy, carry me. I'm tired." Of course, I picked him up.

Jim saw what happened and ordered, "Sally, that boy can walk. Put him down. The walk will be good for him."

Andrew began to cry as I put him down. He clung to me, dragging his feet. "I can't, Mommy. I'm too tired. I can't do it! You have to carry me."

Oh, how I wanted to pick him up! My poor little boy! But fear of Jim's disapproval kept me from doing so. "Andrew, you can walk a little farther. I'll hold your hand to help you."

Andrew continued to cry, but started walking. After a short distance, he sat down. "I can't do it, Mommy. You have to carry me."

Jim took charge. "Sally, I'll take this boy and teach him how to climb the mountain and be a man."

God was answering my prayer! Jim was getting involved. He was going to help instill firmer masculine virtues in my boys. I wanted this for them. I had prayed for it for years—but now I wasn't sure I wanted Jim's help. He was being far more firm than I was accustomed to being, and it made me most uncomfortable!

"Andrew," Jim urged, "you are a big boy with strong legs. You can climb this mountain! Now let's go!"

---

6. Matthew 9:29.

Andrew looked at me with pleading eyes, burst into tears, and sat down on the ground in abject despair. He truly believed he couldn't do it and his father was asking him to do the impossible. Jim knelt beside him and prayed earnestly with him. Then he challenged Andrew again. Andrew continued crying and refused to get up. Turning the little fellow over his knee, Jim gave him a spanking.

"Lord, what do I do?" I cried out in desperation.

"It's going to be all right, Sally. Just trust Me."

"But Lord, this is so far out of my comfort zone! Look at how firm Jim is with Andrew. Mild measures didn't work, so Jim went to firmer measures and spanked him more firmly than I do. Lord, don't let this firmness hurt or scar him."

"Sally, it's going to be all right. Just trust Me. Andrew needs this so he can face the lie he believes—that he can't do it. Don't interfere no matter how much your soft heart wants to rescue him."

"Well," I thought, "my way hasn't done him much good—he is so weak. I want him to be a man—strong, firm, and decisive. I was making him just the opposite. Okay God, I'll trust You against my feelings. I'll watch Jim's results."

"Sally, you take Matthew and hike on ahead of Andrew and me." Jim wanted Andrew to have no hope of rescue, so he would learn that he could climb this mountain. So Matthew and I went way ahead—out of sight up the trail. We sat down and prayed for Jim's patience and for Andrew to learn that he could climb the mountain.

Jim was consistent and firm in his instructions. He delivered consequences when Andrew didn't choose to walk and encouraged him when he did. Jim was very strong under God, but not harsh. His firmness helped Andrew find out that he *could* climb the mountain. Jim's love would not let him believe the lie that he couldn't.

In this manner, we got to the top of the mountain. Matthew and I waited on the summit. When Andrew crested the last little hill, he was hand in hand with his father.

A huge smile spread across his face when he saw me. Leaving his father, he ran up the remainder of the hill shouting, "Mommy, Mommy, I climbed the mountain all by myself. I can do it!" He embraced me with such a happy bear hug.

That was the beginning. Our family continued to climb mountains like this until Andrew, the boy who was sure he couldn't walk very far, excelled in climbing mountains. With his father, he climbed almost all the peaks in Glacier National Park that we can view from our cabin window. Today, at the age of twenty-eight, he still loves long hikes, and there is no place he prefers to walk more than in the gorgeous Glacier National Park mountains that remind him of the God who showed him he could do what he thought was impossible.

What we do in these early years goes with our children for life. Give them a heritage of knowing God and seeing how wonderful that relationship and subjection to God really is. Be the parent God wants you to be to teach and train your toddler how to toddle on to victory in Jesus.

THE LONE EMBRACE
A SPECIAL WORD OF ENCOURAGEMENT FOR SINGLE PARENTS

You, the parent, may feel very much like Andrew—assured in your mind, feelings, and experiences of life so far that you cannot climb the mountain of single parenting. But you will find in Jesus the power, the wisdom, the direction, the companionship, and the guidance you need to meet whatever extremity is before you. In Him you can scale the utmost heights, and if you give Him your permission and cooperation, He can cleanse you of your fears, your misconceptions, even your physical, mental, or spiritual weakness. In Him is life![7] Won't you get in Him?

Take His hand, and you can go anywhere without fear, in confidence of His care for you. You can have peace where there is no peace. You can have the power to do whatever you set your foot to that is according to the will of God. Taste and see that the Lord is good! He awaits your coming to Him that you might have that life.

Jesse Hohnberger.
Toddling on to victory begins with a connection with God.

7. John 1:4, 11, 12.

Chapter 10

A Pleasant Home

Happy is the man who finds wisdom, . . .
Her ways are ways of pleasantness,
And all her paths are peace.
—Proverbs 3:13, 17, NKJV

It was nearly suppertime at the Peters' home. Mother was in the kitchen, humming while she mashed the potatoes. One-year-old Shelly played contentedly with her blocks on the living room floor where her mother could see her and encourage her with little words and smiles from time to time. Four-year-old Justin was doing his best to set the table while eight-year-old Ned washed the dishes his mother had used in preparing the meal.

They lived in a small, but tidy, home a few miles from town. There was a place for everything, and each member of the family did his or her part to keep everything in its place. Chores were done regularly so that the home was kept clean and uncluttered, and yet they were not so morbidly afraid of dirt that they could never have any fun. The yard was trimmed, and flower beds were weeded. The Peters' home was restful to the eye and inviting to the soul.

A car pulled into the driveway. "Father's home," shouted Ned, as he and Justin rushed out the back door, their eager faces glowing. Mother washed and dried her hands, picked up Shelly, and went to meet Father at the door. He came in with Justin in one arm and his briefcase in the other, while Ned chattered away excitedly about all the events of the day. Father put down Justin and his briefcase and wrapped his arms around Mother and Shelly, kissing them both. He paused a moment to look deep into Mother's eyes. "I love you, sweetheart! I've been looking forward to this all day."

"I love you, too, darling! I'm glad you're home."

Ned had paused in his report of the day long enough to let Father greet Mother, but then he picked up right where he had left off. Father chuckled. "Okay, Ned, why don't you tell me the rest of the story when we sit down to eat. Help your mother finish in the kitchen. I have a surprise to bring in from the car."

"A surprise? Oh, Father, what is it? Can we come with you?"

"No. You'll see it soon enough. Finish your chores."

Father walked out the back door, and the boys returned to their tasks. As Ned washed the dishes, he asked Mother, "Do you know what Father's surprise is?"

"No I don't, Ned. He hasn't told me about anything new."

Ned speculated about this and that. Justin did too. It seemed to them an eternity before Father walked back in with a large flat object draped with a blanket. "What is it, Father? What is it?" Both boys stared at the strange package.

"Would you like to see it before supper or after?"

"Before!" shouted Ned. "Before!" lisped Justin.

"What's your vote, Mother?" Father asked, winking at Mother.

"Well, everything is ready to eat except the corn bread. It will come out of the oven in ten minutes. I think we should see your surprise while we wait."

"Okay, everyone. Come sit on the couch and close your eyes."

Everyone giggled as they snuggled on the couch. Father stood before them preparing to remove the blanket from his surprise. "Justin, you're peeking. Cover your eyes." Justin chuckled and put both hands over his eyes. "Hurry, Daddy!"

Father paused dramatically, lifted the blanket, and said, "Now, open your eyes!"

Four sets of eyes opened quickly followed by a series of *oohs* and *aahs*. There before them was a nicely framed painting of a father and son paddling their canoe across a placid lake surrounded by majestic mountains.

Father explained, "I noticed a garage sale at our neighbor's place on my way home and stopped to have a peek. Most of what they had didn't interest me, but I liked this painting. I thought it would look nice here in our living room. We need something on that wall over there."

Just then, the kitchen timer rang. Mother got up to take the corn bread out of the oven while the two boys studied Father's new picture. "How do you like it, dear?" asked Father.

"I think it is a very nice painting," Mother paused as she tested the corn bread. "It looks like you with Ned or with Justin when he gets a little older. It's very peaceful looking. I think you got a good deal." She paused again. "But to be quite honest with you, I don't care for the colors. They seem rather bold to me for our living room. I think the picture would stand out too much."

Father looked disappointed. He didn't say anything for a moment. "Let's put it aside for now and talk about it later."

Mother smiled at Father, and he winked back at her.

"Time to wash up for supper, boys," called Mother. "Then come to the table."

Later that evening, after the family had done their evening chores, played hide-and-seek for a little while, and enjoyed a short but sweet family worship, the children were tucked in their beds. Father and Mother snuggled together in the living room, sharing their thoughts about the day. Their attention turned to the new painting. Father thought it would look stunning in the living room, but Mother disagreed. They each shared their different viewpoints and finally decided on a compromise. They would keep the painting, but instead of hanging it in the living room, they would hang it in the hallway.

The Peters family has a pleasant home—one that is pleasurable and works through difficulties. It conveys warmth, security, companionship, and belonging. The atmosphere surrounding such a home makes you want to be there. Children are drawn to this kind of home. Father and Mother, brother and sister are their dearest friends. There's no place they'd rather be. Infants and toddlers who live in this kind of home are more content and easier to work with than those raised in an unpleasant home.

The attitudes and atmosphere of the home are powerful influences to mold the character of the child. When we are content and assured in Christ, our infants and toddlers feel safe. When all their needs are taken care of in a timely manner, they learn to trust. When the home feels pleasant and happy, our infants and toddlers partake of this too. When selfishness rises in their hearts, their parents understand how to help them give it to Jesus and cultivate contentment in its place. This brings a peaceful atmosphere into the home that the agitated child needs to feel and sense. With God we can give the best atmosphere to encourage our little ones to cultivate self-control.

What does it take to make such a home? Why do so many homes experience just the opposite? Why are so many disagreeable, distasteful, and even obnoxious? Those who grow up in an unpleasant home tend to experience discontent, insecurity, and rejection. Children endure until they are old enough to get away. If your home is unpleasant, it doesn't have to remain that way. With God, your home may become the sweetest place on earth for you and your little ones.

How do I get there?

Disorderly Deana invited me into her home to talk over a meal. She wanted input for parenting her little boys, ages two and four. As I walked up to the home, I couldn't help but notice that toys littered the yard, garden tools lay next to weed-filled flower beds, and the lawn mower had been abandoned in the middle of the yard.

I rang the doorbell, and Deana greeted me warmly. As I stepped into her entryway, a cat dashed by my feet, and Sparkle, the family's golden retriever, jumped up on me to add her enthusiastic welcome. Deana's stern scolding seemed to fall on deaf ears as Sparkle bounced eagerly around me. Deana finally grabbed her collar, locked her in the laundry room, and escorted me to a nicely decorated, but rather cluttered, living room. Stern Stanley and his little brother, Mild Micah, were playing together with Lego bricks on the floor, and judging by the unhappy looks in their eyes and the angry words they were exchanging, they both wanted the same Lego piece.

"Boys! Boys! Let's not argue. You need to be nice to each other. Stanley, let your little brother have what he wants. We have a guest today. This is Mrs. Hohnberger."

She tried to draw both boys to her, but Stanley pushed away angrily and stomped off into the den. She didn't try to stop him. Micah took one look at me and disappeared behind his mother.

"Hi, Micah!" I peeked around Deana. He scowled and pulled farther back. I thought he looked more afraid than shy, so I tried to play peekaboo. He began to cry. His mother picked him up to comfort him, and he buried his head on her shoulder, refusing to look at me.

Deana looked embarrassed and began, "It's like this all the time. My house and yard are always a mess. My kids are unhappy. I'm trying to teach them to obey me, but all I seem to get is more frustration. My husband is usually upset with me, because I can't seem to get my act together. Even my dog won't obey me. It's all so overwhelming that I feel like giving up. I know God doesn't want me to do that, so I keep trying, but nothing ever changes."

Deana explained how the home she had grown up in was much like the one she now managed. She had hated her homelife as a child, and as she grew into her teen years, she could hardly wait until she could have a home of her own. She was sure it would be different—that it would be pleasant. She married a man she thought was her "knight in shining armor" after knowing him for only a few short months. She had expected bliss to begin, but it didn't.

Now, five years later, she carried a lot of fear and resentment toward her husband. He worked long hours, and she was never sure when he'd be home. When he did walk in the door, she and the children would cringe. He was almost always unhappy about something and continually criticized her while either ignoring the children or issuing sharp commands to them. He told Deana she was a lousy cook, a disorganized housekeeper, a poor excuse for a mother, and a disappointment to him as a wife. He expected her to run the home, raise the children, and be there for him when he wanted her—and to expect nothing from him in return.

Deana was devastated. Her emotions were all tied up in knots. Her anxiety and distress were easy to sense. She feared conflict and felt she didn't dare attempt to talk things out with her husband. So instead of confronting him, she withdrew like a turtle into her shell and tried harder to please him. She would determine to clean the house, prepare his favorite meal, and make the children mind, but her fear and anxiety would overwhelm her, and she would find herself incapable of getting anything done. Her lack of accomplishment heightened her fear of her husband's displeasure—it was a vicious cycle that was pulling her down into depression.

She was rightfully concerned about how all of this was affecting Stanley and Micah. She knew her boys behaved poorly. She saw and felt it daily. Stern Stanley imitated his father's disposition, and Mild Micah was timid and anxious like Deana. In her frustration, she was often irritable with them. Then she would feel guilty, swing to the opposite extreme, and indulge them in whatever they wanted—snacks, desserts, new toys, skipping their nap, not having to pick up their things, or watching cartoons on TV. She hoped that these little indulgences would give them a bit of pleasure to make up for the misery they were going through. She was heartbroken that they were experiencing the same kind of childhood she had so hated in her early years, but she didn't know how to change it.

"Oh, Sally, this last week our family was invited to the Peters' home for dinner. We go to the same church, you know. Their home is so different than ours. The parents really seem to love and respect each other, and their children are so happy and well behaved. After the way my children acted, I don't think they'll ever invite us again. And their home is so neat and tidy. I know they're not wealthy; her husband makes less money than mine does. But their home is so . . ." She searched for the right word. "It's so . . . pleasant! I didn't want to leave. I would give anything or do anything if only my home could be like that. It doesn't seem possible. Do you think it's impossible?"

The first step

As Deana poured out her heart to me, I had been silently praying. "Lord, there are so many things that could be addressed in this situation. What is the one issue this mother needs to face that will give her a lifeline of hope and a workable starting place for lasting change? I don't have the wisdom to know. Please help me to help her. Help me to give just what she can handle for the first step that will start her on the journey of breaking this family dysfunction before it is passed on to yet another generation. What shall I do?"[1]

"Sally, she needs to experience Me changing the direction of her thoughts. That will redeem her from her negative emotions—which are her greatest bonds. She needs to risk trusting Me and allowing Me to direct her. I may ask her to speak one time and to be silent another. She will find this hard. But she needs to let Me be her Lord, Savior, and Guide. I'll bring her out of her prison of fear and anxiety. Then I'll show her how to teach her children to come to Me and learn better ways."

I began, "Deana, with man it is impossible. But *with God*, all things are possible. But you must begin with what you can change. You can't change your husband. You can't control how he treats you or your children. Neither can you change your past and the homelife you experienced growing up. You can't even change the cycle of anxiety and depression that you are experiencing by yourself.

"The one thing you can change, Deana, is who you serve. Right now, you are trying to serve your husband. You long for his approval and love, to be valued for who you are, not constantly demeaned for your lack of performance."

Tears filled Deana's eyes as she slowly nodded her head. I continued. "Satan is using the demeaning behavior of your husband to sell you a lying thought, Deana. He is repeating to you over and over again that you have no value, that your worth is based in your performance, which will never ever be good enough. You have heard this lie so many times that you believe it is true, and it becomes a self-fulfilling prophecy that cripples your ability to work and to be organized."

Deana was listening closely. "Sally, I think you're right. I believe that I have no value because I never do anything right, and I go down into hopeless anxi-

---

1. Acts 9:6.

ety. I understand that, and I've tried so many times to overcome it by just doing better. But it doesn't work. What else can I do?"

"What you need to recognize, Deana, is that there is Someone who is a Higher Authority for you than your husband or yourself. It's God. He made you; He died for you; and He has the final word on your value. Your worth was decided on Calvary long before you were born, and it is *nonnegotiable*.

"God wants to become your heavenly Husband.[2] He wants you to come to Him just as you are and let Him love you. He regards you with great tenderness, and He longs to help you. The weaker you find yourself, the more He knows that you need Him and the more He longs to wrap His arms about you. Where His thoughts about you are different than your husband's thoughts or your thoughts, He asks you to believe Him.

"When you choose to believe Him over your lying thoughts and filter through Him what you will say or not say and do or not do, He will work inside of you to give you peace in place of anxiety. His perfect love for you will cast out your fear."

I paused for a moment, and Deana looked thoughtful. "That sounds like a lot of hard work, Sally. I'm not used to even thinking about what I'm thinking. But I understand what you're saying. If I allow self-devaluing thoughts to run through my mind unchallenged all the time, I will feel anxious and fearful because 'as he thinketh in his heart, so is he'.[3] But if I truly believe that my value is already established by the price of Calvary, I will feel secure and at rest. But isn't it hard to challenge old ways of thinking?"

"Yes, it is," I agreed. "It will cost you determined effort to trust God and act on His thoughts about you instead of the ones you're used to obeying. But as you persevere, it will get easier with time, and eventually there will be a new you. You've been working awfully hard on this old program, and you're not happy with the outcome. Why not give God's program a chance and see what happens?"

"You're right, Sally! Nothing could be harder than what I'm doing right now. What do I have to lose by trying God's way—except my misery! Help me understand just how to start."

"You start by going to God and giving yourself to Him, all your thoughts, emotions, and anxieties, even your history and your health, everything that is a part of you. Then you put into His hands your marriage, your home, and your children. You tell Him that you are no longer in charge. He is! And that you choose to serve Him rather than your old ways.

"Then give Him your time and your ear. Make it a priority to spend a few quiet moments with Him and His Word each day. Talk to Him about the things that concern you, and listen for Him to direct you. Search for texts in the Bible that tell you about your value in God's eyes.[4] Think on these things

2. Isaiah 54:5.
3. Proverbs 23:7.
4. Psalm 17:8; Isaiah 13:12; 43:4.

throughout the day. Learn to recognize that you are never alone. God is always by your side to help you. Filter through Him everything you think, everything you say, and everything you do. When you recognize He is asking you to do something, trust Him, and choose to do it.

"All of the effort you have been putting into trying to perform to prove your value needs to be redirected into staying connected with God. When you are connected with Him, He will supply all the direction and power you need to face the things that seem so overwhelming to you right now. You will begin to taste freedom!

"Now, in this process, you are like a little baby learning to walk. You will stumble at times. Just remember that God is not standing over you to criticize you, but to offer His helping hand to you. Just take His hand, get back up, and step forward again. He will never leave you nor forsake you!"

Deana was quiet for a moment. "I understand what you are saying, Sally. I'm determined to try God's way—by His grace!"

"Letting God have you is the key to making your home pleasant; and it doesn't have to take years to start seeing results. As soon as you experience Christ changing you, you can share that understanding with your infant and toddler. They need Jesus too. When you teach them how to make a vital connection with God, they can find real power to make real changes. There is nothing too hard for God.[5] Letting God have you is where you will learn how to raise your children to follow God above the pull of their fleshly, selfish ways."

Looking into Deana's eyes, I saw that hope had been kindled. She was ready to try a new way—God's way. I rejoiced because I know that if just one family member truly allows God to redeem him or her from the bondage of lying thoughts, they become His agent to help the rest of the family.

Persevering in the process

I didn't see Disorderly Deana for a number of months. I met her again at one of our meetings and was delighted to see the change in her countenance. Instead of being clouded with unrest and anxiety, I saw her face reflecting peace and contentment. We found a few moments to visit. She told me that she had done just what we had talked about. She had filled her mind with Bible texts that challenged her long-held view that she was valueless. She had also listened to a number of our seminars on CD that helped her solidify these new thoughts and concepts. She was experiencing God as a tender heavenly Husband who didn't give up on her because of her sins; One who was there to guide her out of her wrong ways and to be her God and change her heart to be His obedient child.[6]

She told me with tears in her eyes, "Sally, Jesus is now my best Friend. He

---

5. Jeremiah 32:27.
6. Ezekiel 36:25–28.

is always with me, and I am finding that my insecurity and fear are being replaced with trust and peace. It does take effort—but it is so worth it! Sometimes I catch myself wallowing in a pity party. I see that God doesn't force His ways on me—Satan is the one who tries to do that through my emotions. As soon as I recognize what I'm doing, I can cry out to God and choose to have Him rule over me. As I choose with my will to serve Him, in time, He subdues my negative emotions, and I feel content.

"What really excites me about all this, Sally, is that as I am finding freedom from my emotional confusion on the inside, God is helping me bring greater order to the physical confusion in my home. I listened to your CD seminar, *The Making of a Woman,* and God helped me step by step to begin to make some changes. First, He helped me work out a skeleton schedule so that we get up in the morning at a regular time, have our meals at set times, and go to bed at night at a predictable time. Just that one change reduced the stress level in our home markedly. Now, everyone knows what to expect.

"Then God put it on my heart to bring general order to my house. There are still a lot of closets and drawers that need to be cleaned out, simplified, and organized, but God helped me to clean up the clutter. At the same time, He started prompting me to put away things when I finished using them. When I change Micah's diaper, I throw it away immediately instead of leaving it to pick up later. When I do the laundry, I fold it as soon as it comes out of the dryer instead of waiting until five loads are all wrinkled up together. After a meal, we wash the dishes right away. Before the boys go outside to play or eat a meal, they have to put away whatever book or toys they were playing with. I've had a hard time getting their cooperation with that—I'd like to talk with you about that in just a moment.

"I still have a long way to go to become the housekeeper I think God wants me to be. But knowing I'm loved and valued by Him is giving me the freedom to begin taking little steps forward under His direction. And do you know what? Having the home picked up makes it seem more restful. It's not so stressful to be there!"

"Deana, I'm so happy to hear how you and God are working together. I see the light of hope in your eyes, and that thrills me. And you're right. God does care about how we manage our physical surroundings.

"When Moses brought the children of Israel out of Egypt into the wilderness, the first lesson God wanted to teach His children was to sanctify themselves and wash their clothes in preparation to meet God and receive His commandments. God wants us, His children, to wash our clothes, to put our tents in order, and to cleanse our hearts also. The inward work and the outward work complement each other.[7]

"As we learn how to bring physical order into our homes under God's tutorship, we will also learn the parallel lessons of how we can have a *neat, orderly*

---

7. Exodus 19:10, 14.

mind. As we discard the excess clutter in each room, we learn lessons of how God wants to help us identify and discard unwholesome, self-serving, or unkind thoughts. As we bring order to the physical structure of our home, God wants to bring order and peace to our thoughts. Everything in our home and in our minds should be pure, sweet, and uplifting.

"Keeping a neat, orderly mind requires *little attentions often* in surrendering, cleansing, and replacing good for evil. These are just the habits needed to keep a neat, orderly home.

"Physical cleanliness and order bring *outward peace* into the home. Ordering the mind to follow God brings an *inward peace* to all who submit to God. Without Satan driving our emotions we can eliminate discord, friction, disputes, chaos, confusion, turmoil, strife, conflicts, contention, and all selfishness. And when those nasty things are replaced with love, joy, peace, gentleness, self-control, and patience, our home becomes a little bit of heaven, doesn't it? A peaceful home is one where God is at the helm."

"Oh, I'm getting the picture, Sally. It takes a lot of work to keep filtering my thoughts through God and making the changes He asks me to. But it is so much better than the old way of floundering through each day, overwhelmed and depressed. Oh, I still have my bad days. But, as you said, I find that God is there to pick me up and help me move forward again."

Love has two sides

"But I wanted to ask you about my boys. I still find myself swinging back and forth between being irritable and overindulgent. When I lose my temper, Stern Stanley gives it right back to me. Oh, he can be so disrespectful—even at the age of four! But poor little Micah is just crushed. He withdraws and cries and sometimes is inconsolable."

As Deana shared, I silently asked God for wisdom. "Deana, our children, especially our infants and toddlers, are very much affected by the emotional climate we project to them.

"When you are peevish, the infant and toddler take in your emotions and react to them. You see this very clearly with your boys. I think you already know that your emotional climate needs to change, and you are beginning to understand how to go about this. The key is recognizing the lying thoughts that are driving your emotions and replacing them with God's truth. In this case, I sense that your definition of love is unbalanced because of your history."

Deana looked surprised. "My definition of love? I hadn't thought about that. I know I love my boys. There isn't anything I wouldn't do for them. They are the center of my day and the focus of my prayers."

"Yes, Deana, you love your boys in the best way that you now understand. But we all need to compare the way we love with how God loves us. His love for us is the model for how we love our children. God's love is a balance of the softer virtues and the firmer virtues. God gives unsparingly to meet our genuine needs, and He sets very firm limits on evil.[8]

"Our children need the same from us. They need us to give unsparingly to meet their needs for belonging, for safety, and for a pleasant home. They need to be nurtured and patiently taught everything they need to know for life. But they also need the firmer side of love. They need us to set consistent limits on what is wrong. It is love to say 'No' to something that they want that is not good for them. It is not true love that leads us to allow our children to form destructive habits."

Deana was quiet for a moment, and tears filled her eyes. "Sally, that's a very different picture of love than what I've had. I can see that I'll need God a lot to grapple with this. But it makes a lot of sense to me."

I continued, "A baby or toddler that knows his boundaries and is introduced to Jesus to empower his choices for right is a happy child. As the child learns the lesson of yielding to his parents and God, he will demonstrate Christ-like characteristics. He will be content because he trusts his parent, whether the child is a timid girl or a rambunctious boy. You are God's instrument to help direct and create your child in the way of God and heaven. Your hand in Christ's makes this possible for your home.

"Don't be discouraged, Deana. The best success for building a pleasant home is to deal with the tiny beginnings of Satan's characteristics, such as anger, fear, bossiness, selfishness, impatience, or sassiness. These faults are much easier to correct now than any time later. Replace the wrong responses with the right ones, one by one.

"God will direct your steps to the right or to the left in your character growth, in making your home a peaceful place, and in dealing with your infant's or toddler's negative character traits. God is there for you. Period. He has all the answers to every problem you may encounter. With Him, we can create this heavenly spirit in our home regardless of our past."[9]

Deana and I talked for some time about this genuine kind of love that calls a child to self-denial while encouraging his connection with Christ, so he can taste grace empowering his choices. Deana recognized how necessary this element is for creating a pleasant home atmosphere.

Then she asked me, "Do husbands need this kind of love too? I mean, I know I need to respect my husband and not treat him like a child . . . but when he comes home and launches into one of his tirades, I find myself doing anything he wants me to do to try to appease him. I always thought that was my Christian duty as a wife. But as we have talked, I'm beginning to wonder. It's almost like I'm rewarding his destructive behavior."

I sent another prayer heavenward and then began, "Both father and mother contribute to the home atmosphere. God intends for each to do their part and be a team together. The husband needs to support his wife physically by helping

8. Leviticus 26.
9. Romans 12:21.

with the many home duties, such as cooking, doing dishes, emptying trash, or caring for the children, so that his wife isn't worn out by overwork. At the same time, the wife needs to do her best to run the home without his help. Neither the husband nor the wife should be a slave to the other. God meant them to be a team! The husband needs to support his wife emotionally by praying for her, affirming her, taking time to listen to her, and being her true friend. Christ can empower the husband to be all that God designed him to be.

"A moody, unpredictable, or unsupportive father places a burden of rejection, shame, and unhappiness upon his wife and children. The mother then has a double burden that she must take to her Savior in order to rise above such negative feelings for her sake and that of their children. That is what you are dealing with in your situation. Because of his deeply ingrained negative habits, your husband is not only depriving you and your children of what God intended, but he is also depriving himself of the joy and fulfillment of true intimacy with you and connection with his children.

"God wants to use you as His agent to reach your husband. God has a plan for reaching your husband's heart and leading him to be a true father to your children. Your part is to cooperate with God. That means you must be willing to return good for evil to your husband when God asks you to—and to cross your husband and endure his wrath when God asks you to. Staying close to God and filtering all you say and do through Him while seeking for His approval is your key once again."

Deana took these principles to heart and began to apply them in earnest. She continued to experience God's power changing her thoughts and feelings. She learned to recognize God's inaudible voice to her conscience through the Scriptures, the lessons of nature, providential leadings, and the impressions of the Holy Spirit upon her mind. Her confidence in God grew. She began to train her children how to overcome their anger, their timidity, their insecurity, and their wrong views of God.

Her husband was severely challenged by the changes Deana made and the resulting freedom she found. She was becoming the wife he had demanded her to be, but he didn't like it. His manipulative control tactics no longer worked on her. She remained calm and peaceful in spite of his tirades and let him own his own emotions. For a time, conflicts increased in the home as he tried to goad her back into her old ways of responding to him. Deana found this painful, but now the pain drove her to God for His power over destructive emotions. As she submitted to Him, He was faithful to deliver her.

Over time and through many painful interactions, Deana's husband realized that his wife had found something that he needed too—a Savior who can redeem us from the inside out. He made the decision to put God in charge and to begin to filter his thoughts and responses through God. By little steps, he became a husband and father in every sense of the word. He learned to regulate his schedule, to come home with kind words for his family, to anticipate their needs and to deny himself to meet those needs. His family no longer cringed when they heard his car pull into the driveway. Instead, they would run out the door to meet him with big smiles on their faces!

What could God do for your home if you gave Him full control over your life? You cannot overestimate the value of a pleasant home. It is worth every denial of self, every sacrifice, and every change you may have to make in order to gain it. And the investment you make of yourself to achieve this result will bring rich dividends in the lives of your children and your children's children. Why not begin today?

THE LONE EMBRACE
A SPECIAL WORD OF ENCOURAGEMENT FOR SINGLE PARENTS

A pleasant home may seem unattainable to a single parent. The heavy burdens you carry and the endless needs that confront you can make pleasantness seem like a luxury. Believe me—it is not! It is fundamental to your happiness and the well-being of your children. It can become yours when you make the same decision Deana did. When the big *I* steps down from the throne in your heart and *God* rules there, you will begin to experience positive changes.

Put your hand in God's hand and begin the journey with Him. Your destination may seem obscure and far away, but remember that you complete the longest trip by taking one step forward. Trust God, and keep taking the next step He points out to you.

Landon Hohnberger.
A pleasant home shows in the face and eyes of our toddler.

Chapter 11
A Predictable Home

And the work of righteousness shall be peace;
and the effect of righteousness quietness and assurance for ever.
—Isaiah 32:17

Tara rolled wearily over in bed as the sound of a car backing out of the driveway awakened her. She peered through bleary eyes at the clock on her bedside table. "It's seven thirty in the morning. Bill must have left for work. Wish I were doing the same. I used to have a fairly productive life. Now I've become an antisocial milk machine who never accomplishes anything." Tears of resentment and frustration spilled onto her pillow. The reality of being a first-time mother was nothing like what she had envisioned when she first found out she was pregnant.

Tara was a very capable young woman who had breezed through school with little effort. After graduation, she had married Bill and accepted a position as an office manager for a busy medical practice. She and Bill had delayed having children for several years to build their financial security so that Tara could be a stay-at-home mom. Tara had looked forward to motherhood with dreamy expectations and assumed she would be able to "wing it" the way she always had. She never thought of studying or planning ahead of time for being a mother. "Doesn't motherhood just come naturally to a woman?" she asked herself.

Now she could hardly bear the thought of facing another day—and nights were even worse. During recent months, had she ever slept a full night without being awakened three or four times? Visions of her kitchen paraded through her head: dirty dishes stacked all over the counter. "And I have a dishwasher," she chided herself. The laundry room—she shuddered at the mental picture of two weeks of dirty clothes piled in a heap. Soon they'd have nothing left to wear. And she couldn't remember the last time she had scrubbed her bathroom or sat down for a full meal. There had been a time in the distant past when Tara had prided herself on her tidy house. Now she couldn't seem to accomplish anything—except trying to pacify six-month-old Tirzah, and she wasn't even successful at that. Feelings of hopelessness and despair washed over Tara, and tasks became impossible.

She had chosen to breast-feed Tirzah, but found the whole experience extremely frustrating. She spent an hour every two hours feeding her baby. A breast infection made the whole experience so painful that she developed a very negative attitude toward her sweet little Tirzah. In turn, Tirzah sensed Tara's resentment and frustration and became increasingly fussy. Both mother and daughter seemed to feed on the same negative thoughts and feelings.

The antibiotics Tara had taken to treat her breast infection decreased her milk, requiring her to spend more time feeding her daughter or supplementing the breast milk with a bottle. Tirzah had refused the bottle, so Tara finally asked for help. Her well-meaning advisor encouraged her to feed Tirzah "on demand"—and things went from bad to worse! Tirzah was now six months old, and Tara was ready to quit being a mother!

An all-too-familiar wail reached Tara's ears. "Oh no! She's awake. Will I ever have a life again?"

Reactive or proactive?

Poor Tara is caught up in a reactive mode of parenting. By *reactive* I mean that she reacts spontaneously and emotionally to events and situations as they occur rather than taking the initiative to educate herself regarding feeding, character development, and communion with God for wisdom to overcome these difficulties. Tara is a slave to her circumstances rather than the queen ruling over them. Her frustration increases Tirzah's confusion, which feeds Tara's frustration. The more Tara reacts, gives up, and withdraws from God, the further she gets from finding the peace and stability she so longs for.

Tara would find a well-planned schedule to be her key to taking the bull by the horns. It would be a tool to help her take control of her life instead of allowing her situation and emotions to control her. Time for the essentials of life is the foundation to productivity and peace. A schedule for the home means that home is dependable, and dependability makes for a happy infant, child, spouse, and mother.

A scheduled home is a *predictable* home. Positive predictability builds trust. When there is a defined time to eat, your infant learns by experience that he is faithfully fed on time. The little one comes to know when it is time to work and exercise his limbs, when it is time to nap, and when it is time to be cuddled and sung to—because these things are scheduled and occur with regularity. When predictability is combined with pleasant attitudes, contentment and trust grow. Our babies' needs are met consistently. They don't have to scream for food, because they are fed before that big empty feeling comes and desperation sets in. Neither do they struggle with the digestive problems that come as a by-product of being fed when they don't need food.

God Himself has established order and regularity as a law of our beings. The sun rises and sets at predictable times. Days, months, years, and seasons are all based on order and regularity. He has built a circadian rhythm into our bodies that is important in determining our sleeping and feeding patterns. This circadian rhythm is clearly reflected in the rise and fall of core body temperature, brain wave activity, hormone production, cell regeneration, and other biological activities. A disturbance in the human circadian rhythm is associated with a number of health problems, including seasonal affective disorder (SAD) and delayed sleep phase syndrome (DSPS). The key to treating and preventing circadian rhythm disorders is a consistent daily routine. God says, "To every thing there is a season, and a time to every purpose."[1]

A schedule for feeding, waking, and sleeping teaches the infant that Mother and Father are dependable. When parents consistently help their babies work through their fussy times, fearful times, anxious times, impatient times, or gassy times, the baby feels more secure, knowing that she will get help when she needs it.

"So," I hear you asking, "how do I make a schedule work? I've tried schedules before, and I always end up frustrated."

How to develop a skeleton schedule—the first layer

The *first step* to a successful schedule is to take some time out with God to list the essentials of life. God is very interested in the details of our lives. "The steps of a good man are ordered by the LORD."[2] He wants to help us live controlled, ordered lives. He does not design that our lives should be in perpetual chaos. He encourages us, "Let all things be done decently and in order."[3] In communion with Him, list your essentials.

- Time to get up
- Time for personal and family worship
- Time for personal hygiene
- Time for family meals and feeding the baby
- Time to care for the baby
- Time for house duties
- Time for my spouse
- Time to go to bed

The *second step* is to create your skeleton schedule. Just as the bones of the body provide the underlying structure that gives stability to the other organs, your skeleton schedule will provide stability for the functioning of your home. To begin, map out the hours of the day in half-hour or hour increments. Then, create a column for each member of your family and schedule the essentials. If you are the mother, include a column for your husband—not to schedule his life for him, but so you can see what his routine is and adapt your schedule to meet his needs as far as it is reasonable to do so.

	Father	Mother	Baby
5:00		Feed Baby	Breast-feed
5:30	Time with Baby	Shower	Time with Father
6:00	Time with God	Time with God	Sleep
6:30	Prepare for work	Meal preparation	
7:00	Breakfast	Breakfast	

1. Ecclesiastes 3:1.
2. Psalm 37:23.
3. 1 Corinthians 14:40.

I encourage you to consult with your husband and older children about what you are doing and why—and consider their input. If you are able, make this a team project! Remember, a schedule should be your friend, guide, and helper. It is a tool to help you remain proactive. Build in some flexibility so that the schedule does not take over and become a pushy taskmaster. Don't try to schedule every fifteen minutes. If you do this, I can promise you that you will end up frustrated.

The *third step* is to implement your schedule. Turn off the TV if you need to; mute the phone if necessary; cancel your trip to the mall. But make it a priority to follow your new routine. As you find the essential things consistently being accomplished, it feels so good! With a time set aside for each thing, you can feel in control again. The clouds of despair and despondency vanish. You have time to talk with God, time for peace and quiet, time to sleep—enough time, anyway—and time to eat regularly. You'll be surprised how much more positive each trial looks under the sunshine of a schedule. A peace will enter your soul with God's residing presence.[4]

The *fourth step* is very important, and I will address that a little later in this chapter. First, however, I'd like to share some ideas for scheduling that are unique to having an infant in the home.

The baby is better with routine

Babies like routine—so do toddlers. If you followed a routine while your baby was in the womb, your infant will already be accustomed to regularity and will flow right into a schedule. If following a schedule is new to you and your baby is older, it will be more of a challenge for both of you, but the benefits of a predictable home far outweigh the effort required to establish regularity. With Christ, you can accomplish this. Divine power combined with human effort brings success. Seek God, make a plan, and then go forward with Him.

I'll give you a brief and simple plan that works if you work the plan with God leading. (For further ideas, see the resources on scheduling listed in the resource section.) An easy overview of the baby's schedule is to rotate eating, awake time, and sleep time.

Newborns generally need to be fed every three to four hours. If you opt to feed every three hours at first, plan to switch to four-hour increments by the time your infant reaches four months of age. At four months, babies need fewer feedings since they are eating more each time. Feeding times should last twenty to thirty minutes, including burping. If the baby consistently wants to suck longer, try giving him a pacifier.

---

4. See Isaiah 32:17. For more information regarding a schedule that will give you guidelines for your home after the first year of raising your infant, read the chapter "Does Your Schedule Match Your Priorities?" in my book *Parenting by the Spirit*. Here you can read a more detailed explanation of the concept of a skeleton schedule and learn how to include *your* absolute essentials—those things that should be done daily and in their appointed time for your family.

If you are breast-feeding your baby, you are giving your baby more than milk. Your milk carries antibodies to your child that gives his immune system a boost and helps to protect him from colds, influenza, and other diseases. It's still a good idea to protect your infant from exposure to sick people, to eat well yourself, and to stay close to God. This is another way to give your child a dependable home.

Another interesting fact that is nice to know is that for the first five minutes of feeding, a mother's milk is like skim milk. For the second five minutes, the mother's milk is like regular milk. And for the last fifteen to twenty minutes, it is like cream. If a baby is breast-fed often, he will not nurse as long and may not get as good quality milk as the baby who is nursed longer but less frequently.

The feeding schedule should be flexible to a point. For instance, when the baby has a growth spurt, he will be fussier and may need a longer feeding time or a temporary increase in frequency. If you stay close to God, He will put the thought in your mind when change is necessary.

The first year of life for the breast-feeding mother is a real adjustment. Satan will imply that you are doing nothing important because you can't review your day and list any tangible things getting done. In reality, you are bonding with your child—which is extremely important. Use the time to pray for and with your infant. Ponder the high honor of motherhood and what your work really involves. Commune with God for wisdom about how to connect your baby to Him, and grapple with what character development consists of. Don't expect the first six months to show tangible evidences of your investment of time and energy. But the next six months will reward your efforts with a happy and secure child.

An important lesson for the baby to learn in those first few months is the difference between night and day. Daytime is for activity, and nighttime is for sleeping. Of course, newborns sleep much of the time, day and night, but schedule some awake time for them following their daytime feedings. Start with just ten to thirty minutes at a time, but increase it as the baby gets older. Awake time is anything other than sleeping. It includes diaper changes, baths, massages, interaction with parents, and playing or exercise time. During the day, you should wake up the baby for feedings if he is still sleeping. At night, let the baby sleep until he wakes up or you sense God directing you to alter the schedule. Realize that not every thought is from God. Each idea must be weighed, measured, and judged as to its source.

Sleep time follows awake time. It's best to have awake time between feeding and sleeping times, because we don't want the infant to associate eating with sleeping—that can cause bigger problems down the road. Avoid using the breast or the bottle to put your child to sleep.

Some mothers find that swaddling their newborn mimics the womb and helps the infant not to wake himself by jerking his arms. Babies that like this consider swaddling to be snug and cozy. Experiment with your baby.

You can expect a newborn to sleep for two to three hours at a time. This is the time for you to do what you need to do, including resting and taking care of yourself. Seek God's input to find the proper balance of rest and activity for you. Some mothers overload their to-do list and wear themselves out, while others lazily leave off all duties. So, set reasonable goals with God guiding you. As your baby grows older, his sleep time during the day will decrease, and he will have more awake time that you need to direct.

I think all parents celebrate the day, or rather the night, when their baby sleeps all the way through the night. Some babies learn to do this easier than others. Many mothers find it advantageous to put their baby down to sleep after the last feeding of the night—for many that is 10:00 P.M. They just change the diaper, eliminate awake time, and put the baby down to sleep.

By about eight weeks, the baby should have only one feeding during the night and should sleep between six and eight hours. By working with your schedule, you can train your baby to eat more and be more active during the daytime and to be ready to eliminate the night feedings by the time he is four months old—or sooner.

Should your baby not wake until 4:00 or 5:00 A.M. and you have scheduled your first feeding at 6:00 A.M., try to hold the baby off to keep him on the daytime schedule that fits your family routine. If you can't put him off, give him a small feeding just to hold him over. Then wake him for the first morning feeding at the scheduled time. This will bring in schedule and routine as a tool to help you have a consistent, dependable schedule.

As you set up a dependable schedule under God's direction and wise counsel, you will develop habits of regularity, and your baby will settle into that schedule as well. You will be developing mental attitudes of contentedness, trust, and faith. Your baby will feel that his parents take care of his every need and that they are dependable. A bond of trust will develop. These are key factors in a happy baby and a happy home.

As the infant grows older, he spends less time eating and sleeping—and more time awake, learning about the world he lives in. Infants need wise management to meet their growing physical needs. By the time they are a year old, they can begin to learn small but useful occupations, which we will address in a later chapter.

From ages one to four, a child's character development becomes the major occupation for both mother and child. Teaching your child how to respond to right and wrong thoughts, feelings, and emotions is your work under God's tutorship. Be a predictable parent by taking your infant or toddler to Christ consistently to exercise choices for right according to his or her age.

Flesh out the skeleton schedule

This brings me back to the *fourth step* in establishing a schedule as the backbone of a predictable home—the step of frequently evaluating your routine and adjusting it under God's guidance. As you find a workable, simple, yet flexible schedule that accommodates the skeleton necessities of the home, then you can add whatever other priorities you may have, such as tending to your housekeeping, laundry, mending, cooking, cleaning windows, shopping, yardwork, watering the flowers, gardening, or whatever else needs regular attention. These things can be added at your discretion.

Are there other siblings in the home? They will take a piece of your schedule in this secondary layer, and something else will get crowded out. Plan time in the schedule for them—for training, playing, and homeschooling, if that is part of your priorities.

Maximize your resources. Divide up home duties between you and your husband—if he is willing and able to help. Maybe on special occasions your mother or a friend has some time to help you. Consider hiring a responsible schoolgirl to do the major cleaning and housework once or twice a week if your budget will allow.

Or try this organizational tip. Divide up your home duties throughout the week so that the cleaning doesn't funnel itself all into a single day. Do a load or two of laundry every day so that it never becomes a huge chore. Dust and iron on Wednesday. Clean the bathrooms on Thursday. Do the floors on Friday. Daily straighten your living room and bedroom while you are talking on the phone. Straighten up the laundry room with those five extra minutes you have right now.

Teach your older children to be part of the team. Train your two-year-old to pick up and put away one toy before he gets out another. Teach your two- or three-year-old to help fold washcloths or match socks, then add to their responsibilities. They get to work side by side with you, which is what they desire, and you can have a pleasant conversation during this play and work time. Have the older siblings run to get a diaper or a toy for you. Helping makes for a happy home. Be grateful for their true and honest help. Teach and train them in good service and give honest praise.

Don't overfill your schedule or expect great accomplishments the first year of your baby's life—that is what brings stress. Be realistic. There are only twenty-four hours in a day. Do what you can. Turn to God to improve your efficiency, but don't try to be a superwoman or compare yourself with another mother who seems to be able to accomplish more than you do. If you do, you will live in perpetual unrest. Pace yourself for what you can do!

A *schedule is to be your tool* to help you accomplish the basic tasks of your day. It takes time to learn to use a tool properly, so be patient with yourself. Look for progress, not perfection, in your habits. It may be that you were not trained as a child how to be organized. You may find that the habits of disorder are very strong. You don't have to stay in bondage to these habits. Jesus is your personal Friend and a powerful Savior who can teach you heavenly ways of order. Learn to recognize and follow His voice.[5] You can choose God or Satan as

---

5. Jeremiah 32:27. See also chapter 4, "The Voice of God" in *Parenting by the Spirit* and *Parenting Your Child by the Spirit.*

your master by your God-given freewill choice every moment of your day.[6] No one can force you to remain under the rule of disorder. Satan may try by stirring up distaste for order, a dislike of disciplining yourself. But you can say "No" to all his tactics. God will empower you when you choose to come out of disorder and into orderly habits, and your home will reflect these choices.

Remember that your schedule is a tool—it is not your savior. Life will often present circumstances that tend to throw us off balance. We can look at these situations as frustrations or as opportunities to call out to God for help to identify the problem, name it, and choose a reasonable response.

A common frustration for a parent—one that can throw off the whole schedule—is a baby who cries when he should be sleeping. I don't believe in letting a baby just cry and cry for long periods of time. I wouldn't do this unless I was assured God was leading me with a specific purpose in mind. In most cases, letting a child continue to cry becomes a source of insecurity for him. But neither do I believe in rushing in and scooping up the baby every time he whimpers. So, seek God for His wisdom.

First, *listen* to the cry in order to evaluate why the child is awake during a sleep time. Is it a cry of pain, frustration, or working up a bowel movement? You will learn to tell the difference between pain, fear, gas, or "I'm working on something."

Second, *look and observe*. Look at the face and body movements to understand the possible reason for waking. Maybe the baby's foot is caught in the slats of his crib. Consider what happened during the previous cycle of sleep/feed/awake time. Is the baby overtired? Is it a bowel issue?

Third, *pray for wisdom and respond*. Ask God to direct your thoughts and reasoning to the right conclusion to act upon. Follow your reason with what knowledge you have. God will be directing in the process—you will recognize it in hindsight more than at the moment. How you and your infant are taught to respond to these trials is character development.

Tired little lamb

Three-year-old Laura couldn't go to sleep without a struggle. From the time she was a newborn, her mother had to lie down with her, feed her, sing to her, and pat her before she would finally go off to dreamland. The long protracted effort frustrated Mother, which Laura sensed. Both mother and daughter dreaded nap time and bedtime.

This struggle with sleep made keeping a routine very difficult. Not only did Laura not go to sleep or wake up on time, but her missed naps also produced an irritable disposition that took more time to deal with. Mother's friends told her not to worry about it—that Laura would grow out of it. Mother wasn't so sure about this. She had talked to God about it, but it seemed that God was not answering her prayers or giving her any special ideas for correction. Laura's rest

---

6. Joshua 24:15.

time seemed always associated with a struggle.

One morning, God told Mother, *"I want you to think back on what the history of nap and sleep time has been with Laura."* As Mother pondered, another thought came to her mind. *"I want to teach you—both mother and child—how to rest without struggling."*

She liked the thought, but didn't see how that could be. Family members happened to be visiting in the home right then, and Mother knew Laura wouldn't sleep. "We've struggled for two days so far, Lord, with no nap, and Laura so desperately needs her nap." Just then, someone called from the kitchen, and Mother got into her day without finishing her time with God.

By the afternoon, Laura was very irritable and unreasonable. She was tired, but she fought going down for a nap. Mother finally took Laura into her room and tried the usual ways to get her to sleep. She felt desperate and could feel her frustration level rising. Crying silently to God in her desperation, she begged, "Help me use love as my power and success!"

Just then, Laura made a profound statement. "Mama, I don't know how to go to sleep!"

Mother was floored when she heard that, because she had never thought about going to sleep as a *learned skill*—a trained behavior. For three years, Laura had associated sleep with stress. Mother had never thought to teach her how to relax and go to sleep. So she asked Jesus, "How can I help Laura learn to go to sleep?"

"How would you put a little tired, restless lamb to sleep?"

She thought for a moment and then gathered Laura into her arms. "Sweetheart, pretend that you are a tired, little lamb. Just close your eyes and imagine being in Jesus' lap. You are safe, tired, and comfortable in His arms. You can relax, close your eyes, and fall asleep as one of His little lambs."

After a little while of talking, praying, and helping Laura relax, Mother laid the little girl in her bed, and within ten minutes Laura was asleep! The next day, Mother tried this technique again, and it worked.

God has the solution to all of your anxieties and frustrations. As we place our wills in God's hands and deal with the destructive character traits that come up in ourselves and in our children, we can learn to rest without a struggle. We are to restrain the wrong and cultivate the right. Each victory brings greater joy and stability to our home. Parents, we need to be dependable and not let Satan rule over our children in thought or word, habit or deed. We must consistently bring our infant/toddler to Christ to be changed. God will teach us—and our infant—how to be His child and rest from self's tyrannical rule. He will teach us how to rest from the humanism of doing what Christ asks us to do in self. We must each come to Jesus that we may have life and have that upright life more abundantly!

It really will make a difference!

Tara awoke at 5:00 A.M. Two-year-old Tirzah and two-month-old Andrew were still sleeping. Tara had slept for seven hours straight and felt good. She got up to use the bathroom, and as she was washing her hands, she talked with God. "Thank You for helping me make my home predictable. I actually like being a mother now. Things have changed so much since Tirzah was a newborn!"

"Why don't you go ahead and start your day?" God posed the thought to her. *"You could feed the baby and have time for an exercise workout. Haven't you wanted to do that?"*

"Well, yes I have. It would feel nice to sleep some more, though, since the baby is sleeping." As Tara pondered her options, she decided to stay up.

"Come on, little one, wake up. It's time to eat. Mommy is full. You can nurse, and then you can go back to sleep while I do my exercises this morning to work off this extra fluff that I have. Won't that be nice, precious?" And the baby responded happily.

Mother situated herself and the baby in the rocking chair. She felt wide-awake and continued her conversation with God. "You know, Lord, this might be a good program. I think I could do this. Tirzah doesn't get up until 7:00 A.M., and this would give me two hours to exercise, shower, and have my personal worship time with You without a rush. I need all of that!"

Mother fed the baby in a leisurely manner while continuing to converse with God as with a friend. She made the choice to connect with God. He would be her Lord all day and she promised to respond when she was convinced He was prompting thoughts in her mind. "Interrupt me when I'm heading in the wrong direction," she prayed. Mother burped baby Andrew, told him how much she loved him, and then turned again to God. She gave Him permission to be her baby's Lord and surrendered his will and way for him, as though it were her own. All too soon, she noticed half an hour had passed. She tucked the baby back in his crib to sleep. He drowsily, happily, and willingly went off to sleep, secure in his mother's care.

Exercise time was great! It felt good to get back into this routine again. She used her stair stepper for twenty minutes and did some stretching. She enjoyed a leisurely shower and then sat in her quiet spot in her bedroom with her Bible and her Lord. "Lord, I too easily get irritated with my children and myself. I want to do better. Help me to be aware when I'm about to slip into the wrong attitude. I want to think Your thoughts and feel Your feelings instead of obeying these wrong ways. I want You to re-create me in Your image after Your likeness." Then she prayed for her immediate family individually, her extended family, and for special needs.

Next, she opened her Bible and began to read in Deuteronomy, asking for God's direction. She read a little, then talked to God. He helped her see parallels between her life and what she was reading in the Bible that she had never seen before. She had barely read half the chapter this way when she heard two-year-old Tirzah climbing out of bed and opening her door. Sure enough—it was 7:00 A.M. How time flies when you are having fun!

We can cooperate with God just as Tara learned to. Her heart and mind were sensitive and aware of the inaudible voice of God speaking to her reason, intellect, and conscience. His voice may not have any unique earmarks indicating which thoughts are from Him, but with reason, evaluation, and experience you will come to know when He is speaking to you. Everything good comes from God. As Tara repeated this routine, it worked well for her. She felt connected to God, had peace in her heart, and trusted God to keep her. That attitude brought more confidence that change was possible. And most importantly, she responded to the promptings of the Lord in her day. Without our permission and cooperation, God cannot keep us, change us, or direct our steps. So this connection is the most important part of any parent's day.

With this beginning, Mother was patient when her two-year-old was fussy, and she took her over and over to Christ to decide to follow the right over the pull of her flesh. When the toilet bowl backed up—no problem. She turned automatically to Jesus, much like the flowers turn to the sun. God brought to her mind where her husband had told her he'd put the plunger.

Tara sang while she made some homemade bread during one of the baby's sleep times. She felt good and wanted to use her energy to do something special for the family. The house was picked up and in order. This alone time brought such a peace to her soul. Tirzah helped Mother organize her toys. She liked being with her mother and aimed to please her. The schedule Tara had laid out and modified with each new phase of parenthood was a big help in directing her energies, and she knew just what to do each day. She was so much happier.

God was giving Tara His power and wisdom at each step of her day. She expressed gratitude to Him often, and her mental spirit was like a sunny day. She was tempted on several occasions to give way to irritation, but God interrupted her thoughts at just the right time, and she yielded to Him. Victory— how sweet it is with Jesus at your side! Tara gave a good example of dying to self and following God instead. She instructed her toddler in new depths of helping, neatness, and order, and it was a wonderful day—heavenly, in fact! God was at the core of her life, keeping her heart and mind as she cooperated with Him.

This is being a dependable parent, fostering a pleasantly predictable home in the power of Christ—not self's willpower unaided. Wouldn't you like to have a home such as this? You can. Take hold of Christ and begin today.

THE LONE EMBRACE
A SPECIAL WORD OF ENCOURAGEMENT FOR SINGLE PARENTS

God is your faithful Instructor and your Savior from self. He will teach you how to parent by the Spirit, how to bring happiness into your heart and your home and make your life doable. A schedule for your life is not an enemy. It is your friend, if you embrace it under God's direction. Educate yourself with all the suggestions in the referenced books, picking and choosing with God which you will try to do in your home. Take one little step today, and soon you will see that you are miles from where you used to be under the yoke of fear, insecurity, and unworthiness. Remember, you are not alone in heart and mind if you marry Jesus as your heavenly Husband. You and God are the majority and no longer in the minority. Your attitude and faith in Jesus—not your circumstances—will determine your attitude in life. Try God!

Matthew and Angela Hohnberger are striving to
make their home predictable.

Chapter 12

Faith Building

For we walk by faith, not by sight.
—2 Corinthians 5:7

ow faith is the substance of things hoped for, the evidence of things not seen."[1] In other words, faith *is an act of believing without seeing*. It is trusting God—believing and following Him. It is learning that we must yield to do His will. He is very real, although we can't see Him. The ability to trust God and believe that He loves us and knows what is best for us is one of the most precious gifts parents can instill in their children. This will go with them for life.

Faith is a thought muscle that is developed through exercise. You can begin to develop that faith muscle in your little one even before he or she is born, by exercising your own trust in God and allowing His peace and presence to rule in your thoughts, feelings, and emotions. When your newborn experiences Christ in you, his faith is nurtured. Trust grows in an environment of trustworthiness. As God has earned our trust by being trustworthy, so we must earn the trust of our infants and toddlers.

Exercising trust

We can begin to teach faith to our infants and toddlers by playing peekaboo and commenting to the child that "Mommy is here—even when you can't see her!" Carry the lesson a little further for your toddler by closing your hand around a small toy. As the child opens your fingers to search for what you have said was there, you can say, "You trusted me. I said I had a toy for you, and you believed that what I said was true. You can believe and trust God in the same way. What He says, He will do—even if you can't see it at first." Point out how you can talk to someone on the phone and know who that person is by his voice, even though you cannot see him. Animal tracks, too, are evidence that the animal was there, although we did not see it.

Trusting Tommy, aged two, just loved it when his daddy came home. Daddy was so much fun to play with. He was much rougher and more exciting than his mommy. His father would lie on the floor while Tommy crawled up on the couch. Then Tommy would jump right into his daddy's faithful arms. When the two of them were out feeding the horses, Daddy helped Tommy climb a bale of hay and then jump to Daddy. Daddy never dropped him. At the swimming pool, Trusting Tommy cast himself fearlessly into the water where his daddy waited for him. He was secure, knowing his daddy would catch him safely.

---

1. Hebrews 11:1.

Your presence, actions, and responses can build faith in your little Tommy. Are you faithfully there for your toddler to physically jump to your arms? Are you there when your child needs you? Are you there emotionally for him? Are you faithfully available to bring him to know Christ in a practical way according to his age? As a child learns that he can safely love, trust, and obey you, he is prepared to love, trust, and obey his heavenly Father. This is the beginning of faith.

Faith is closely linked with prayer. You can illustrate to your toddler how prayer is like a key in the hand of faith that unlocks heaven's storehouse. Have your child use a key to open a locked door and teach him the parallel with faith. For a toddler, things that he wants are often out of reach. You can use these moments as opportunities to teach him that prayer is asking God for what we need and that God will give these things to us if they are good for us right now. If not, we trust God knows best. You can make this truth real by hiding things out of the reach of your toddler and then, after he prays, you can lift him to get the desired object. You can also teach him that sometimes his prayer is answered right away and sometimes he has to wait. Another time, he might desire something that could hurt him—like a sharp knife. When he prays or asks Mommy, and the answer is "No," he can learn to trust that "No" is best. Let him touch the knife to see it could hurt him. Learning reasons for "No" in the physical world helps your child be content when God says "No" as well. This is building faith.

There are endless object lessons like these that you can use to point your child to God and to teach lessons in the Christian walk. Let God become your Teacher and open your mind to see teaching opportunities all around you. He will not disappoint you.

A favorite game for my boys when they were three and four years old was "I am Hiding."[2] Matthew or Andrew would go hide in the living room and then start singing, "I am hiding, I am hiding, can you tell me where?" Then I'd sing in response, "I can't see you, I can't see you, but I know you're here." Then together we'd sing the second verse: "God is watching, God is loving children everywhere. I can't see Him, I can't see Him, but I know He's near."

Andrew's favorite hiding place was amidst the living room drapes. He would push his head and upper body behind the drapes and think that he was all hidden. He thought that if he couldn't see me, I couldn't see him either! Of course, I would chuckle and play along with him.

God builds the parent's faith first

It has often occurred to me that, as parents, we often do something similar with God. We think we are hiding from Him, when everything about us is plain and obvious to Him. We often hide from Him because deep down inside we have misconceptions about Him. We may think of Him as a harsh

2. Ladder of Life series, Teacher's Guide.

dictator to be dreaded or as a permissive parent who gives us what we want but who can't be respected. These misbeliefs about God may not be conscious, but they still affect us deeply. God comes looking for us. He wants us to come out of hiding and see Him as He truly is—our tender heavenly Father who doesn't give up on us because of our sins, rather He wants to empower us to change.

We owe it to ourselves, our children, and to God to step back from the curtain of false ideas and give God an opportunity to show us who He really is. As we get to know Him through His Word and as we experience His tender, helpful ways in our daily life, our faith muscle begins to grow, choice by choice. We believe what His Word says about Him instead of what our feelings and emotions tell us. If the Bible says it, I believe it, and that is good enough for me. "Faith comes by hearing, and hearing by the word of God."[3]

Faith in Christ's power, even if no larger than a grain of mustard seed, which is very small, can move mountains of misconceptions, mountains of opposing emotions, and the rock-hard places of old habits. If it can do that for us as adults, what can the exercise of faith do for our infants and toddlers?

Faith often conflicts with feelings. My feelings tell me that God is stern and unjust, but my faith in God's Word tells me that He is loving and just. When I choose to act in accordance with my faith, my feelings will, in time, come into line with my faith. At first, it doesn't seem real, but as faith is exercised it becomes very real and changes us.

For instance, at times my emotions tell me to be unhappy. My faith in God's Word tells me that God's will for me is to give thanks in everything. Which path I follow tells me whom I believe. If I choose to nurture my unhappy feelings, I'm following Satan and will reap sadness. If I choose, instead, to give thanks in accordance with my faith, asking God to make my choice real by His power, I'm following God and will find happiness. Choosing to follow God gives Him permission to work on the inside of my mind, removing the cobwebs of unhappiness. You can't see Him working, but in time your feelings will come in line with your faith. God can change your negative or wrong emotions. You will know God is there—first by faith, not by sight. Our feelings and emotions are not to be trusted when they oppose the truth of God as found in His Word.

God can be trusted fully, and He does what He says He will do. Let's see God only as the Bible portrays Him. Exercising our faith *in Him* will bring us freedom from our misconceptions and negative emotions. Parents, as we come to experience God's transformation of our misconceptions, we will be able to simplify this deliverance process and train our little ones to takes Jesus' hand, follow Him, and experience this freedom much earlier than we did. They will experience God as the loving Father He is.

---

3. Romans 10:17, NKJV.

How God builds the parent's faith

I recall our own timid beginnings of believing and following Christ. Jim and I were in the early stages of taking Bible studies to come to know God. While studying what the Bible says about prayer, I found a growing desire being expressed at last.

"Lord, heal my Matthew's crooked feet." Matthew was two months old and had been born with his little legs and feet deformed. When I'd lay him down to change his diaper, his legs bowed out and the soles of his feet touched each other. The problem was even more obvious when I put him in his swing. Our physician had prescribed a special brace for Matthew and predicted it would take several years to correct the problem. Every time I put Matthew down to sleep, I had to lace his little feet into a pair of sturdy baby shoes that were positioned flat on a bar with the toes pointed out at a forty-five-degree angle. He would cry and cry. No position was comfortable for him in that brace. I would shut the door but could still hear his cries of discomfort. It broke my heart.

As Jim and I studied about prayer, I finally uttered my plea to God for my child. I did not pray in full faith. Doubts mingled with my hope. I didn't even tell Jim about my prayer, because I was afraid he would disapprove.

A week went by. I continued to apply the brace and to pray, but nothing happened. One day as I was pulling the brace out of the closet, a thought came to me. It was God, although I didn't yet recognize His voice to my heart at that time. *"Sally, if you put the brace on and pray, how will you know if it is I who healed his feet or if the brace did its work?"*

God gave me time to mull that one over. I decided to put the brace into the closet and just pray. Again, I didn't tell Jim, for my faith was too small.

Some time went by. Matthew was now almost four months old. One morning, after breakfast, I put Matthew into his swing in the living room and wound it up. I headed for the kitchen, and as I reached the entry, I turned around to look at our precious Matthew. That's when I noticed it! Matthew's legs hung straight and normal with the bottoms of his feet toward the floor. I could hardly believe it!

I repositioned him in the seat—his legs were still straight! I pulled him out of the swing and lay him on the floor—the same thing was evident. His feet were down and straight! I got so excited I called Jim, and through tears of excitement, relayed my finding, telling him of my prayer for God to heal Matthew's feet and how I hadn't been using the brace at all for a long time—just prayer.

Jim didn't believe it until he came home and saw it for himself. God had chosen to heal those crooked feet. What a tender heavenly Father we serve! We can never earn or deserve such blessings. He freely bestows them at key times to get our attention or to draw us to Him and for us to be encouraged to exercise more faith.

Well, I can tell you that this expression of God's love for us drew Jim and me to Him as nothing else could have done. We wanted to know this Father. Who is He? And why does He care for us? We pass on to our children the stories of these experiences, telling them of the personal God who cares for them. What a joy that God does come down to this earth, to little insignificant me, to answer prayer! God is an awesome God when He answers. And when He does not answer in the way that we think He should, He is with us to empower us through this experience as well.

"And the Lord said, If ye had faith as a grain of mustard seed, ye might say unto this sycamine tree, Be thou plucked up by the root, and be thou planted in the sea; and it should obey you."[4]

Wild eyes

It happened one evening when Fred and Gina's firstborn son, Mark, was only four weeks old. They were in the family room, and Gina was nursing the baby. Suddenly his eyes went wild, jerking uncontrollably from side to side. In a few seconds they focused normally. Minutes passed, and then it happened again. Fred and Gina were alarmed.

Over the next few days, they saw their pediatrician and some other specialists. The diagnosis was nystagmus—a congenital condition that would last for life. The doctors predicted it would worsen as their son got older and would prevent him from learning to read, drive a car, and any other activity that required the ability to focus.

They were devastated. Gina cried out to God, "Lord, I can't believe it! Why? Why? Take my health, my life, but please let this little newborn baby be healthy." That night she thought a lot about sin and the originator of it all—Satan. She told him he could not have her baby—that he belonged to Jesus. Satan attempts to claim even newborns as his own. But we, their parents, can dedicate them to our loving God.

As the weeks went by, the erratic eye movements continued at unpredictable times. Gina sank deeper and deeper into despair. She needed strength from above, because she had none. At night, when Fred was asleep, she would claim the promises of God. "This poor man cried out, and the LORD heard him, and saved him out of all his troubles."[5] Oh, what a promise! She knew that God could heal Mark's eyes. God brought to her mind similar texts that also promised deliverance. She kept repeating these promises; they were her lifeline.

It is hard for a parent to see his or her child suffer. It's probably the worst thing that can happen to a parent. Gina reflected upon her heavenly Father—what enormous pain it must have been for Him to see His Son being crucified.

Gina felt she was walking "through the valley of the shadow of death."[6] She

---

4. Luke 17:6.
5. Psalm 34:6.
6. Psalm 23:4

knew that Jesus wanted her to trust Him fully—not by sight, but by faith—whether or not He healed her son. She wanted to do this, but she could not bring herself to accept this health condition in her son. She struggled with that issue for days and weeks.

Finally, she surrendered saying, "Lord, whatever is Your will, let it be so. If Mark will have this condition for the rest of his life—it is well with my soul. You will be with me through it. I surrender it *all* to You."

This was very hard to say, but what a burden was lifted from her shoulders! Peace from above filled her heart and soul. The Lord was waiting for this moment of faith. It was then that a miracle took place. Mark was touched by God's divine healing hand. God freed Mark from the eye disease, and it never returned again. Praise God!

I don't know why some children are healed and others aren't. In heaven, we will find out the reasons for these mysteries. But God used this experience to purify Gina's faith and to lead her to depend fully and wholly upon Him. She learned that only by continually holding on to God's outstretched hand, could she raise her son according to His will.

God takes us through various experiences calculated to build our faith in Him, because it is only by exercising our faith to connect with Him and to trust Him that we can become agents to build faith in our children. God doesn't always perform these kinds of physical miracles, but He always rewards faith. There is no greater miracle than a changed heart—of a parent or child!

The deeper faith-building miracle

Sandy was a young mother with a genetic disorder called Tourette's syndrome. Her case was mild enough that she was not aware she had it until after her youngest daughter was born with a severe case of the disease.

As an infant, Nicole was hyperactive and obsessive-compulsive. As a toddler, she struggled to learn. By the time Nicole was four years old, Sandy and her husband thought their daughter might be autistic and had her evaluated. That's when she was diagnosed with Tourette's syndrome and was placed on medication. Parenting difficulties included behavior problems, obsessive-compulsive disorder, attention deficit hyperactivity disorder, and sensory issues. As a nurse, Sandy educated herself thoroughly in all the treatment options and was very consistent in keeping Nicole in the proper therapies and on all the right medications. But in spite of her efforts, Nicole's behavior continually disrupted the peace of their home.

Sandy was frustrated. She cried out to God to heal Nicole. She had her anointed, but God didn't answer her prayer in the way she hoped. Sandy continued to search for better answers, because the traditional methods were not working. That's when God led her to attend an Empowered Living camp meeting. As Sandy listened to the principles of parenting by the Spirit that I presented, she argued with me in her own mind. "You don't understand, Sally. My child is disabled. These principles won't work for her."

Still, Sandy remained open for God to guide her and felt strongly impressed to purchase the CD seminar, *The Indulgent Parent Delivered*. As she listened to that series at home, the Holy Spirit began to teach her, and she began to understand what God was trying to tell her. She was too indulgent with Nicole, which made her condition worse, not better. Sandy recognized that she had been parenting *in self* rather than *in Christ*. A longing desire for *real* victory in Christ began to rise within her. That, in itself, is the work of the Holy Spirit—and the desires He implants within us He is fully prepared to fulfill.

Sandy asked the Lord to help her make a change and for the strength to persevere. What a challenge! By faith, she knew it was possible with Christ, but her emotions told her it would take too long, be too hard, and might not work. She chose to act on her faith.

The first hurdle was to make Nicole the top priority of her day. That meant that whenever Nicole had an attitude or behavioral problem, Sandy would have to stop whatever she was doing to deal with it—whether she was cooking, on the phone, or even driving. That was not an easy feat!

The second hurdle was devoting as much time as necessary until a *true heart surrender* was accomplished.

The third obstacle was for Sandy to learn to surrender and ask what God would have her to do instead of disciplining according to her own impulses. She asked herself, "How can I teach my child to surrender if I'm not surrendered?" She began to see that when she parented *in self*, Nicole didn't truly surrender. *In Christ* was different. God would impress her with what to say or do, and Nicole's surrender would transform her into a happy, pleasant little girl. When Christ is on the throne of the heart, the light shines forth for all to see. Sandy began to see herself as God's tool to train Nicole. She saw that God was the One changing her daughter—not Sandy or her methods. Her faith in Christ grew.

This new program was difficult at first for both mother and daughter. Nicole was not convinced. She rebelled, resisted praying, and argued at every step. She would say, "Do we have to pray again?" They discussed how these attitudes gave Satan the upper hand and that they needed to call on someone stronger to fight their battles. Sandy explained her God-given responsibility as a parent to ally herself with God and not let Satan have dominion over their home. "We will come to Him as many times a day as we need," she told Nicole, and Nicole began to realize that Sandy was not going to give up. Her mother refused to let Satan have Nicole and was willing to fight in her behalf because she loved her.

At times both Sandy and Nicole would be in tears when they were at odds with one another. Sandy would explain to Nicole that she was ready to act in her flesh. She would go to her room with tears flowing down her cheeks, asking God for strength and wisdom. When she was surrendered, she'd return to bring Nicole to surrender.

After one month of this program, there was a notable change in both Nicole and Sandy. Surrendering to God's will was quicker and easier. Soon they were able to surrender as soon as a problem would arise—instead of laboring for more than an hour. God impressed Sandy to reduce Nicole's medications, and God became the strong medicine that changed their hearts, minds, and home.

The greatest of all blessings was that negative attitudes were diminishing. Sandy's husband and other daughter noticed the difference and began to enter into a deeper walk with God themselves. They were learning how to stay surrendered to God continuously, and home became a happy place. Nicole's biggest handicap was being apart from God.

In hindsight, Sandy believes that God allowed this trial to happen in her life because she needed to come closer to God. If He had healed Nicole, she and her family would not be spiritually where they are today. God doesn't allow anything that isn't for our good. Someday we will understand more than we do today.

Even though Nicole and Sandy still deal with the liabilities of Tourette's syndrome, their faith in God is growing. They are experiencing the miracle of being "kept by the power of God through faith unto salvation."[7]

Faithfulness instills security

Little Nelly's parents were not there for her. They were so caught up in their lifestyle of alcoholism and promiscuity that Nelly was often not even fed—much less cleaned and cuddled. At six months of age, she was placed in a foster home. She was a bundle of fear, nervousness, and insecurity that whined and fussed a great deal—day and night. Nelly's foster mother took little Nelly to God to dedicate her to Him. She committed herself to seek from God the wisdom necessary to bring Nelly out of all her troubles.

The foster mother committed Nelly to God at night, in the morning, and at every situation that arose throughout the day. God led her to surrender Nelly's fear and insecurity for her when it arose. The mother would instruct Nelly very simply, "You are all right. I'm here. I won't leave you." After weeks of consistently doing this, the mother began doubting God was leading, for she saw no change in Nelly.

"Mother, be not weary in well doing. This will take some time," God encouraged her. Another month passed. The twenty-four-hour battle was wearing the foster mother down. She longed for just one full night of sleep. The temptation to give up was strong.

"Lord, I feel so weak and frail. I can't handle this much longer." The tears flowed freely. She needed comfort and security herself.

God impressed upon her mind, *"Mother, be strong and of good courage. Be not afraid for I am with thee. Faith grows the greatest in the dark, when you have no evidence that what you are doing is working. Continue to trust Me."*

The mother cooperated with God. In her mind's eye she saw herself crawling up into Jesus' lap and feeling safe and cared for in His loving arms. God subdued her doubting thoughts and emotions. Cheerfully she took up her work

---

7. 1 Peter 1:5.

of taking this child to Jesus again and again. "Trust God, Nelly. He's here. I'm here. You are all right. Calm down."

Very soon after that, Nervous Nelly had the breakthrough her foster mother had worked and prayed for so long. Her strong negative emotions began to give way to trust. She began to relax and smile. She actually began to sleep through the night consistently. Security grew. When Nelly was a year and a half old, her favorite story, which the mother repeated over and over, was the story of how safe Jesus is and how she could go to Him at any time and crawl up into His lap and fall asleep.

Once again, God stretched a parent's faith, enabling the mother to call forth the exercise of her child's faith.

Faith unlocks God's treasures

Three and-a-half-year-old Johnny was acting like a terror. It started at breakfast. He didn't want to eat pancakes—his favorite meal. He argued about everything and talked constantly, interrupting everyone else. No one enjoyed the meal. Johnny was following his impulses while his faith muscle remained inactive.

Mother's emotions hit her hard with thoughts such as the following: "I'm a lousy mother. I can see what this day is going to be like—one hard battle after another with no joy or rest. I wonder if I could hire a babysitter and go somewhere quiet for the day." Unfortunately, Mother wasn't exercising her faith muscle either.

Johnny looked into Mother's eyes and sensed her feelings toward him. He could not reason how his behavior affected others. He only knew that Mother didn't like to be with him, and that spelled out rejection. He reacted to that rejection with more irritation and uncooperativeness. He didn't want to help Mommy wash dishes or fold clothes. He threw his toys around the room and refused to pick them up. Mother sent him outside to play, and he wet his pants. Mother sighed in disgust, "He's been potty trained for a year; why now? This motherhood idea is not all it's cracked up to be!"

Six-month-old Tyler had a cold and was miserable too. The afternoon nap time finally arrived. Mother was desperately hoping for some quiet time to put herself back together emotionally. She had been parenting *in self* all morning unknowingly. Her unconscious self-talk repeated to her what a bad mother she was and that God was not there for her. As far as she could tell, her prayers went no higher than the ceiling, so she didn't bother to call out to God. This was misery. Maybe someone else could raise Johnny and Tyler better than she was doing. Hopelessness took root in her thoughts.

Putting Johnny down for a nap became a war of the wills. Mother's disposition stirred up Johnny, and Johnny's disposition stirred up Mother. Finally, after an hour, Johnny resigned himself to look quietly at some books. Mother went downstairs and collapsed on the couch. "What's a mother to do on days like this?" she cried out in desperation. To her surprise, God answered her question.

" 'Come unto me, all ye that labour and are heavy laden, and I will give you rest.' 'My yoke is easy, and my burden is light.'[8] Serving these negative thoughts and feelings is a cruel bondage. Do you want Me to come in and help redeem you?"

The mother was caught off guard. As she pondered this new thought, she remembered an article she had read recently that suggested journaling one's prayers. The idea was to record your requests to God and write down how He answers your prayers and is with you in difficult times. Then you can review all this during the times of despair that are bound to come along.

"Yes, oh yes! Why didn't I think of that before? I did journal about some really good days I had recently. Where are those papers? I need to read them right now." As the mother read what she had written earlier, a flood of memories washed over her—memories of another day just like the one she was experiencing. A cloud of lying thoughts and negative emotions that seemed so real had oppressed her. She had written down Psalm 50:15, " 'Call upon Me in the day of trouble; I will deliver you, and you shall glorify Me' " (NKJV). As she had cried out to God and chose to praise Him in spite of her negative feelings, He had delivered her from her pit of despair.

She turned her face up to heaven. "Lord," she prayed, "You've delivered me before. I believe You can deliver me again. How can I glorify You?"

"Turn your thoughts from the dark picture Satan is painting for you to the bright picture in Me! In Me, you are the best mother in the world for Johnny and Tyler. In Me, your home can be heaven on earth. In Me, you may have joy and rest in the midst of your home—even when Johnny is misbehaving. I am here. I will never leave you nor forsake you. I can direct you how to win Johnny's heart if you'll let Me have your heart."

Mother chose to cooperate with God and think His thoughts. As she focused on the bright picture of God's presence, power, and love for her, the despair melted away, and contentment filled its place. God delivered her out of that pit of despair and put her feet on solid Rock—Jesus Christ. Soon she was up cheerfully folding the laundry and talking further with God.

Johnny came out of his bedroom with a scowl on his little face. "Lord, what do You want me to do with Johnny?"

"Ask him to help you with the laundry. Draw him into My presence."

"Johnny, come help Mother fold the laundry," she invited sweetly.

"Don't want to," Johnny responded in an irritated tone.

"Now what?" Mother prayed silently.

"Bring him to Me in prayer."

"Johnny, Mother realizes that she has let Satan come into our home today and make us all unhappy. But I've asked Jesus to come in now and make our home happy. God changed my heart from sad to happy. He wants to make your heart happy too. Why don't we pray? You can ask Jesus for a clean, happy heart too."

---

8. Matthew 11:28, 30.

They knelt together, and Mother helped Johnny ask for deliverance from his irritation. Johnny got the victory, and love reigned between them. The rest of the day was sweet—because Mother exercised her faith muscle and so was able to help Johnny exercise his.

At the end of the day, Mother recorded her new experiences in her journal and added some new promises that she found in her Bible. "Grace and peace be multiplied unto you through the knowledge of God. . . . According as his divine power hath given unto us all things that pertain unto life and godliness."[9] "But my God shall supply all your need according to His riches in glory by Christ Jesus."[10] "Rejoice not against me, O mine enemy: when I fall, I shall arise; when I sit in darkness, the LORD shall be a light unto me."[11]

As the days went by and Mother exercised her faith in God's Word in opposition to the negative thoughts and strong emotions that pressed upon her from time to time, she found freedom. As her faith in God grew stronger, she imparted the same to her children. Johnny learned to be thoughtful and unselfish instead of irritating others to get attention. Through Mother's example and leading, Johnny learned to go to God for a change in his heart and disposition.

Faith grows with exercising choices on the side of right. One day, Johnny lost his temper with his little brother Tyler. Before Mother could intervene, Johnny ran to his own bedroom and closed the door. Mother followed him quietly, sending up a prayer for wisdom. She knocked softly and then gently opened the door to Johnny's bedroom. There was four-year-old Johnny on his knees, telling God about his temper and asking for help to be kind to Tyler. In a few moments, he looked up from his prayer with a sweet smile on his face. "Jesus is my best Friend, Mommy. Now I want to go say I'm sorry to Tyler."

Truth, uprightness, and purity are the secrets of life's success. It is faith that puts us in possession of these principles. Faith opens our eyes, turns us from darkness to light and from the power of Satan to the power of God![12] Faith is best built in infancy and toddlerhood. God will teach you how to build your own faith and the faith of your little ones. Trust Him!

THE LONE EMBRACE
A SPECIAL WORD OF ENCOURAGEMENT FOR SINGLE PARENTS

Do you deal with fear? Do you doubt God's care for you? Do you know intellectually that God loves you but emotionally you don't really believe He

---

9. 2 Peter 1:2, 3.
10. Philippians 4:19.
11. Micah 7:8.
12. Acts 26:18.

does love you? As a result, you don't think you can have faith, trust, or a belief in God as this chapter encourages you to. Feelings of inadequacy loom up before you, broken promises of past commitments discourage you from trying, and helplessness overwhelms you like a tidal wave.

This is an entirely new concept for you, and you fear to try. Your fear is based in not knowing God as a personal Savior to you—just you. God can change that when you come to Him just as you are. He is the Redeemer! How can you be redeemed from lying thoughts, misconceptions, and fearful feelings unless you come to Him just as you are? By yourself, you cannot change your feelings and disposition, but you can commit yourself to God's keeping. He can change these things. You can learn to recognize His loving voice calling to you. You can risk trusting Him by climbing up into His lap and finding security and comfort there by experience. If you don't come to Christ, your debilitating fears will never change. But if by faith you do come to Him and begin to know Him as a Friend and Redeemer, I guarantee you He will become your best Friend like no one on this earth you have ever met.

Christ wants to come into your heart and dwell there by faith.[13] He wants to clean up the ugly misconceptions you carry and free you from addiction to your negative emotions. God will teach you what to do and how to do it. Then He wants to fill your heart with all His goodness, confidence, courage, happiness, and love—yes, true love, a safe love. Won't you try God today? Taste and see that the Lord is good!

Jesse is being taught how to enjoy the snow and not fear it.

---

13. Ephesians 3:17.

Chapter 13
Worshiping God

O come, let us worship and bow down: let us kneel before the LORD our maker.
—Psalm 95:6

What is worship? Noah Webster's 1828 dictionary defines worship as "to adore; to reverence with supreme respect and veneration." The only One worthy of our supreme respect and veneration is God. He created us and is willing to redeem us. We belong to Him, and He is entitled to our worship. Coming to know and follow God is the basis and object of parenting by the Spirit.

How do we worship Him? Giving God supreme respect involves more than simply attending church services once a week. Paul puts it this way, "to offer your bodies as living sacrifices, holy and pleasing to God—this is your spiritual act of worship."[1] To worship God is to obey Him, to be under His guidance. It means that God leads and directs our lives. Worship is giving God permission to enter into our hearts, to cleanse our wrong thoughts, to challenge and replace wrong feelings. Worship involves yielding to His way and will. Following Him is worshipful obedience. "Do you not know that when you present yourselves to someone as slaves for obedience, you are slaves of the one whom you obey, either of sin resulting in death, or of obedience resulting in righteousness?"[2]

God promises, "And I will walk among you, and will be your God, and ye shall be my people."[3] We can choose to be God's people, and He can be our God. This is the choice you and I have to make each day of our lives. If we don't covenant with Him to be our God, Satan steps in to keep us under his forced bondage to obey our flesh. Satan becomes our lord. As we yield to obey his promptings, we are worshiping him. When we are obeying Satan's feelings to hurt others, to be angry, hateful, or selfish, we are obeying our inheritance to serve sin and self. This is worshiping Satan. When we choose to cooperate with Christ in our thoughts, feelings, and behaviors, we are worshiping God. We have a daily choice—to worship God instead of self. Learning to choose God is saying, "You are my God today, no one else. Satan, I am no longer yours. Instead, I belong to Christ and will obey Him today. This is my freewill choice." Choosing God to be our Lord is worship.

Making this choice real involves time—time to "be still, and know that I am God."[4] The Scriptures invite us, "Come, let us worship and bow down: let us

---

1. Romans 12:1, NIV; emphasis added.
2. Romans 6:16, NASB.
3. Leviticus 26:12.
4. Psalm 46:10.

kneel before the LORD our maker."[5] We do this in personal, family, and church worship.

Personal worship

The purpose of our individual worship time is to reinforce, develop, and enlarge these concepts of worship. It is to follow the Bible's counsel to "acquaint now thyself with him."[6] It is to come to know His voice, to know how to connect with Him for power. These thoughts should be kept uppermost in all that we do in our personal worship time with God.

My personal time with God includes kneeling to pray and studying His Word. Kneeling physically makes me keenly aware that I am subservient to my Maker. I bow to yield my will to His. He is over and above me. I am to trust Him and His direction instead of my own. All of my behavior—even my thoughts and responses in life—are to be subject to Him. Am I responding, feeling, and thinking as Jesus would if He were me in this situation? Don't be afraid to do this kind of self-evaluation.

For example, ask yourself, "Is my response according to God's character and will for me? Is it His will to cherish hatred in my heart toward someone?"

"Obviously not!" you say.

Well, then, for God to be my God, and for me to be His child, I must choose to follow Him and not my old way. Following God brings freedom—not bondage.

I can give hateful thoughts and feelings to God, and He can take them away.[7] He can create in me His heart, which represents His feelings and emotions, His responses and thoughts toward the erring person. Hatred need not rule over me and push my behavior in a wrong line. As I allow God to challenge me like this, and as I choose to follow Him, He will re-create me into His likeness. As I think right thoughts, God nurtures right responses too. I learn to think and do the right, depending upon Him to change me inside—something I cannot do of myself. By repetition, one day all the hatred and hurt toward this person will be replaced with pity and love by the power of Christ working redemption in me. I contemplate and choose these things as I kneel before Him.

Various forms of study

Rising from my knees, I sit in my chair at my desk or table and prepare to study. One morning several years ago, I reflected, "Lord, I come to You in need of Your presence, Your wisdom, and Your power to direct my studies. Things are getting a bit rote and boring. I don't look forward to studying like I used to. What shall I do?"

I sat back in my chair, hoping God would direct me somehow. If not now,

---

5. Psalm 95:6.
6. Job 22:21.
7. Jeremiah 32:27.

I trusted He would do so at another time of His choice. He is a trustworthy and communicating God. I began to review in my mind the different types of studies I had done so far.

I had really enjoyed reading through an inspired book on the life of Christ. It had helped me to grasp that Christ understands my struggles, because He struggled too. I wanted to remember some of those treasures I had encountered that had helped me with my struggles at the time, but I didn't remember the details. A friend told me that she wrote down inspiring thoughts as she read and put them in a three-ring binder by topic for future reference. Another writes down at the end of each chapter what God has revealed to him as he reads.

I thought about my many attempts as a new Christian to read my Bible through from start to finish. I always bogged down soon after Genesis. Maybe I just didn't understand enough. Maybe it was my superficial experience and not recognizing God's voice to guide me. Or it could be that the misconceptions I carried were confusing me about what the Bible was saying. I wasn't sure, but God impressed my heart to try again.

The *word study* approach had been intensely interesting to me for a while. I would look up keywords in my text for the day in Webster's 1828 dictionary. This dictionary painted a detailed understanding of the individual word and helped me make a practical application of it. So, I tried to read my Bible through again, using the word study method; it was interesting for a time. But I bogged down in so many details that I missed the overview of each chapter. Again, I abandoned reading my Bible through. I realized that the word study method has value and a place, but it needs to be balanced with the overview method too.

I'd have to say that I found the *topical study* method was the most helpful in meeting my specific needs. Using my dictionary, concordance, Bible, and other trusted Christian literature, I'd look up topics such as surrender, cooperation, submission, faith, works, communion with God, and what it means to be *in Christ* versus in self. I recorded the texts and my thoughts into various categories so that I could refer to them easily. My largest files were related to parenting principles, the Christian walk, and communion with God. In this way, I received practical direction for my life, and it was life changing as I applied it.

I also read several books by *safe* authors that really gave me insights into how to cooperate with God in my redemption. I began to read my Bible through again, and this time I underlined in red what God does to redeem me. Then I marked in blue what I must do to cooperate with Him. Understanding this distinction is vitally important. The Bible came alive in a new dimension. My part was to surrender to do His will, and His part was to change my wrong thoughts and emotions inside as I cooperated. This clarity brought notable success in my daily walk with God. I stopped trying to do God's part to change my emotions apart from His divine power accompanying my efforts. I stopped expecting Him to surrender my wrong will or desire for me. Instead, I made the choice to surrender my will to His. He cannot surrender for me—I must do this. My Bible became more practical and interesting as my understanding and experience grew. Now I've read my Bible through from Genesis to Revelation twice, enjoying and understanding so much more. This concept transformed my Bible reading, making it fulfilling again.

This summary of the various forms of study I did in my personal worship time was very good for me. But then God brought this thought to my mind.

"Sally, haven't I promised you that I would be your Teacher [8] *as you open My Word? I have promised to be right beside you always. I am with you as your God. Keep Me in that position and heed my directions. You will learn greater things than these."*

At this point in my life, I was beginning to understand that God was speaking personally to me through my Bible. At times, I'd just read one verse or a whole chapter—then I'd sit back for the Lord to instruct me and teach me its meaning through His Holy Spirit's presence. God brought clear and simple applications of the text to my mind. Often I'd write them down. His Word and Spirit were teaching me of a personal caring God.

When I'd recognize in myself a spirit of opposition or confusion, I'd test my thoughts by the Word of God. I'd prayerfully evaluate with God the spirit of my thought or concept. Was it compelling and forceful like Satan, or convicting and encouraging like God's Spirit? The Bible says to test what we think, feel, and believe by the Spirit *and* the truth. [9] This process helped me to recognize Satan's thoughts from God's thoughts—so I could know which to abandon and which to experiment and work with. Personal worship is a time to connect with God and to learn practically how He directs my life and to know His voice and learn to follow Him. At no time in life do we need this kind of relationship with God more than when we are parents—and finding the quiet time to make it meaningful can be a challenge.

Learning on the job

I lay in bed awake, fearful to move lest my husband, who is a light sleeper, be disturbed. I was hungry for God and seemed to have so little time alone with Him. Everything in my life seemed designed to crowd Him out. I felt that I was losing ground in being Christlike with my two-year-old Matthew and infant Andrew. I needed the healing, transforming touch of Jesus in my daily life. I needed His strength, which seemed connected to my time with God. I thought of my morning quiet time as a chance to refuel my character tank with God's power of Christlike manners. That time kept getting crowded out, and I was running on empty!

"Lord, I'm going to try again," I prayed silently. "I'm determined to spend time with You alone. Please keep my babies asleep! I've tried several times before to get up and they always seem to wake up. When they are awake there is

---

8. John 6:45.
9. John 4:24.

no hope to pray, study, or listen to You. I need this time."

I climbed slowly out of bed, silently wrapped myself in a warm robe, and crept down the stairs, avoiding the creaky spots along the way. Reaching the couch, I knelt to pray. Five minutes passed. I cuddled up on the couch and opened my Bible, ready to drink in the words of life when a wail from Andrew's crib shattered the stillness.

"How can this be? It's only five thirty in the morning, and he doesn't usually get up until seven o'clock. I believe Satan is behind all this! I made no noise. This isn't fair!" Resentment, frustration, and disgust flooded my emotions as I quickly went upstairs to soothe Andrew before he woke my energetic two-year-old. Thankfully, he settled down, and I returned to my Bible.

But as soon as I started reading, *Whaah!* came forth from my Andrew again. This time, I didn't get to him fast enough. Matthew was awakened and wanted to get up. "Oh, this is hopeless, Lord. What do I do now?"

I believe Satan was the instigator of these circumstances to keep me from having true union and communion with God. He hoped I would give up trying to seek God. But God is able to bring good out of Satan's devices. Although Satan appeared to win that day, God directed my thoughts to see and feel how important my morning time with Him is. My hunger became an insatiable desire. Instead of yielding to discouragement, I became more determined than ever to do whatever it took to get back into my morning time with God for power to become the parent I longed to be.

In that process, God led me to redefine love. I had believed that love meant I had no choice but to submit to the circumstances before me and permit my children to rise when they felt like it. God led me to see that true love keeps a schedule, expects my child to obey me, and teaches them the art of surrender to Mother's and God's wills through prayer and connection with God. My boys had to learn that they could not get up so early. I learned to set boundaries and to balance my softer virtues by exercising the firmer virtues without harshness and anger. With each new step of proper firmness, I gained greater heart obedience from my children and was able to spend time with Christ consistently. Home was happier.

This experience was a worship of God. I submitted to Him, evaluating my concepts, giving up those that were not of Christ and embracing those that were of God according to the understanding I had at the time. I took one more step toward allowing God to be my God and to being His child, following Him in trial.

The toddler's personal worships

As parents make quiet time with God each morning a habit of life, they are setting a worthy example for their little ones to follow. As infants grow into toddlers, they can be taught to spend quiet time alone with God each morning.

Initially, this time will be brief, but make it as pleasant and cheerful as possible. Teach your children that Jesus loves to hear their prayers and that His

Word is the most wonderful Book in the world. Your positive attitude will make worshiping God attractive to them.

The object is to teach them to have alone time with God, but at the beginning, they will need you to be with them at least part of the time. However, they should understand that this time is not primarily story time with Mommy or Daddy, neither is it playtime. It is time for them to learn to commune one-on-one with God and to think about Him.

Three-year-old MaryAnn lay quietly in bed. She knew her mother would tell her when it was seven o'clock and time to get up. Soon Mother stepped into the room, turned on the lamp, bent over to hug her daughter, and planted a kiss on her forehead. "Good morning, MaryAnn," she greeted cheerfully. "It's time for you to get up now."

MaryAnn stretched and sat up. She got out of bed and knelt on the floor beside Mother. "Dear Jesus, Thank You for a good night's sleep and a happy new day. Please be my Shepherd today and help me to be a good little lamb. In Jesus' name, amen." Mother added a short prayer to MaryAnn's and checked to see that MaryAnn remembered what she was going to do for her personal time that morning.

MaryAnn went to the bathroom. A few minutes later, she came back to her room, cuddled up in a corner with a cozy blanket and some cushions, and put a cassette in her tape player. Mother waved goodbye and left MaryAnn's room. Opening her Psalm 23 book, MaryAnn turned on the player. As the tape played the Psalm 23 song, she listened for the bell to ring to tell her when to turn the pages of her book. She had listened to this tape many times before and knew the songs well, so she sang along.

When the tape clicked off less than ten minutes later, MaryAnn lay her book down, got onto her knees, and prayed quietly. Then she jumped up and ran downstairs to find Daddy. He was finishing his own quiet time and welcomed MaryAnn with a smile as he drew her up onto his lap. "What did you learn in your quiet time this morning, MaryAnn?"

"I listened to Psalm 23 again, and I learned that I am Jesus' little lamb and that He will shepherd me. What does it mean for Jesus to shepherd me, Daddy?"

"Do you remember the story of Jabel the shepherd?"

MaryAnn nodded.

"Remember how he took such good care of the sheep? He would lead them where they could eat and drink. He told them they had to wait to eat and the sheep waited patiently, although they were hungry. When the shepherd had made sure there were no snakes or poisonous weeds in the pasture, the sheep could eat. Jesus will lead and direct you too. And you must trust and obey Him.

"Remember when the wolf came to attack them, the shepherd protected them because the sheep obeyed and huddled together? Satan is like that wolf who wants to hurt you, but Jesus, your Shepherd, is with you to protect you too. You must follow Him.

"You can't see Jesus, but He is here. He is your Shepherd. He wants to lead and direct you in all you do. You will be happiest following Him. Is that what you want to do today?"

MaryAnn nodded as she pondered these thoughts.

"Then let's pray together," Daddy said, "and thank Jesus for being our Shepherd to lead and protect us and ask Him to help us be good sheep."

MaryAnn followed this routine, because she had been trained consistently. It was a habit for her. As a one-year-old, her quiet time had consisted of looking at some special books for a few minutes and then praying with Mommy or Daddy. As she got older, her parents varied her quiet time activities with Scripture songs on tape, Bible stories or other spiritual stories on tape, a quiet felt book, Bible storybooks, or a beautiful picture Bible. They stayed involved with what she was doing and worked with her when she got distracted. One of her parents always helped her get started, and the other would spend a little time with her at the end, answering her questions and making some practical application to her life. Some toddlers do better with their parents. You choose.

God wants to help you build these kinds of habits for yourself and your little ones. (In the resource appendix at the back of this book, I've listed some resources for personal worship and quiet time.) God will help you choose what's best for you. Strive for consistency as you instill these habits in yourself and your children and remember to seek for progress, rather than perfection.

Family worship

If ever there was a time when every home should be a house of prayer, it is now. Nearly everything in our society is geared to cause one to forget God or to regard Him as irrelevant. Far too often, sin is glorified while godliness is considered old-fashioned. As a result, the family unit, which forms the bedrock of society, is crumbling and leaving behind empty individuals and disconnected hearts.

We need God's hedge of protection around our homes and little ones. The help of the angels is essential for us to care properly for our children. It is our privilege morning and evening to gather our families together to worship God—to thank Him for His blessings and to ask for His help. This should be a priority. Don't allow it to be crowded out by guests or extra work. Demonstrate to your children that you will "seek first the kingdom of God and His righteousness" and trust God that all the other things "shall be added to you."[10]

Family worship can be the happiest and most helpful time of the day—if parents make it that way. I've been in some homes where the father reads a long chapter from the Bible—uninterrupted—followed by a long explanation and an equally long prayer. The family members are detached and disinterested, and the father doesn't seem to recognize how tedious and boring this manner of worship is to them. The children learn to tune out the parent. I've not been surprised in these situations that the four-year-old is eager to get down and play

---

10. Matthew 6:33, NKJV.

and dreads worship time. It need not be this way.

Family worship should be short, relevant, and full of life, involving every member of the family. It is a time to worship God in song, to express thankfulness, and to realize our deep need of Him. We connect with God and with each other. It should be understood that this is a special time to meet with Jesus and that no troubled, unkind thoughts should be allowed to intrude and sour the atmosphere. Making family worship all that it can be requires some thought and planning on the part of parents.

"Oscar, it's seven-thirty. Time for family worship!" called Father. Three-year-old Oscar pulled on his last sock and ran for the living room. Mother was already sitting in the rocker with baby Mae. Father was seated on the couch with his Bible open and the felt board ready for use. He smiled at Oscar, and Oscar snuggled up beside him on the couch.

"Today we are going to begin learning about how God made everything, so let's stand up and sing about some of the things God has made."

They all stood—Mother with baby Mae in her arms—and began to make the motions of what they were singing. Father and Mother planned that this part of worship would be active and that the next part would require the children to learn to sit still.

"The trees are gently swaying, showing 'God is love.' The flowers are lightly nodding, telling 'God is love.' The birds are swiftly flying, singing 'God is love.' " Oscar and his family swayed back and forth like trees, nodded their heads like flowers, and flapped their arms like wings. Baby Mae took it all in and gurgled happily.

"Now let's kneel for prayer," said Father. Everyone knelt down, and Oscar folded his little hands. "Dear Father in heaven," prayed Father, "thank You for giving us this new day. Please be our Teacher as we begin today to learn about Creation and help us to remember what we learn all day long. In Jesus' name, amen."

The family sat back in their seats, and Mother began to nurse baby Mae.

Father picked up His Bible and read, "In the beginning, God . . ." He asked Oscar to repeat those words after him, then he discussed that the beginning of our day needs to be a time of becoming connected to God. Father asked, "Oscar, do you like to hold Daddy's hand while we go for a walk?"

"Oh, yes, Daddy!"

"Well, God wants to walk with you as well." Father gave Oscar some felts of Jesus walking with a little boy and girl. Oscar put these on the felt board to picture this thought. "God wants to help us when we feel agitated and naughty inside here," Father pointed to Oscar's heart. "Today, we want to let Jesus keep our hearts clean. We must choose to be willing to do the right. God knows it isn't always easy to do this. So He wants to help you. He knows you can't change your heart yourself, but He will clean it for you whenever you ask Him to. Come to Him in prayer, asking for His hand to help you walk in the right way."

The felt illustrations involved Oscar and helped him to understand what Father was talking about regarding "In the beginning, God . . ." and God wanting to walk and talk with us. Worship lasted between five and ten minutes. The family closed their worship time with prayer, committing themselves to God's keeping and to listening for His voice and responding by taking His helping hand today.

It was easy to prepare such simple lessons. Throughout the day, God brought these lessons to Mother's mind when she crossed Oscar's will and he wanted to argue like a lawyer. When he didn't want to submit to Mother's wishes and started to retort to her in a sassy manner, she was able to remind Oscar of what he had learned during worship time. Mother took him to God in prayer and showed him the choices he needed to make. She gave him the opportunity to make a good decision without pressure. As Oscar remembered the lesson of the morning, he chose to take God's hand and find power to obey. Family worship was a definite help to both Mother and Oscar.

This style of worship is simple and easy and teaches children practical lessons about God, awakening in them a desire to connect with this loving heavenly Father, and developing habits of walking and talking with Jesus throughout their day. It teaches and trains them to turn to God in their troubles and joys, and God becomes real to them in this way. You can't start too early. While newborns and infants can't participate in the same way that toddlers can, they will absorb everything that goes on in worship. They fit right into the program and learn that family worship is a normal part of life. Their little hearts are made sensitive to the influence of the Holy Spirit very early. Worship is a discipline and calls forth self-denial and self-control. In Christ, we can teach right responses and even train a Wiggly Willy how to be empowered to sit still, which we will cover in the chapters on discipline.

Felts provide an excellent way to illustrate the stories and lessons you are learning. And illustrated Bible storybooks can work equally well. I love the set *My Bible Friends*. These books are written so well and provide many opportunities to make applications and parallels to your children's day. You can plant good thoughts and knowledge of God in their minds and hearts—just like planting good seeds in a garden. You can point out character traits that are to be esteemed and developed. In these ways, little attentions often make for an excellent learning approach.

If leading out in singing is not your forte, you can use recordings of Scripture songs or hymns and sing along with them during worship. In the resource section at the back of this book, I list some other resources for personal or family worship.

I remember Peter, aged two, whose parents had accustomed him from infancy to morning and evening family worship. One evening, circumstances crowded out worship. Father and Mother were busy, and Peter sat on the couch feeling very uncomfortable about not having worship. Soon Peter got an idea and disappeared to his bedroom.

His father missed him a few minutes later and went in search of him. He found Peter sitting on his bed looking at a Bible storybook with pictures and telling himself the story out loud.

"What are you doing, Son?"

"Worship, Daddy. I pray, I sing, and now I read Jesus story."

Who gave Peter this idea? I'm sure that God did. Do you see the power of example, habit, consistency, and teaching our children to recognize the voice of God in their little hearts—even at the tender age of two?

Elijah was the three-year-old child of a single mother who made persevering and consistent efforts to have morning and evening family worship. She wanted her children to have a practical understanding of God. Elijah was an exceptionally gifted child, but his mother had not yet recognized this. One evening, she chose to read a vivid description—about three paragraphs long—of the battle between the good and evil angels over one soul. The evil angels crowded around the individual to smother him with darkness. Not until the tempted one cried out to God for help could the good angels who excelled in strength come in and drive away the evil angels. Mother made the point very clear that Jesus loves for us to call out to Him and that He will answer this prayer every time. When she finished reading, she asked Elijah to repeat the story to her.

To her amazement, he repeated the whole story nearly word for word. "Could you tell that to me again?" she asked. She opened the book she had read from and saw that his recitation was almost verbatim. As she questioned Elijah about the story, his understanding of the meaning of the reading was very clear in three-year-old terms.

Our children's minds are like sponges—some more than others. What goes in at this age forms the core of who the child will become! We need to be led of God to discern what to put in the minds of our children at this stage of life, for truly these ideas will go with them for life. Elijah's mother was thankful that she was filling his mind with thoughts of God.

Church worship

" 'Remember the Sabbath day, to keep it holy. Six days you shall labor, and do all your work, but the seventh day is the Sabbath of the LORD your God.' "[11]

The Sabbath is a sign of God's creative and redeeming power. It points to Him as our Source of life and knowledge. It reminds us of how God originally created us in His own image and of His purpose to restore that image in us. By keeping the Sabbath, we acknowledge that God is in charge of our lives and that we are utterly dependent on Him. This is worship.

While the first six days of the week are task-oriented days, the Sabbath is a special day set apart by God to focus on relationships—with Him and with the members of our family. God, in His mercy, has set a limit to the demands of

11. Exodus 20:8–10, NKJV.

work. On His own special Sabbath day He preserves for the family an opportunity for communion with Him, with nature, and with one another. The opportunities God has made available with the Sabbath are unlimited.

Carl and Karen were conscientious parents who worshiped God as their Lord, Maker, and Savior. Sabbath was the most delightful day in their home—but it didn't happen that way by accident. All week long Karen made plans under God to make Sabbath special. Usually, she and Carl planned a theme for the day based on the interests and needs of their family. These themes featured one of the fruits of the Spirit or character qualities, such as courage, kindness, perseverance, diligence, love, sharing, listening, surrender, cooperation, or other virtues. They wanted to teach their children to live these virtues in the power of Christ and not in the power of self-will alone. Other times, they would choose a hymn to sing and discuss. Or they might choose a songwriter like Fanny Crosby and discuss how even though she was blind, she clearly saw Christ as her Redeemer. They made these lessons and activities simple and pleasant for their two-year-old and four-year-old to understand and enjoy.

Karen planned each Sabbath meal to correlate in some way to the theme of the day, and Carl would plan something special for the worship time. They found often that what they learned at church could be tied in with their theme as well. The children learned that their parents were available to them on Sabbath in a very special way.

Sabbath morning, following a simple but special breakfast, the family would go to church. Carl and Karen worked with their children to help them participate in the services and to sit still to listen. This was challenging, because their church faced the same thing most churches face—a dearth of reverence and quiet in the sanctuary. This is not God's plan. The din of noise from our children shows their lack of knowing a redeeming, caring, powerful God who can bring willing silence to incessant noise and chatter. God can change the hearts of our children. The willful child may become surrendered, the overactive can become self-controlled, the fussy can be contented, and the easily distracted can become peaceful. At church we need the wisdom of Heaven in how to manage and direct our children to serve God in their thoughts, feelings, and emotions. They are free in Jesus to obey the Spirit instead of the flesh. When we connect to God, we are the branch connecting to the Vine. This connection gives parents wisdom and guidance, while it gives understanding, self-control and self-denial to every yielded infant and toddler's heart.

At church or at home, we worship God with our voices in song. We sing about who God is—Wonderful, Counselor, Prince of Peace, the Almighty God. He is the God of the impossible! What lofty themes to point our children to in such a lovely way.

At church, Karen encouraged her infant to participate in the cradle roll activities and stretched him to sit still when Mother asked him to. When he resisted, she'd take him in prayer to Jesus to empower his surrender—taking him outside to accomplish this if necessary. Her two-year-old was trained at home to know his memory verse and to obey the teacher's requests to speak and participate. This training commenced at home in family and personal worship times. It was continued at church. Karen used the mothers' room at church to continue this education and training for surrender of the will.

Karen laid her infant down to sleep on a blanket on the floor during the worship hour. She taught this surrender and scheduled habit at home, and with Christ, so can you. Many of our infants' problems with disposition are due to insufficient sleep. So follow God in being sensitive to the needs of your infant and train to have self-control.

Sabbath afternoon was spent out-of-doors as much as possible, exploring the wonders of creation and enjoying an activity that tied in with the theme for the day. In the evening, the family reflected and shared what they had learned according to their ages. The precious hours of the Sabbath would close with family worship. Each person was refreshed and encouraged to worship God by following Him through all the activities in the coming week.

What we learn in our homes about worshiping God in truth, in character, in spirit, and in life is what we share with our infants and toddlers. All this builds the sure foundation in Christ Jesus. We can share and teach only that which we ourselves have learned. Our young ones learn in our family worship how to behave, sit still, find God, and learn more about Him. These habits we then bring into our churches. The church furthers the training we have begun in our homes.

Parents, God has called us to worship Him in truth and in spirit—and in turn, to teach our little ones to do the same. May God inspire you and bless you to this end.

THE LONE EMBRACE
A SPECIAL WORD OF ENCOURAGEMENT FOR SINGLE PARENTS

Do you want to find the experiences described in this chapter—but still hold back in fear of being able to actually accomplish it? Worship and communion with God is the beginning of the Christian journey. We must come to know the God we want to serve as a kind and just God who loves us and who has been wooing us all our life. Satan, the alternative ruler of our lives, uses fear, misconception, and superstition to keep us from God. A vital connection with God—knowing Him as He truly is—will bring us out of serving fear, confusion, timidity, and failure into a power-filled experience that will transform our homes and families into His likeness. This is Satan's biggest fear. This is why he keeps pressing those wrong emotions of ours to hold us back and chain us up in fear of the decision to follow Christ, instead of Satan.

Begin your worship by reading just one Bible verse and ask God to teach you what is in that one verse for you. In this way, you can begin to gain experience with the Holy Spirit being your Teacher, helping you understand and apply what you have just read. I encourage you to read the books of Deuteronomy, Exodus, and Leviticus. Let God redirect your principles and concepts to reflect what these books teach you. Ask God to be your personal Teacher. Strive to learn His inaudible voice to your conscience. A thoughtful hour spent with God's Word is excellent and needful, but if you can't put in that much time, begin with even a few minutes and build from there. Let God show you how He can change your weak character traits into the stronger traits by connection with Him. Learn to worship God on your knees first, then on your feet, and then in the moment. God bless you!

Jim (Opa) with his grandsons.

Andrew with his son.

Personal and family worship is learning more about God working in our life.

Chapter 14

I Can Help!

Help, LORD; for the godly man ceaseth;
for the faithful fail from among the children of men.
—Psalm 12:1

"Help you, Mommy?" little Grinning Gordon, aged three, asked.

"No, I'm doing the laundry right now. You go play with your Noah's ark." Gordon wandered off to the living room to play. A little later, he came back to his mommy.

"Mommy, come play with me?"

"No, I'm peeling potatoes. You go play by yourself." Later, Grinning Gordon found Mommy making a crust for her potpie. So he pulled a chair over to the sink, climbed up, turned on the faucet, and started pouring water from one dirty dish to another—of course, missing the sink once in a while and splashing water on himself and the floor. "Gordon help Mommy!" he exclaimed enthusiastically. Mother's concentration was broken, and she glanced over at Gordon.

"Oh, Son, you are making such a mess! Get down from there! Leave Mommy alone. Why don't you go look at a book?" She abruptly lifted him off the chair and returned to her work. Gordon looked rather crestfallen but obeyed her.

A few moments passed in silence as Mother finished rolling out the crust. She was interrupted this time by a loud crash in the living room. She dropped her rolling pin and ran to see what had caused the noise. There was Gordon picking up the broken pieces of an expensive porcelain lamp. "Ouch!" Gordon cried as a piece of porcelain sliced his tender finger.

Mother was furious. She picked Gordon up and carried him to the bathroom to clean and bandage his cut, scolding him all the way. "Gordon, can't you stay out of trouble for just a little while? Can't you leave Mother alone to get her things done? Why can't you just play quietly by yourself like other children?"

Grinning Gordon wasn't grinning anymore. He was thinking, "Why doesn't Mommy like me? I tried to help her in the kitchen. She does something like I was doing in the sink. I thought I was helping. I was trying to occupy myself and look at a book, but I needed light to see. When I tried to turn it on by myself, it fell to the floor and broke. I tried to take care of the vase by myself like Mommy said, but I cut myself, and it hurt. I don't mean to bother Mommy."

So what's a mother to do? You have work that needs to be done. You can't spend all day playing blocks on the living room floor. There are meals to be prepared, laundry to wash, a house to be kept clean. You can accomplish these tasks a lot faster without a youngster underfoot. Young children should be left to play and entertain themselves until they get old enough to work—right? Wrong!

A child left to play without parental training develops selfish play habits. Self is like a weed that grows up without any help. Toddlers get into trouble because they don't know better. Without supervision or direction, they follow curiosity. Many children play in wrong ways with other children, because Mother is in the other room working. She's just glad to have them out of her hair. If parents neglect their children physically, you can be assured they neglect them emotionally and spiritually. Idleness is the devil's workshop where selfish, bad thoughts and feelings are built. Children get used to making choices to do what *they* want. Satan educates these toddlers as he thinks and feels, and he will marshal them as his subjects.

Some mothers I've known don't send their children off to play by themselves. They play with them—most of the day. And their meals are poorly prepared or entirely missed, and the house is dirty and cluttered. Children never learn the value of order, regularity, and cleanliness.

Yet still other parents place unrealistic expectations on their little ones. They think that they should be able to wash the dishes or clean their room when they haven't been taught sufficiently. Toddlers don't have the focus, direction, or skill in work habits to stay with the task to completion unless they are trained to do so. They are left to themselves for long periods, and as a result, they naturally develop playful, nonproductive, and nonthorough work habits. Mother returns to find the work not done and scolds them harshly. What happens to such children? Does this kind of program draw them to God?

Quite the contrary. Their spirits are crushed. They feel unloved. They conclude that work is not fun and that Mother hates them! In time, the seeds of resentment spring up into rebellion. Satan faithfully nurtures all this negativity to hurt the child, to develop lying thoughts he'll build on through life.

Can you imagine Gordon at the age of six when his mother decides it is time for him to do some chores? She will find herself dragging him into the kitchen and using stern measures to get him to work, because he is no longer inclined to do so. Furthermore, he doesn't really want to be with his mother. His negative thoughts would have been exercised for three additional years. This treatment would certainly convince him that his lying thoughts were correct—wouldn't they? "Mother doesn't like you. Better stay out of her way." These wrong feelings become the building blocks of the child's attitudes and concepts, and a wall comes up between parent and child. Trust is damaged! Is this damaged trust the reason why God's people fail in their Christian walk? I believe it is part of the reason.

Is there a better way? Yes, there is! Gordon was pleasant. He wanted to help. Like most children, he just wanted to be with Mommy or Daddy and do whatever they were doing. Gordon would have loved learning to help put the dirty clothes in the washer, the clean clothes in the dryer, or how to fold the laundry. He could have helped his mother peel potatoes, and they could have talked together and bonded. Oh sure, he wouldn't peel the potatoes perfectly. But if he were a welcomed helper, he'd learn, and within the year he could peel the potatoes for the family supper! Gordon is old enough to do more than just let the water run and play in it. He could be taught how to rinse the dishes.

So what is wrong with a little child working? To a child, your work seems more like play than work—depending on your attitude.

"I think I can!"

"The little engine that could" had the right attitude. You may remember the story. A long train must be pulled over a high mountain. Several larger engines were asked to pull the train, but for various reasons, they refused. The request was sent to a small engine, who agreed to try. This little engine succeeded in pulling the train over the mountain, while repeating its motto: "I think I can."

To think of hard things and say, "I can't," is sure to mean "nothing done." To refuse to be daunted and insist on saying, "I think I can," is to make sure of being able to say triumphantly, by and by, "I thought I could. I thought I could." Let's teach our children to say, "I think I can. I think I can. I think I can. I *will* follow God!" We want to communicate to them by our words, actions, and facial expressions, "I love you. I like you. You are welcome in my presence. I enjoy being with you. I believe you can learn to be a good worker. I will teach you how. It will be fun to do it together. I will honestly affirm your good efforts and lovingly correct your errors."

Many mothers today don't recognize the opportunities before them every day to teach and train their little ones and to instill in them God's character traits of upright manners, self-control, and good work habits. They see before them the tasks *they* want to accomplish and wrongly think it is easier to do the work themselves than to have their little one underfoot. As Satan blinds mothers, he seeks to cripple their children so that they enter the adult world without honest work habits, organization skills, perseverance, and faithfulness. They are weak in endurance and determination. They instinctively look for the easiest way through life, doing as little as possible to get by.

I was one of these mothers when we moved to the mountains of Montana to find out if there was a *real* God who could empower us to change and do the right. That was in 1983—twenty-six years ago. My boys were four and six years old. One of the first lessons God gave me was to face my misconceptions and myself. He set me on a course to begin to change. He wanted me to adopt new and better ways. I needed to cooperate with Him by replacing my old ways of thinking—and respond with His ways. For a time, doubts about myself held me back. But I began to believe "I can do all things through Christ who strengthens me."[1] The more I entered into His program and changed, the more joy I discovered in parenting.

One of my erroneous concepts was that it was easier for me to do all the housework while my children played. Truly this was a lie. In the long run, it's harder. God had to show me that I was a slave to my house and child care.

1. Philippians 4:13, NKJV.

Allowing the children to play—and only play—exercised their selfishness without interruption. While I worked, the boys would get into a terrible argument. I would have to stop working and go settle it—only to find self so strong that it was not an easy thing to resolve. Their hearts wouldn't surrender to right and getting them to admit wrong was like pulling teeth. I eventually learned through this hard school that my boys needed to work beside me and cultivate good attitudes under God.

God led me to bring them to Him in prayer, to tell them how to yield their selfish hearts to God, and discover the lesson of yielding their will to do gladsome work, which made for happy hearts and home. Work actually curtailed the growth of self. They played better together. They became more aware of *others,* feelings, hearts, and needs. More loving attitudes towards each other grew as a by-product of work discipline. They came to know God's voice to their minds and how to make right choices.[2]

God wants us and our toddlers to be like the little engine that could. We can learn, through His guidance, the attitude of "I think I can. I think I can. I will with God." When we and our children connect vitally to Christ, all the power of heaven enables us to do whatever we choose to do for God and right—to rinse and stack the dishes, to sweep or vacuum the floor. Through communion with God, we may be supremely successful. Let's give our children the true beginnings of a power-filled Christian walk with God through teaching and training them in the skills and attitudes of working in the practical daily duties of the household, while facing and changing wrong traits of character. To do this, Mother will need to be under God's direction, *in Christ,* and as consistent as the sunrise.

Our children as *the little engines that could* can spread the gospel of the power of God that is sufficient to change self-serving individuals into self-controlled, enduring workers. They can be like Samuel, Naaman's little maidservant, and Joseph, demonstrating to others God's power to make our characters noble! Good work attitudes and ethics give glory to God.

Bible examples

Samuel, so very young and tender, was taught by his mother to know and follow the voice of God to his conscience. He had learned this lesson well by the age of four when Hannah took him to the home of Eli, the priest. Samuel did not associate with Eli's sons nor participate in their evil ways. He was a dependable worker for Eli and served God in the work of the sanctuary. He already had an excellent attitude toward work and serving God instead of self, and Eli entrusted him with greater and greater responsibilities.

How did Samuel come to possess that kind of character so early in life? It

2. For the rest of the story, my emotional struggles, and how God led me out of them, I refer you to my book *Parenting Your Child by the Spirit,* chapter 16, "Useful Labor." Imbalanced parenting is a galling yoke to all, and God has a solution for each of us.

didn't happen by accident. With his first wrong thoughts and feelings, Samuel's mother began training him about God. She took him to God in prayer and taught him to replace wrong responses with right ones. She welcomed him at her side and taught him how to work willingly. She lovingly corrected wrong attitudes while consistently nurturing right habits *in Christ*.

Today, every mother can train her toddler in the same way under Christ's leadership. As our toddlers learn to walk, then run and skip, they can also learn to be Christians by listening to and obeying God through their mommy and daddy, by learning to work, by serving others, and by being faithful in daily household duties. This training will give them the stamina to stand for right against peers who do wrong.

The little maid was taken captive as a young girl and made a slave in a foreign land. In spite of her forbidding circumstances, she revealed a rare strength of character and a tenacity to follow God. How did she develop these qualities?

I believe that she was trained at her mother's knee to believe right thoughts, to practice pure habits, and to trust and follow God. She learned to be content with less and to do her best at whatever task was given her. As the priest of the home, her father portrayed a worthy example to her of what God is like and taught her right concepts about God. It was these humble little beginnings that inspired her to turn to God for comfort and direction in the awful crisis of her life. She turned to the God her parents had taught her about and given her experiences with. By trusting Him, she learned to be content as a slave—and God used her and made her life happy.

Joseph turned to God in his youth in the midst of very troublesome times—very much like the little maid. He could have yielded to despair and hopelessness, but Joseph didn't! Instead, he turned to God as he had been taught from his earliest years. He had been trained to seek counsel, to yield to God's direction, and to make the best of where he was. It was this beginning that gave him the habit, the inclination, the courage, and the inspiration to choose God at such a terrible time as this. This was the foundation of his choice to be a faithful worker as he managed Potiphar's possessions. It was his work ethic that got Potiphar's attention, and this was the reason Joseph was advanced to positions of greater and greater trust. It all began in the toddler years.

Knowing God's guidance, recognizing His voice to their minds, and yielding to follow it is what made these Bible characters great—and makes them an inspiration for our lives. There are many more individuals in the Bible who illustrate right work attitudes, ethics, and faithfulness. I think of Moses, the great leader; David, the shepherd; Paul, the tentmaker; Nehemiah, the contractor; Jesus, the carpenter; and many others. All these were truly successful because their work abilities were founded on seeking and following God's will for them. God was able to mightily use their cultivated abilities to demonstrate to heathen nations, and to Israel itself, the joy and freedom that results from serving God rather than serving self.

Are you seeing the far-reaching importance of the humble beginnings of our little toddlers? There is no work more influential than teaching our little ones from their earliest moments the right attitudes of following God, serving others, and working faithfully. These traits don't sprout up like weeds. No, no! They must be taught under God before they become part of one's character. God is waiting to help you today. Call upon Him to enable you to raise another little maid or Joseph.

Age-appropriate occupation

A two-month-old infant is fully occupied with a schedule of sleeping, eating, and awake time. He has his earliest experiences of yielding to Mother's will and direction when ill feelings crop up. Routine brings comfort, security, and trust, which build an essential foundation for later stages of learning. With God as your Guide, provide your infant with a consistent awake time, swing time, tummy time, exercise time, bath time, cuddle time, feeding time, nap time, and bedtime. It is important for us to see this as their occupation. Over the next four months, this occupation changes little. The time awake increases, but regularity remains the greatest preparation for what is to come.

By six months, the feeding times lessen notably, and the baby's schedule fits closer to the family schedule. His or her occupation broadens. Mat time—with objects to reach for—develops hand-eye coordination. The infant learns to turn over from his tummy onto his back with great joy, then back to tummy. He needs to move all his limbs to develop muscles so that he can learn to sit up—first wobbly, then securely.

The infant becomes more social and interactive. He smiles, laughs, and responds to your attentions. Character growth deepens in trusting his parents. Security grows, and the bud of patience begins to break ground. All this happens wisely under God's leadership.

At some point, the infant learns to crawl, and from then on, gaining mobility is the chief pursuit. For example, infants love to climb the stairs. This really exercises their leg and hip muscles. Have you ever noticed how high they lift their leg to reach that next step? The steps in our house are very high. I imagined climbing a step and having to reach as high as my hip to reach the next step. Wow! This develops good muscles. Yes, and the infant needs supervision here, doesn't he?

Pulling themselves up to stand is an exciting time for infants and their parents. Usually around twelve months of age, the infant begins to take his first steps, and soon he is walking with confidence. Parents find themselves in need of plenty of prayer to set healthy limits for the exploring child without quenching his delight of learning about the world around him. Another occupation for infants is learning how to surrender willful attitudes to God and do the right instead of the natural wrong. True success is accomplished as we are connected to God's power.

From eighteen months to two years of age, the infant's social interaction continues to enlarge. He can learn to help put away his toy before taking out another. He can follow directions and throw objects into the trash for you. His excellent mobility calls for the training of self-denial and self-control under God. He needs to be taught proper ways to express his individuality under God rather than as self or nature prompts him, and he can begin to learn right and wrong. Mother's need to say "No" increases, and she can teach the child to respond positively to her loving restraint. God will personally teach her how to do this.

I've known some toddlers who help their parents rinse the dishes at eighteen months of age and who joyfully look forward to participating in the work of the home. Inviting a child to work side by side with you is thrilling to him. Encourage it! Yes, it is mostly play and a nonproductive activity at this stage, but look at the attitude toward work that you are formulating in your child's mind. Look at the team spirit that you are engendering. Your child's will is exercised to "help Mommy." Don't let Satan instill the lie that your child is in the way. That is not true. Your child is trying to help—how wonderful! Let's begin in very little ways to show him how to rinse one dish and put it on the counter or drainboard. Thus, you are forming the beginning of a pattern of how to work, and soon your child will be a real work force and help to you! Don't hinder your helper. Instead, work with him under God's direction. Let him be with you!

At eighteen months, my grandson, Landon, loved being with his father. In fact, helping Daddy was his greatest desire. Andrew was building his house at the time, and Landon was with him almost all the time he worked. When Daddy picked up a hammer, Landon picked up his little hammer and did his best to work just like Dad! When Andrew used his drill, so did Landon. Side by side they worked—inseparable! When Daddy climbed a big ladder, his son climbed a little one. When Daddy took a measurement for the next piece of lumber, Landon measured to the same spot Daddy did and expressed his view of the matter distinctly.

Parents, our example, our love, our availability—physically and emotionally— make home secure for our toddlers. Trust, confidence, and respect continue to grow. This is our work and their occupation. Isn't this why we have children— to show them the way to go, to work, and to do?

Occupation for a two-, three-, and four-year-old

Our children need direction, and much of their occupation at this age is doing whatever you are doing. They can help with the dishes, sweep the floor, put the dirty clothes into the washer, put the washed clothes into the dryer, fold the clothes, collect the trash, help with making the meal, clean up the table from the meal, rinse the dishes, put the silverware into the dishwasher, put their toys away, pull weeds, rake the lawn, pick up sticks around the yard, and so many other things. True, much of this is more of a hindrance than a real help (don't let them know that), but they are learning the process of whatever task you are doing. Start with general instructions and add greater detail as they get older and more skilled. They need restraint, instruction, and direction, but it is important that they are right there with you. You know what they are doing. They like being with you and are learning by observation and modest participation what it takes to work, to clean, to build, and to do yard maintenance. As they grow older and become more proficient, they will have developed the attitude that work is fun, is expected, and is rewarding. They will come to feel, "I love being with Mother and Father."

I pray this inspires you to go to God to ask, "What can my son or my daughter, do to learn the practical duties of life at his or her age?" The fact that the child does not do it perfectly yet isn't the issue. The issue is that he or she is getting the unsaid message, "Mother loves to be with me. Father wants my help. I like helping. Work is fun. How can I help?" This is an attitude of the little engine that could, an attitude that can take them over many of the mountains of life. Isn't that, in itself, worth the time and effort? And more than that, very soon your three-year-old—well trained in both attitude and skill under God—can take a little task off your duty list that he can do from start to finish and truly help you.

Three- and four-year-olds continue to grow in usefulness—provided you model the right attitude and encourage them cheerfully to participate in what you are doing. Let God challenge your misconceptions—perhaps overprotection or underprotection—so your child can grow up in a positive environment.

When they were three years old, I let my boys help me cook. They loved to dump this or that into the bowl or go get this or that from the pantry. I always thanked them for their help, and they liked being in the kitchen with me.

At the age of four, my boys would stand on a stool to help in the kitchen. I decided to let Andrew cut vegetables for the salad. He was used to helping in the kitchen and loved doing new and different things—especially making bread. I had allowed him to do more than other children we knew, and he liked it. He did a great job cutting those vegetables. I was right there watching that no harm came to him. One day I told a friend how great it was to have Andrew cutting up vegetables, and she reproved me for letting a four-year-old cut with a sharp knife.

Each parent needs to consult with God what is and isn't best for his or her family. When other people give you advice, don't be militant or defensive. Don't react like a whipped puppy, either. Find your comfort and confidence in God because He will challenge you in what you are doing wrong. But He will also give you room for your individuality. He wants you to be you. Do what's right, knowing that in some cases your methods and attitudes may be different from others. That can be Okay. Differing opinions don't make one right and one wrong. So sort it out with God and be honest!

If one woman honestly believes that allowing her four-year-old to use a knife is dangerous, she doesn't have to do it. But if another woman honestly doesn't see it as dangerous, shouldn't she be allowed the freedom to view things differently and to conduct her family in the way she feels is best—under God?

Yes, we must give each other freedom to be different. It's not safe to compare ourselves among ourselves. Jesus is our only safe Example. Honestly evaluate your differences as a family under God and follow Him.

A visit to Opa's house

My grandsons, Landon and Jesse, came over for a weekend visit while their parents had some time alone. Landon had just turned three, and Jesse was one. Our son Andrew said, "Now don't spoil the grandchildren. Landon does chores at home."

"Don't spoil the grandchildren" meant don't nurture self as the center of what activities they will or will not do. It meant "nurture them in the right ways," as their parents see things. As much as possible, we would stay on their usual schedule. Grandparents are to be helpers and supporters of their children's children. They are not to encourage selfishness in their grandchildren which the parents will have to undo after their visit. It's fun to be a grandparent and to help our children in the work of training their children to follow God, assisting in developing good attitudes.

The first thing I did after Andrew and Sarah left was to get a hammer and take Landon with me to the pantry room where we hang up our coats and take off our shoes. I pounded in some nails at the height he could reach—one for his jacket, another for his hat, and a third for his sweater. Then I showed him where and how to place his shoes. He willingly hung up his things and put his shoes away. The first few times he came in from outside, we reminded him where and how to put away his things. We didn't hang up his things for him—we had him do it. We affirmed him when he did it right and encouraged him when he didn't. By the second day, he'd come in, take off his coat, and say, "I'll put my coat in the pantry. I'll put my shoes here." Regularity and routine is good for us. Each person, taking responsibility under God, makes for success.

Landon loved playing in the sandbox with Opa, his grandpa. As I had done with my own sons when they were little, I would interrupt Landon's play by calling him in to do some little task. These exercises gave him the opportunity to yield self's will to the parent's will, which should be the same as God's will. He came in cheerfully. "Landon, I need you to help me set the table for lunch." Step by step, I instructed him in what to do. And he did it. First he set the plates for each person, then knives for adults, then spoons, forks, and napkins for everyone. He needed assistance to know how to place the silverware with the handles down and which side of the plate to place them on. He did very well with no attitude problems. Then he put the margarine, crackers, soy milk, and a few other items on the table.

"Thank you very much, Landon. You did a good job! You may go back outside and play some more in the sandbox with Opa." And he did.

At lunch, I served him first the things that he *needed* to eat—the things that are not his favorite foods. We prayed to help him surrender to God, and he cheerfully ate what was on his plate. Then I served him small amounts of the other items until each was finished. That way I knew he had eaten a sufficient amount. It worked very well. When his plate was empty, we served him a dessert, which was a positive motivator for him.

After lunch, Landon helped clear away the entire table. Opa took the dishwashing position. While I put the food away, Landon picked up each plate, with silverware on top, and delivered it to the kitchen counter for Opa to wash. He needed supervision to stay on task, but we were all cheerful and enjoyed working together. In good time, the table was cleared. "Landon, go get the step stool from the bathroom, and you can rinse the dishes with Opa."

Oh, what joy! He ran to get the step stool and climbed up beside Opa to rinse the dishes and stack them in the drainboard. This was a new experience for Landon. At his home there is a dishwasher. First, we showed him how much rinsing was necessary. Then we taught him how to put the rinsed dishes in the dish rack. He got it close. When he'd get distracted with the running water, we just nurtured him to move forward, and he did. Smiles and encouragement are excellent motivators for doing right. He got behind in rinsing, so Jim stepped away from the sink for a few minutes until Landon caught up. Returning with a smile, Opa said, "I like doing dishes with you." Oh, what beams of joy filled Landon's eyes, heart, and hands. Children love to please us. Soon the dishes were all done and put away.

"You play with the Lincoln Logs with me, Grandma?" Landon asked.

"We need to sweep up the kitchen floor first. Would you like to help? I have a broom for you too. Then we can build with the logs," I said.

"I don't know how," Landon responded honestly.

"I'll teach you," I said.

And teach I did by demonstration, by instruction, and by a helping hand to get the right angle and the right feel of the pull of the broom. Soon he was pulling that broom here and there. He wasn't very effective, but with some practice, he soon will be! A three-year-old can do many more things than you might think.

When the kitchen was cleaned up, we brushed our teeth together and went to the living room to play. Building a Lincoln Log cabin was his occupation now. Landon already knew how to stack these logs successfully. Oh, what fun we had together building different kinds of homes! When we work together, we have time to play together. This is a reward for everyone.

This experience went so smoothly because of the day-by-day effort of our son Andrew and his wife, Sarah, who both take seriously developing a godly character in their little ones. They have worked hard with Jesus to instill good attitudes, to establish a routine schedule, to make worship a part of daily life, and to correct their children in a positive manner. As grandparents, Jim and I encourage them forward and are there to care for the children when the need arises—to augment their work and to build on their foundation.

The next morning, I had personal worship with Landon and Jesse on the living room couch. Following prayer, we went to the bathroom, and I gave them water to drink and supervised Landon brushing his teeth. Then I gave each boy a bath in Grandma's sink—oh, what special fun!—and got them dressed. Breakfast preparation was next, and Landon ran to get his step stool to help me make pancakes. I enjoyed having him work beside me. Opa came into the kitchen, and Landon was excited to see him. Opa started the wood cook-stove, and Landon helped him. As I began to cook the pancakes, Landon helped Opa unload the wood carrier into the wood stacker by the stove. He just needed a little help getting the wood stacked neatly. He was a trooper and didn't stop until he couldn't add one more stick of wood. Then he helped set the table again. He was catching on to how things go in Opa and Grandma's house. We gave him a few corrections, and some cheerful help when needed. All of us were happy. Family worship began with prayer. Then both children climbed into Opa's lap while he read them a Bible story from a lovely illustrated book. We said their memory verse, knelt for prayer, had our hugs, and went to the breakfast table.

Breakfast was such a cheerful time with fresh and dried fruit, homemade jam, and sweet cream over the pancakes. Following breakfast, the routine to clear the table began again. Landon could hardly wait to get up on the step stool beside Opa to rinse the dishes again. He was motivated to work efficiently clearing the table. He needed a little assistance to keep his mind on track while he rinsed the dishes. Playing with water can be so much fun! With cheerful encouragement, he kept the dishes flowing onto the drain rack. After only two days, we were working together like a well-oiled machine. Already, new routines were quite well established.

After the kitchen was all cleaned up, Opa took Landon with him to collect all the burnable trash and burn it in the pit. Landon loved being active with us in whatever we were doing. We worked together. We played together. We prayed together. This loving environment created an atmosphere in which a child learned that correction is a part of life, and he has so much evidence he is loved that correction does not devastate him!

I know you want this for your family. God wants it for you too. But you need to come to Him, learn of Him, communicate with Him, and He will direct your path so that this can be your home. This is not theory, but reality. We find ourselves in many situations in which we need not only instruct and correct our children, but discipline them as well, because of attitude problems. What do we do then? In the next three chapters, we will discuss some ideas to help you with some how-tos in the area of discipline as a helper and motivator for right doing under God.

THE LONE EMBRACE
A SPECIAL WORD OF ENCOURAGEMENT FOR SINGLE PARENTS

Perhaps you didn't learn good work habits as a child. Don't despair. God will re-parent you so you possess good character traits and habits. Then you can teach these skills to your toddlers and children under God's tutorship. Perhaps you are a harsh, critical mother. You don't know how to correct except in anger. God can teach you how to change, to be positive and kind in Him, and get real results in the hearts of your children.

Learn how to let God into your mind and then into your heart. Let Him touch those tender or fearful areas. Don't be afraid. God touches these areas not to crush you with your shortcomings and failures, but to offer you freedom and healing from them. You don't have to continue the family dysfunction that was passed on to you. In Christ, you can give your toddler better than you had. But this work must begin with you. God must become your Companion and Friend before He becomes your child's Friend. You must learn self-control as it is in Jesus before you can teach the same to your child. Let God be with you, and by your permission, God can be *in* you, and you, too, can have that new heart to be all the parent you want to be.[3]

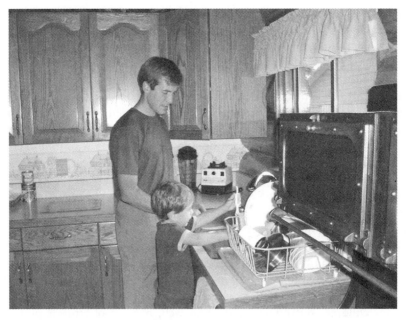

Landon was trained very young with the joy of "I can help."

---

3. Ezekiel 36:25–28.

Chapter 15
Discipline to Deliver:
Overview and Mild Measures

I do nothing of myself; but as my Father taught me, I speak these things.
—John 8:28

This chapter and the two that follow explore the subject of discipline. *Discipline* is a word that conjures up negative images for many people. They think of rules and punishment as synonyms for discipline. I'd like to suggest that when you are parenting by the Spirit, discipline is not negative. Rather, it can be the key to freedom!

True discipline is not a method whereby you can ensure that your infant or toddler will always obey and never irritate you. The purpose of discipline is to develop in the child the ability to control himself under God. It is to deliver him from the tyranny of lying thoughts, negative feelings, and destructive habits, and to develop his true individuality under God. In the broadest sense, discipline is that process that molds the character of the child to be like Christ, and it is multifaceted. This process begins at birth.

Discipline overview in the first year

The first year of life is the time to nurture, mold, shape, and fashion the infant's character—his thoughts, feelings, emotions, and responses. Providing a predictable and pleasant home develops trust in the infant and teaches him that there is a time for everything and everything should be done in its time. He learns that if he has a problem, Mother or Father will figure it out and fix it. When negative or fleshly emotions come up, we help our infant learn to respond properly under God through instruction, prayer, distraction, and modeling the right responses. Providing dependable care and fair parental government makes God real to our child—as He truly is.

Discipline overview for the one-year-old

The child learns to crawl, then to walk, and then to run. He wants to venture out and explore the world around him. He may crawl into your cupboards and pull out everything. Discipline includes setting limits for the youngster to keep him from danger and to teach a proper respect for property without quenching his delight in learning. Tell him, "You can go here" and "You can't go there." He needs to learn that correction is positive even when it crosses his will. As his mind is molded under God and he learns to yield to his mother, it becomes the cheerful norm.

Who is in charge? is a vital lesson continued from the first year of life. The discipline of routine deepens as the child's eating schedule changes to fit better into the family's schedule. The child can begin simple personal worships, while family worship should already be part of his or her routine. Knowledge of God is gained in worship time and implemented throughout the day as wrong emotions are dealt with. When milder measures don't reach a stubborn heart, a prayerful spanking should be used—not to hurt the child—but to get his attention and motivate him to obey under Christ's leadership. This makes following self and being stubborn distasteful to him. Use spankings wisely.

Discipline overview for the two-year-old

With God, the second year can be a pleasant experience of seeing growth in self-control and a sweet, innocent toddler emerging.

Teaching obedience to Mommy's and Daddy's directions is the main class for the child at this time. "Come." "Sit still." "Repeat after me." "It's time for bed." His increasing independence and ability to express himself make us aware of our need for ideas and direction from God in how to direct him. The garden of the heart needs to be filled with good plants—activities and interactions that feed positive thoughts and responses—and the weeds of self and its wrong expression must be kept pulled up before they grow strong through indulgence.

Routine is still your friend, and regularity is your teacher to build trust in the child toward the parent and ultimately toward God. Be reliable, dependable, and fair. Give your child choices within the parameters of what is acceptable. "Would you like to wear a red shirt or a blue shirt today?" "Would you like to eat your peas or your salad first?" This builds within the child a proper sense of autonomy.

Prayer and wisdom are necessary, especially for the active two-year-old, as his emotions and stubbornness are gaining more strength. If self is allowed to be in charge and unrestrained, you will experience the "terrible twos" and have a little tyrant. Taking your child to Christ is the only way to subdue self. Be God-governed rather than flesh-driven. Be fair, and under God, find a proper balance in your government. Softness needs to be added to the firm parent. Firmness needs to be added to the soft parent. Both need God as their Director to rightly represent Him.

Discipline overview for the three-year-old

The child is a bit more mature now—a little gentleman or lady can be forming. Continue to lead and mold the thoughts and feelings after God and right. If self is allowed to reign and rule in your home and in your child's heart at this age, you will experience the "trying threes," because wrong traits indulged now will grow with the child's growth and strengthen with his strength. But you can change that through connection with God by cultivating the opposite trait.

The habit of obedience should be well established by now. If it isn't, the child will run the home, and you will obey him. This is out of God's order and makes life difficult. I'm not suggesting that you should punish your child in anger or rule over him with an iron fist, but under God you must establish yourself as the proper authority. In Christ, with consistency and no variableness, you are to be the one in charge, just as Moses was the leader of the children of Israel. His word was honored and accepted. Moses' real authority was that he was under God, exercising self-control and self-denial to provide a character pattern worthy of imitation.

At this age, children continue learning what belongs to them and what belongs to others, as well as finding the joy of sometimes cheerfully sharing what belongs to them. Their social graces and manners can be developed in unselfish, thoughtful ways.

Any undesirable habits you have overlooked will become more evident now. Excessive shyness or sensitivity to correction may need to be challenged and brought into balance. Habits such as talking too much, hitting others, giving way to angry outbursts, and negotiating like a lawyer to avoid obedience become obvious and can be changed with Christ. Consider what you have done or are doing to contribute to your child being this way and make the first step under God to change it. Then make plans to cultivate the opposite—the right to overcome and replace the wrong habits of response.

Discipline overview for the four-year-old

The child continues to mature. His social manners are well learned. By now, submitting to parents should be a well-established habit, and you should have a successful program for dealing with character weaknesses. Otherwise, the child may become unruly, which breeds frustration in the parent.

Under God's direction, you can begin to correct wrong ways now, if you haven't begun to do so before. Jesus is your Source of strength, wisdom, and self-control. He can reveal to you the lying thoughts that are ruling over your child and that push these wrong behaviors, and guide you to a solution.

Your child can begin to see God as a real Helper for emotional, physical, or spiritual trouble. For example, some children get angry with themselves when they don't learn something new the first time they try. We need to teach them better ways of handling such disappointments by God-led thoughts, which will replace the lying ones and connect them to Christ for power to change.

If you experience the "frustrating fours," realize it is because Satan is leading your child in what to think and to obey his fears, his anger, his unwillingness to submit, his unreasonableness, his peevish spirit, or even his obsessive-compulsive behavior. Without God leading, instructing, correcting, and calling us to a decision to come out of wrong ways, Satan is the child's true leader by default. Satan uses our child's misbehavior to lead us to give up trying to help our child or give up to hopelessness and despair and be crushed. You don't want this. All you need is God as your personal Savior and Companion, directing you in what to do to gain the heart of your toddler for Him.

Definitions of discipline

As you can see, discipline encompasses many aspects. It is a broad subject and consists of calling self into control and doing things that may not be comfortable, yet are good for our spiritual, mental, and physical life. True discipline is found only in Jesus' power and wisdom. I've summarized into short phrases the various facets of discipline that I have come to understand over the years. I'll list them here and then illustrate some of them in the remainder of this chapter and the two chapters that follow. Discipline is

- receiving wisdom from God;
- becoming pliable in the Potter's hands;
- finding control of our emotions through Christ;
- maintaining regularity;
- being gentle instead of forceful or harsh;
- giving proper instructions;
- discipleship of my child to Christ;
- training in habits of self-control;
- giving the child nothing for which they cry;
- subduing all the child's passions and tempers;
- saying "Yes" to God and "No" to self;
- yielding my will to God;
- evaluating who is in charge and changing masters;
- allowing no wrong habit to go uncorrected;
- giving mild consequences to motivate a decision for right;
- using firmer measures when mild measures do not work.

Discipline is receiving wisdom from God

In child rearing, we can give only that which we possess. We can teach only that which we have learned. We can instruct only in the way in which we have been educated. And often we discipline as we have been disciplined—in either a controlling or punishing attitude or an instructing and training approach.

All parents bring to parenting their history, misconceptions, and imbalances. Every one of us tends to use either an approach that is too soft or too firm. Thus, every one of us needs to be re-parented by Christ in order to bring us into balance. First, we need to come to Christ so He can teach us and so that we can impart His teaching to our children. We must speak Christ's words and be in His spirit. To teach discipline, we must be under God's discipline ourselves. That is parenting by the Spirit.

My Andrew was about nine months old and didn't like to lie still while I changed his diapers. Diaper changing was becoming a contest of wills, and I tried to hurry through it as fast as possible. My friend Jane had a son the same age. While we were both changing our sons' diapers in the mothers' room at church one day, I noticed that her son, Joel, liked to wiggle like Andrew did, but her approach was much more successful than mine.

She would fold Joel's little hands in hers and pray, "Dear Jesus, please help Joel to lie still so that I can change his diapers properly. I place his will in Your hands." Then she would look Joel in the eye and tell him calmly, "Joel, you can hold still while Mama changes your diapers." If he continued to squirm, she'd give him three mild pats on his leg and—presto!—he'd promptly surrender and settle down for a quiet diaper change. If he resumed his protesting disposition— even a little—she'd repeat this process a little more forcefully, and again he'd quickly surrender and become content.

Well, I wanted the response Jane got and began to implement her method right away! I skipped over the prayer part because that seemed insignificant to me and proceeded to tell Andrew, "You can hold still while Mama changes your diaper!" Instead of settling down, Andrew squirmed all the harder, so I gave him three mild pats on his leg, expecting a miraculous surrender. Instead, his resistance became more determined. Not being one to give up easily, I repeated my instructions and the three pats to the leg several times with greater firmness. Andrew protested loudly and wrestled to get away. My frustration level rose exponentially. "What's wrong with me? Why doesn't Andrew respond to me the way Joel responded to Jane? I did exactly what she did!"

Or did I?

What was wrong with this process? I was *depending upon a method* instead of relying on the Creator God to transform my son's heart. I didn't recognize the spiritual battle going on behind the scenes[1] and didn't seek God's will and power.[2] I attacked the giant Self without my General to guide me, without His wisdom to instruct and direct me, without my Creator to empower my son and me in this warfare against self. Without Christ in the battle, I'm no match for self or Satan.

Satan must have laughed while he orchestrated all this negativity in the thoughts and emotions of both my son and myself. My failure to actively choose Christ as my Guide made me easy prey for Satan to step in and insinuate his ideas. He inspired both my son's selfish desire to get away from me and my resultant anger. I learned the hard way that my wisdom—trying to do right and to convince my infant to do right in my own strength—is futile. "But the wisdom that is from above is first pure, then peaceable, gentle, willing to yield, full of mercy and good fruits, without partiality and without hypocrisy." This kind of wisdom comes only from God. Remember the parenting pyramid from chapter 2? "If any of you lacks wisdom, let him ask of God, who gives to all liberally and without reproach, and it will be given to him."[3]

The step that I had skipped—asking God for the wisdom from above that

---

1. Ephesians 6:12.
2. Acts 9:6.
3. James 3:17, NKJV; James 1:5, NKJV.

would subdue my disposition and my infant's disposition—was the most important step! Linked to Christ, my attack against sin and Satan ruling in my infant's heart would have lead to success because Satan must leave when Christ comes on board.

"Give me the knife!"

Selena and Kari lingered at the lunch table enjoying pleasant adult conversation while their two little boys played happily with their blocks on the living room floor. They didn't notice, at first, that three-year-old Sam and two-year-old Paul were getting rather wound up.

"I can throw this block very far!" boasted Sam, and he hurled his block across the room into the sofa. Not to be outdone, Paul threw his block too. That was fun! Both boys started throwing their blocks and running to get them so they could throw them again. Screaming only added to the delight of the whole thing.

"Sam," called Selena, "come to Mother." Sam came running over with a mischievous glint in his eye. Before Selena could give him the good instruction she had in mind, Sam grabbed a sharp knife off the table, and quick as a wink, ran back into the living room waving his prize over his head, laughing gleefully. Paul caught sight of Sam's treasure and immediately wanted it. Grabbing Sam, he stretched as tall as he could, trying to wrestle the knife out of Sam's hand as he swung it back and forth.

Selena immediately recognized the danger and called out authoritatively, "Sam, stop running right now! That knife can hurt you!" Getting up, she prayed silently for God to save everyone from harm. "Lord, be with me. What shall I do?[4] I must get that knife."

First, Selena snatched up Paul and handed him over to his mother to settle down. Then she turned to look into the wild eyes of her son. He smiled back at her, daring her to chase him. He thought this was fun! Satan was stirring up Sam's unreasonable excitement. Selena was instantly tempted to get angry, grab Sam, take the knife, and paddle him. But just as quickly, God called to her heart. *"Selena, don't do that. You want to discipline by the Spirit, not the flesh!"*

Selena chose to listen to God. "Lord, what would You have me do? How can I teach my son self-control in this situation?"

"Connect him with Me. Call his heart to surrender. Make your request calm but clear. I am with you," God directed her reason.

Selena said very calmly, but firmly, "Sam, you must calm down. That knife can hurt you or us very badly. You don't want to hurt anyone. Now give Mother the knife gently."

Instead of handing the knife to his mother, Sam lunged at her as if he would stab her. Selena grabbed his little arms and restrained them firmly. She realized that Sam needed to come to Jesus for help to subdue his wild flesh. "Sam, let's

---

4. Acts 9:6.

pray to Jesus. You are out of control right now. Fold your hands."

Sam looked around, confused for a moment. Prayer was a common thing to do, and that was a good thing in this instance. Sam chose to fold his hands while still clutching the knife protectively.

Selena folded her hands over Sam's and prayed out loud, "Dear Jesus, help Sam to give Mother the knife willingly. Help him understand that what he is doing is not funny but very serious and very dangerous. Take his mind and heart, and may He follow You."

Then she stood back and calmly said again, "Sam, you must give Mother the knife softly." She reached out her hand.

Mother could see that Sam was wrestling in his mind. He didn't want to give up this treasure, but somehow it didn't seem to be as much fun as it had been in the beginning. He looked into his mother's eyes. He could see that she loved him.

Selena was talking silently with God simultaneously, "What next, Lord?" The picture was clear to her now that this was an important lesson for Sam in willing surrender that would have been lost if she had used her superior strength to force the knife from him. He must make a choice for the right without being forced—that would develop real character. She was prepared to give Sam a spanking if necessary while he clung to the knife rather than grab it forcefully. She wanted to gain this treasure of willing obedience under God rather than use Satan's tactics of forced surrender.

Sam's steam was gone now. He looked down at the knife and then back to his mother. Calmly, he placed the knife in his mother's hand. Mother put the knife safely away in the kitchen and then picked up Sam for a big hug while she explained about how dangerous a knife can be and what a good choice he had made to follow God.

Because she sought and obeyed the wisdom that is from above, Selena was prepared to respond correctly in this situation. She disciplined her son in such a way that he learned valuable lessons. Without Christ, we can do nothing.[5]

Discipline is giving proper instructions and directions

Often, calmly instructing our toddler in the proper response, coupled with seeing to it that he does what he knows to be right, develops good manners, proper behavior, and self-control. Instruction must be given in Christ, while we are under His supervision and guidance. We want to be God-governed not self-managed. We want God's power working in us.

Aaron, age two, was in the kitchen with Mother enjoying his new work-bench—a Christmas gift. Father had taught him how to twist the toy screws and pound the large pegs into the holes provided in his workbench. The hammer was Aaron's favorite tool. He had spent many hours outside with Father pounding real nails into real wood. Just thinking about it made him want to

---

5. John 15:5.

hammer all the more. He pounded away energetically while his mother went about her work.

Just then the phone rang, and Mother picked it up. Seeing that Aaron was playing nicely—though loudly—she stepped into the other room so that she could hear the caller. She was fully engaged in her conversation when she noticed that the lights in the kitchen were blinking on and off. That seemed odd, so she went to investigate. When she saw what was happening, she ended her phone conversation very quickly.

There was Aaron, hammering on the light switch with all his might. The boards from his workbench were strewn all over the kitchen floor, and little chips of paint scattered along the base of the wall were telltale evidence of other places he had tried out his hammer.

Immediately, Mother felt angry. But instead of venting her anger, she cried out to God in her heart. "What shall I do with this child?" Before we are ready to discipline a child, to call him to self-control, we must be in control under the guidance of God ourselves. Discipline begins with me.

"Mother, have you taught Aaron what is proper to hammer on and what is not?"

"I guess not. It never occurred to me that he might hammer on anything but his workbench. It seems like common sense to me. Why shouldn't he just know that?"

"Your child needs patient instruction to develop that 'common sense.'"

"Son, come here with Mother." Aaron didn't come, so Mother walked over and picked him up without harshness and anger and took him to the couch to sit down. He was wound up and tried to get down from her lap. "You need to calm down first, and we need to talk." He continued to squirm.

"Lord?" Mother called out silently again. Following the logical and Christ-like idea that came to her mind, she said to Aaron, "Okay, Son, you need a time-out before we can talk. Sit right here on the steps for two minutes."

He obeyed and sat there for one minute before he asked, "Get up now?"

"Not yet." During this time she was collecting her thoughts and looking over the damages. They weren't too bad. That was good. "Thank You, Lord, for getting my attention with the lights so that this situation isn't worse than it is. Give me wisdom now!"

"Okay, Aaron, come to Mother. We need to pray to Jesus so you can listen and understand Mommy." And they prayed. Taking Aaron to the kitchen, she showed him the small pieces of paint that had been chipped off the wall. "Aaron, there are places where pounding your hammer is good, and there are other places where pounding your hammer breaks things. You can pound on your workbench or outside with Daddy, but not anywhere else—not the wall, the light switches, or anything else. If you do, Mommy will take away your hammer and workbench until you can choose to use it properly again. Do you understand?"

"Yes, Mommy," Aaron responded.

"Well, let's play together now," said Mother and proceeded to show him how to put his workbench back together and play with it properly. Over the next few months, Mother repeated the lesson, restraining the wrong and cultivating the right. Aaron's father participated in this education too.

Mother had to remove the workbench from use a few times before Aaron got the picture. She put a sheet over it and pinned a sad face on it to help reinforce the lesson. Often children learn best by experiencing the consequences of poor choices. You can save yourself anguish by enforcing reasonable consequences sooner, in a matter-of-fact disposition, rather than later in anger.

In Aaron's case, prayer, consistency, and proper instructions given in the spirit of Christ bore the fruit of good manners, the proper handling of tools, and a willingness to heed instruction. As the child learns what is expected, he should begin to integrate the instruction into his behavior without repeated reminders.

Internalizing instruction

"Mama, more potatoes?" Paula asked.

"What do you say, Paula?"

"Pweese!" she responded sweetly.

A little later during the same meal, Paula asked, "Mama, more peas?"

"What's the password, Paula?"

"Pweese!"

Paula was always willing to say "please," "thank you," "you're welcome," and "excuse me" at the proper times, but she always had to be prompted. After six months of this, her mother went to God. "I have been very consistent in having Paula say 'please' and 'thank you,' but it's all me and not her. She is three and a half years old. How much longer until she learns to do these things without my prompting?"

Mother didn't sense God answering her personally with any thoughts, so she went looking in some child-rearing books she thought to be biblically based in Jesus. There she read how teaching deals with the mind, but training deals with the will. She pondered what that meant and asked the Holy Spirit to help her make a practical application.

At the next meal, Paula asked, "Mommy, cookie?"

Mother was about to respond with "What do you say?" but a little check in her mind kept her from answering right away. This was God working with her understanding, but she didn't recognize it until later.

She waited quietly, praying, "God, help Paula to understand the purpose for my silence. Help her to engage her will in remembering to say 'please' without being reminded!" Paula's father was about to prompt Paula's "please," but Mother caught his attention and discreetly shook her head.

A few minutes passed while Paula continued to eat. It took a little time to register in her mind that she hadn't gotten her cookie yet. Then she paused, looked up at Mommy questioningly and asked again, "Mommy, cookie?"

Mother looked at her in the eyes, smiled, and tilted her head questioningly. Daddy looked at her in similar fashion. The three of them looked back and forth at each other for a seemingly long time. If children are not expected to respond without a prompt, they won't. If they are not held responsible to act on the instruction they well understand, they will continue in the prompting mode. This situation was different for Paula. It felt uncomfortable, but it engaged her brain to think, "What am I missing?"

"Mommy, cookie?" she repeated more insistently and then added, "Please?"

This was the beginning of Paula's good manners. This is true discipline. Give proper instructions under Christ until the child understands well. Then withhold directions at times to kindle initiative.

Challenging the child's thinking

Three-year-old Stefan and two-year-old Eaton were playmates visiting Mrs. Smith's home while their mothers went shopping together. Mrs. Smith sent them to the toy room to find something they'd like to play with. They each picked two things. Eaton looked at what Stefan had in his hands and exclaimed, "I want!" and reached for it. Just then Stefan took a third toy from the cupboard. Eaton started grabbing for all he could hold, dropping some toys as a result. There was a mad scramble as each boy greedily tried to gather up as many toys as he could possibly hold.

Mrs. Smith was standing in the doorway. She chuckled and then sent up a silent prayer for wisdom and help. Sitting the boys down, she asked them both to let go of all their toys. Both boys wrestled with the request and held on tightly to all they had. "Okay, I can see we need Jesus to help us be willing to be made willing. Let's pray."

They prayed, folding their hands around the toys in their possession. Following a simple prayer, Mrs. Smith instructed, "We are going to put all the toys back into the cupboard, and I'm going to show you how to get them out in a way that is the most fun." As she talked, she was silently asking God to take the lesson home to their hearts. "Now let's start by putting all the toys back where they came from."

The boys slowly put the toys back where they had found them. God was working on their hearts, and they were cooperating. Mrs. Smith instructed, "Now, you each pick out one toy for yourself." After they had done that, she continued, "Now you can each pick out one toy for the other boy." They did that with sheepish grins on their faces. "Now let's go play with these toys. We can try out some of the others later." They went to play with the two toys with greater respect than they would have without this little experience and challenge to their thinking. And they had lots of fun playing together and alone.

We do have a great influence on our toddlers' lives in showing them a better way. We begin by being Christlike ourselves, then connecting our children to Christ so they have the power to choose to live above the pull of their flesh.

"That which I heard of the LORD . . . have I declared unto you."[6] God initiates right thoughts, and we repeat to our children what God would have them to do. What an awesome God we serve! Home becomes peaceable and orderly as we give instructions through Christ.

Dipping cookies, not fingers

My nephew, two-year-old Jared, and I sat together at the lunch table enjoying cookies and milk for dessert. Jared loved dipping his cookie into a bowl of soy milk. And he also loved to dip his hand into the milk and watch it splash and drip onto the table. As we began to eat our cookies, I gave him the simple instruction to dip his cookie, but not his hands, in the milk. While I turned away momentarily, he dipped his fingers into the milk and announced with a big grin, "Look Auntie, I put my hands in my milk."

My first reaction was to ignore it. "It's not really that big of an issue," I thought. "After all, he's not my child, and I don't want to offend his parents."

But the Holy Spirit interjected another thought into my mind: *"Disobedience is a big deal, and I want you to deal with it, even if he isn't your child."*

I asked God what He would have me to do. I wanted to be sure this was God's voice.

"Try mild reasoning with him. Then take him to prayer," came to my mind.

I gently asked Jared if he remembered that I had asked him *not* to dip his hands into the milk. He nodded Yes. I asked him if he had been disobedient, and he nodded Yes. The smile and sparkle went right off his face, and I saw fear rising in his little eyes. I sensed that I needed to deal tenderly. "Jared, would you like to make it right with Auntie and Jesus?" He nodded his head, saying, "Sorry, Auntie."

He willingly followed me in prayer and surrendered his heart to Jesus and accepted a new heart.[7] Then he told me with a smile on his face, "I won't put my hands in my milk anymore." And he didn't. He finished dipping the rest of his cookie and never put even a finger in his milk.

I thought that was the end of the matter, but two days later, we were sitting together in the backseat of the car headed for town. He looked at me and said, "Auntie, you helped me to not put my hands in my milk." The look in his eye told me that God had spoken to his little heart and taught him something about living faith and obedience, and that he liked it! God is so good. There are far-reaching rewards to working wisely with the minds of our children in these situations, for God continues to impress the lessons on their minds.

Often, prayer and tender instruction are all that are needed to put our children on the path of obedience. By consistently correcting them under Christ, we can mold their minds, emotions, and habits after God's ways instead of self's ways. Little attentions often can reform bad manners. Then good manners

---

6. Isaiah 21:10.
7. Ezekiel 36:25, 26.

will grow, because our children are learning the voice of God to their hearts and minds. They will become accustomed to obeying God's ways.

" 'And these words which I command you today shall be in your heart. You shall teach them diligently to your children, and shall talk of them when you sit in your house, when you walk by the way, when you lie down, and when you rise up.' "[8]

THE LONE EMBRACE
A SPECIAL WORD OF ENCOURAGEMENT FOR SINGLE PARENTS

Did you find this chapter challenging? Do you feel the standard is too high for a single parent trying to fill the position of both mother and father? Some single parents who have experienced a failed marriage feel that God is punishing them for their failure. Is that you? Are you weighed down with guilt and loneliness—feeling that Christ is far away from you? Do you feel unworthy of God's help or that He is too busy to hear your cries for help?

If so, I understand. Satan insinuates negative thoughts about yourself and God, and they seem more true to you than does the Word of God, because you are so accustomed to believing them. And as you think, so you are. Through these thoughts, Satan closes you in with a dark cloud. The reality, however, is that these negative thoughts are all lies. God regards you with tenderness, and He is near at hand to help you. He is just waiting for you to call upon Him. He is not punishing you—Satan is. You have the choice to believe God and pierce through the dark clouds of unworthy feelings and to soar free in the sunshine of Jesus' love and willingness to be your General, Guide, and personal Savior. He has faced your fears and won the victory for you. Your negativity need not rule over you. Trust God and cast your vote on His side!

Jim and Landon. True discipline begins with coming to know Jesus, who can change their wrong emotions or responses to serve Him.

---

8. Deuteronomy 6:6, 7, NKJV.

Chapter 16
Discipline to Deliver:
More Mild Measures

"Let the little children come to Me, and do not forbid them;
for of such is the kingdom of God."
—Mark 10:14, NKJV

Discipline is discipleship of my infant or toddler to Christ

*T*anya was eleven months old, the youngest of four children, and liked to be held by her mother *all the time*. She was sweet when Mother held her, but very sour when Mother didn't. When Mother didn't pick her up, Tanya's sour disposition exploded in a bloodcurdling, demanding cry. To keep peace, Mother dutifully held her most of the day while she did her work, but she was wearing out.

Tanya and her family came to visit us, and our two families went for a walk. Andrew carried Tanya in a backpack to give Mother a break, but the baby fussed, insisting that her mother carry her—and Mother gave in. Back at the house, if Tanya was placed on the floor to entertain herself, she'd cry and cry until Mother picked her up. Tanya would accept no one else.

As I observed this, I wondered, "Who is ruling here—God, Mother, or Tanya?" It was quite apparent that Tanya ruled. Although Mother's surrender to the infant's will brought a temporary outward peace to the home, it was not good for Tanya, Mother, or the family.

Mother was embarrassed by Tanya's behavior and asked me for my input. We discussed the basic concepts of the parenting pyramid. God must be at the top of the pyramid. He must be in charge—not the infant—and Mother needed to take her orders from God, not her child. We talked about how to distinguish God's voice from the voice of her flesh. God would teach her the course she needed to take, and as she received directions from Christ, she needed to give directions to her child about what to think, feel, and expect. God would help her to balance her softness with Christlike firmness.

While we were preparing breakfast together the next morning, she asked me, "Where do I start? How do I correct this?"

"Well, first you must disciple Tanya to Christ. We must bring her to Him so He can instruct, nurture, help her understand your instructions, and empower her to obey. This is putting her into God's keeping. It is connecting her to God, like the branch is grafted to the Vine. She needs this connection to receive the Living Water that brings life to the branch from the Vine. Only with this connection can she change from her wrong ways to God's right ways of thinking and reacting.

"Your part is to cooperate with God by telling Tanya what she will do—and then motivating her to exercise her will to act on what she has been told. This must be done in Christ—not in self. To deal with the minds of our little ones, to mold them in the correct way to go, is a vitally important work. Don't fear facing hard things because nothing is too hard for God.[1] Also, recognize that you are not alone. You have Jesus as your Lord and Savior to free you from your wrong thoughts and ways. As Creator, He can bring life out of apparent death in your daughter, and she can change in thoughts, feelings, and reactions."

When we sat down to eat, Tanya continually demanded her mother's attention. She fussed for this, then that, and then something else. It became apparent that she didn't know what she wanted—she just believed that having Mother's full, undivided attention would make her happy. Mother felt that God had been nudging her for a long time to challenge this behavior and decided that now was the time.

"Tanya, you may play with these toys on this blanket while Mother eats," she instructed as she sat Tanya on the floor.

Was this reasonable? Certainly it was. But Satan stirred up Tanya to fuss so loudly that she didn't listen to Mother's direction. All Tanya wanted was to have her mother's entire time and attention. I believe Satan contributed to Tanya's unrest to keep her mother and me from discussing the solution to this problem.

Tanya's mother turned to me and said, "Can you show me how I do what we just talked about?"

At first I pulled away from the task. I didn't have any particular plan in mind, and I preferred to simply coach the mother. But she was so exhausted and needed to eat. I consulted with God and decided to give it a try. "Lord, attend my ways. I give Tanya into Your hands to mold, shape, and fashion after heaven's ways. Give me the wisdom I need and give Tanya the power to choose against her flesh and old ways."

I walked over to Tanya, knelt down beside her, and looked her in the eye. Kindly, but earnestly, I said, "Tanya, you may have nothing for which you cry." I knew I was asking Tanya to deny her selfish desires and to exercise self-control, and I knew she would not like it at first. But I didn't mind challenging her wrong thoughts in this way, because Jesus was with me in the parenting pyramid to help her to understand what I was asking of her.

Tanya continued to fuss as if she hadn't heard me. I picked her up from the floor, and she squirmed to get out of my arms. I snuggled her into a corner of the couch where she could watch us at the breakfast table and supported her with a pillow. "Tanya, you are all right here. Mother needs to eat now. You can wait. You don't need to cry. You can be a happy girl." And I held her hands and

1. Jeremiah 32:27.

had prayer. "Lord, help Tanya choose to be happy here. She can be alone for a while."

She was quiet momentarily. I'm sure she didn't like this new program, and soon she chose to cry again. I went back to her and held her little hands while I prayed again, "Lord, take the thoughts of Tanya's mind and the emotions of her heart and cleanse them. Help her to understand my direction." I picked her up, smiled into her eyes to show her what I wanted her to do, and said, "Tanya, you can choose to be happy!" She stopped fussing, and I put her back on the couch and returned to the table.

Tanya was quiet, but started squirming out of the position in which I had put her. "Lord, what shall I do?"

"Restrain the wrong and cultivate the right. Be not overcome of evil, but overcome evil with good."

I understood. "Tanya, no. You may not do that. Sit up where I put you." I was very kind, but very direct, in denying the wrong and directing her about what she should do instead. I set her back up in the sitting position. Right away, she deliberately wiggled her way back to the slouched position.

"No, Tanya, you may not do this." I smiled. "You must obey me and sit where I put you." Now I saw that this struggle was all about who was to be in charge. I sat her back up again and prayed silently to God for help and wisdom in my further directions.

Tanya stopped fussing and looked at me strangely. This was a new response for her. I felt God was speaking understanding to her mind and that she understood my direction. In my instruction to sit where I placed her, I was looking for a little surrender of her will under God. I knew that when she would surrender to obey, God would come in and cleanse away her selfish emotions and she could be content. She pushed down just a little this time and looked me in the eye to see what I would do.

"No, Tanya," I said sweetly, "you must sit in the position I put you." She started to pout. "No, Tanya." I waved my finger back and forth. "You can choose to be happy. You don't need to cry. You have Jesus with you." This is restraining self, using positive requirements without harshness and anger. Now Tanya made a choice; she stopped her pouting and put her fingers in her mouth and sat contentedly in the position I put her. It surprised me that she surrendered so soon, but I accepted it.

"Good girl, Tanya! Good choice! Now you must sit here until I come to get you." I was establishing my authority under God's direction. God brought the ideas, and I carried them out. I returned to the breakfast table.

Two minutes passed, and Tanya began to fuss again, defiantly slouching and then rolling over to slide off the couch. She was used to having her wishes obeyed, and she didn't want to change. Infants do love consistency—whether right or wrong.

I repeated my instructions and corrections a few more times, and she gradually became content for longer and longer periods. "You can stay here until I choose to come and get you," I said cheerfully. She seemed to understand this new program and put her fingers in her mouth. She sat quietly for five full minutes. This was my plan and goal.

I went over to encourage her with God at my side. "Tanya is a happy girl. Jesus is in her heart." And I put out my hands, offering to pick her up. She frowned and turned away from me. Then she stuck her fingers in her mouth in that position.

Was self subdued in Christ yet? No, Tanya had complied to a degree, but self was still ruling—her reaction told us something about her feelings and thoughts. "Okay then, you must stay here until you can be happy. Choose, Tanya. Jesus is here to help you." We want a full surrender—not a partial one.

Another five minutes passed quietly, and again I came to Tanya to check her disposition. "Good girl, you sat so nicely. Would you like to get up now?" I smiled and offered my hands again to pick her up. This time Tanya responded with a smile and reached back to me. For the first time, she willingly let someone besides her mother pick her up without fussing. I cuddled her a moment and then placed her on the floor to play with the toys on the blanket. "Tanya, you can play with your toys for a little while. You are a happy girl now." Tanya experienced true surrender and found freedom from her selfish disposition. This process took about thirty minutes.

During the next meal, this process was repeated, and Tanya yielded much more quickly. She was learning that when she fussed, her mother and I would train her in right responses—without harshness, anger, or domination. And the Holy Spirit and angels were there to help us all, as well.

Discipline is discipleship of our children to Christ. It is recognizing Christ as the Head of that parenting pyramid and yielding ourselves to Him first. Under His direction, we give the infant positive direction of the right thing to do instead of the wrong, and we give minor consequences as needed to gain her cooperation—never in harshness or anger. As the child yields to do your will, God re-creates her inner disposition to serve Him instead of self. As this experience is repeated, happy obedience becomes the habit. "The Father raiseth up the dead, and quickeneth them."[2] Christ in us can do this in our homes with our children today. Won't you try Him?

Discipline is training our infants to habits of self-control

Nathan was nine months old and his mother, Angela, wanted him to learn to eat cleanly, to not grab the spoon or squeeze food and be messy. She prayerfully reasoned the situation through and made a plan. At the next meal, she put Nathan into his high chair, held his little hands in hers, and looked him in the eye. "Nathan, Mommy wants you to fold your hands in your lap while she feeds you." She prayed for God's blessing on the meal and for this new endeavor.

2. John 5:21.

Then she put Nathan's bowl of mashed potatoes and peas in front of him. Nathan's hand automatically reached for the mashed potatoes.

"No, Nathan, put your hands in your lap." And she moved the bowl to one side. Nathan looked at his mother. She smiled and offered a spoonful of mashed potatoes to his mouth. He took the bite. "Good boy, Nathan," Angela affirmed. She continued to feed him, repeating her instructions and moving the bowl to illustrate what she expected of him.

At some point during the meal, Nathan put his hand in his mouth full of mashed potatoes. Angela reminded, "Nathan, you may not put your hands in your mouth when you are eating." She took his hand out of his mouth and wiped it off, placing it in his lap. The next time his hand went toward the bowl or to his mouth, she held his hand away momentarily, while kindly instructing, "No." After consistent training this way for a few meals, Nathan was catching on. Within two weeks, the habit was established. Nathan would put his hands in his lap and open his mouth to eat.

Training our infants and toddlers in habits of self-control is both instructing them what to do and then also seeing to it that they follow through with what we have said. Be consistent in a Christlike spirit to develop these habits of self-control under God.

You can implement this same process to teach your infant not to touch electrical outlets or to play in certain drawers. Take your child to Jesus in prayer and instruct him, "You may not touch this. You can play with this instead." Christ will lead you as you listen to Him. He is your wisdom and power. He will help your child understand what you are saying. When your infant reaches for the electrical outlet or the forbidden drawer, smile and say, "Don't touch." He will reply to you, "No touch." Repetition is your teacher, so be consistent in what your child can and cannot play with. Infants can learn that "No," said without scolding or irritation, is a helpful rather than a hurtful thing.

When my boys were a year and a half old, I didn't remove the Christmas figurines from my tables. Instead, I taught them they could not touch them or play with them. At first, they loved to grab my figurines and get me to chase them. I gave them something else to play with so that they could learn to obey "No" to touching my figurines without giving up the innocent joy of the chase game.

Don't leave off prayer. It is our secret of success! Christ empowers our direction. Don't do anything without Him!

Self-control in family worship

God intends for family worship to be one of the sweetest times of the day—a time to draw the family near to each other and to Him through song, prayer, and sharing the Scriptures together. However, many families I have worked with find family worship to be a stressful time of the day, in part because their children don't exercise self-control.

Kathy and Terry decided to include their first child, Amanda, in their morning and evening worships. They wanted to establish the routine of worship early in life. Often, they worshiped while Amanda was nursing. At first, the routine worked well, but then it seemed that Amanda would get fussy and irritable whenever they started worship. Her outbursts made it very difficult to listen— let alone participate in the discussion. The Holy Spirit impressed Kathy that the cause of this disturbance was not circumstances as much as it was the devil interfering with their spiritual life and using her little child to steal away their time with God.

Kathy thought about this for days and weeks before she decided what to do. Morning and evening, she would pray and put Amanda into God's watch care and submit her little heart to God's keeping for her. She asked God that Satan be bound and not be allowed to stir up her daughter's agitated emotions. She committed herself to follow God's leading especially during family worship time.

That evening at worship when Amanda began to squirm and fuss, Kathy breathed a prayer for God's help. Then she picked up Amanda so that she could look her in the eye, smiled at her, and said simply, "Amanda, you need not behave this way. This is God's time. You don't need to listen to Satan through your feelings. Worship is something very pleasant. Don't yield to being agitated." We need to tell our infants the truth in order to combat the lying thoughts and feelings Satan is pressing upon them. In this way, you take them out of Satan's hands and put them into Jesus' hands to direct and lead them.

"Let's pray," Kathy said. "Jesus, help Amanda to understand what Mommy said to her. Help her yield up her little heart to God. Come into her mind and heart, and bring heaven's peace to her soul. May worship time become her most favorite, restful time."

Mother smiled again in Amanda's sight. "You can choose to be a happy girl. Now let's sit here for worship. Self-control is a good thing. Listen to Daddy as he reads to us."

Mother sat down again, Amanda looked into her eyes, and a pout began to form. "No, Amanda," her mother instructed. "You are a happy girl. You can smile." Mother tickled her, smiled at her, and soon enough Amanda smiled back. She sat quietly for ten minutes. Then Mother finished her nighttime feeding to the close of worship.

Does taking God into the picture change things? By all means, Yes. Maybe not always; maybe not the first time, but as we stick close to Jesus it will come soon enough. And the next worship, when this process was repeated, it was easier for Amanda to exercise self-control. Soon peace was the routine rather than the exception. Do you want this for your little ones? Take them to Christ that they may learn to exercise self-control.

I don't have to wiggle

Sometimes we don't have the ideas or understanding to bring up our children from the very beginning the way Kathy and Terry did. What do you do if you have a three-year-old that is a Wiggly Willy, distracting and disrupting every attempt at family worship?

While I was presenting a weekend seminar at a church, I stayed at the home of Earl and Edith. They had three children: six-year-old Earl Jr., five-year-old Elise, and three-year-old Eric. The first evening in their home, we sat down for family worship, and I began to notice something amiss right away. Earl Jr. was fidgeting with a toy; Elise was looking at a book; and Eric was squirming in his mother's lap.

"Sally, why don't you help this family with their Wiggly Willies?"

"Oh Lord, can't I just relax and enjoy the worship? I don't want to challenge parents. Some don't want help, You know."

"I'm asking you to do this. They told you they wanted help, and they were sincere—don't you think?"

"Well, yes." Logic fell heavy on my unwilling heart. I surrendered myself to God and asked for His guidance—for myself and for them.

"Is this what your worship is typically like?" I interrupted.

"Well, yes. To tell you the truth, we often don't have worship because of Eric's behavior. We don't seem to find the way to change it." They shared some of their attempts, failures, and frustrations. "We were hoping you'd have some advice for us."

I shared the concepts of the parenting pyramid and the need for courage to experiment with new ways with God. Only by experimentation will we discover that Jesus is big enough for any difficulty we face.

Mother placed Eric in my lap, and I explained to him, "This is worship time. You are expected to sit still and listen to Daddy read and talk about God. God wants to help you to be happy on the inside during worship. He can give you the power to obey Mommy and Daddy, even though at times that may seem hard. Now I expect you to sit here in my lap, and I'll teach you how to have self-control, to listen, and to enjoy worship. Let's pray first so Jesus can come into your heart and help you obey."

We prayed, and Father resumed the story he was reading. Eric sat quietly for about two minutes and then started wiggling, wanting to get down from my lap and play. Father stopped reading, and I repeated the earlier instruction and prayer. Eric sat still another two minutes and started wiggling again.

"Mother, we need to use firmer measures to teach Eric how he can surrender and obey. Let's go into the other room where we can be private and hear God's direction to us. We need God. Father, can you read to your other children in our absence?"

"Sure," Father agreed.

In the other room, I gave Eric to his mother, and we knelt to pray to God. Eric cooperated nicely in prayer, even repeating after his mother who was repeating after me: "Jesus, I want to learn how to sit still during worship. I want to obey You. I need Your power to obey. Teach me, please!"

"Okay, Eric. Now you have prayed for God to help. He will help you, but there is something only you can do. You must choose to cooperate by sitting still. You can trust Jesus to change you inside as you do your part. It will take a few tries to learn, but you will see God helping you only if you cooperate. This will take effort. You can be a happy boy right now by choosing to follow God. Do you understand what you are to do?"

"Yes," said Eric.

"Then let's go sit still in worship. You will be in my lap and must obey whatever I tell you to do. I'll teach you how to be still. You will find your heart will be very happy because Jesus is in there helping you." This worked for a full five minutes. The father read, then asked questions of his children to see if they understood what he had read to them. During this discussion, Eric began to wiggle just a little. He looked right up into my eyes. "No, Eric. You can choose again. Jesus is willing to help you, but you must choose to sit still." And Eric chose to pull away from me and cry for his mommy.

Off into the other room we went again. We went through a similar prayer, explanation, decision, and response—but Eric wouldn't stay kneeling. He clung to his mother, not wanting to obey. "Lord, what would You have me to do now?"

"Because sentence against an evil [selfish] work is not executed speedily, therefore the heart of the sons of men is fully set in them to do evil." [3]

"Okay, I understand, Lord. He needs more motivation to choose."

"Mother, we need to give Eric a consequence for his wrong choice. He knows and understands what he is being asked to do. He's refused twice now. He needs some consequence for motivation. Can you handle giving him a spanking? And can you do it lovingly without harshness and anger?"

The Bible says, "The rod and rebuke give wisdom, But a child left to himself brings shame to his mother." [4] A spanking is given for the purpose of getting a child's attention, motivating him to listen, surrender, and cooperate with God. It should never be given to punish, vent our frustration, or to force our will on him.

Mother reflected for a moment and then said, "Yes, I can." She explained to Eric that when he chose to disobey, he was choosing a consequence, then laid him over her lap and delivered what I would call a medium spanking. He cried, and she cuddled him tenderly saying, "Jesus is your best Friend. He can clean all that yucky old stubbornness out of your heart if you will let Him. Would you like to ask Him to?"

Eric did and returned to family worship with a genuine smile and a willingness to cooperate. The father had gotten the rest of the children into their pajamas and ready for bed while they waited for us. Everyone returned, and we resumed family worship. This time Eric sat for five minutes without a wiggle. He began to squirm as was his old habit, but he immediately turned to me. I

3. Ecclesiastes 8:11.
4. Proverbs 29:15, NKJV.

recognized he only wanted direction and that this was not disobedience. So I encouraged him saying, "Eric, choose again. You can choose. Jesus is here to help you again." And Eric chose. Wiggles returned after a little bit, and again he looked right to me for direction.

"Eric, fold your hands." In this way I gave him something else to think of. "Listen to the story Father is telling." And I sent up a prayer to heaven for God to remain real to Eric and give him strength and decision to do the right.

We finished our twenty-minute worship successfully in this manner. The parents were awestruck and pleased at what God did in such a simple manner.

The next morning, Eric sat on his mother's lap during worship. After a few minutes, he started wiggling again, and we took him out to the other room to pray. That was enough to convince him we were going to act the same today as yesterday. I'm sure he thought obedience was easier than correction. He sat through morning worship very well. Several times he'd begin to go into the old pattern of wiggling, but God made him aware of it, and each time he looked to me for direction. I followed God and encouraged him just as I had the night before. Each time he chose to follow my direction, and he was learning to enjoy family worship. He liked the stories and discussions.

It doesn't matter how old your child may be. The best time to learn self-control is now. Begin to implement this process of teaching—which is telling the mind what is right, and training—which is calling forth a decision to act. As we help our toddlers to connect to God, divine power enables their human effort to obey. This training has far-reaching benefits. Eric learned in a short time that he didn't have to be Wiggly Willy, that in Jesus he could be happy and content to sit and listen. "Jesus can change me; I can enjoy the worship stories." These true thoughts implanted at the core of his life will go with him forever and are truly a blessing. And each child could learn the same victory.

Discipline is giving your child nothing for which he cries

Not choosing God involves terrible curses. I was in Sassy Shawn's home during family worship time. Karl, the father, led out while his wife, Gertrude, sat on the couch next to four-year-old Sassy Shawn. When we opened our hymnals to sing, Shawn tried to grab his mother's hymnal and close it. He didn't want to sing. There was a momentary scuffle, and Gertrude relinquished the hymnal to Shawn and blurted out to Karl, "Let's not sing today. Shawn isn't feeling up to it."

Karl frowned, but let it go. "Let's pray, then," he said. Everyone bowed in prayer, but Shawn wiggled and sighed restlessly the whole time. As Karl began to read, the mother tried to coax and bribe Shawn to sit quietly, but he became more and more agitated and disrespectful. "When is this going to be done? It's taking too long!" He began to jump on the couch. Mother picked up a picture book. "Come sit here, Shawn. Look at the pictures with me." Father's voice grew louder and louder as he tried to read above the distractions. Shawn ventured over to look halfheartedly at Mother's picture book. She put her arm around him and pulled him down beside her. He squirmed and fussed and wiggled off the couch. Father sighed and stopped reading.

I asked Gertrude, "So, is this normal?"

"I'm afraid we don't have regular worships because of Shawn's aversion to anything that deals with God. It started when he was about a year and a half old, as I recall. He was fussy and didn't want to sit still, so we stopped trying to have worship for a while because it was too hard. Then I read a book that said parents should expect to go through the 'terrible twos' and 'trying threes'; so, we figured he would eventually grow out of it and we could reason with him. But it has gotten steadily worse. I don't understand, though. Why wouldn't our little boy like God?"

"Would you like some input? Would you like to help him learn to sit still and be content?"

Gertrude's face turned red, and Karl stared out the window. She hesitated and then said, "Thanks for offering, but no; we'd rather work this through as he gets older and can reason things through better. We'd like to keep home happy and pleasant and not cause him to have an outburst. It's so disruptive!"

What Karl and Gertrude didn't understand was that permitting Shawn to fuss and cry and get what he wanted only set them up for the situation in which they found themselves. Their lack of restraint trained Shawn to think and act as he did. They established these habits by allowing him to act them out. If your child gets what he wants by crying or by being disruptive, sassy, or physically dominant over you, you can be assured he will do it again. His pattern of controlling you—instead of yielding to you—is reinforced. Recognize that Satan is behind this behavior and that the child needs you to fight for his freedom. Anger, hitting, and bad language need to be restrained and replaced by God and right habits.

Satan didn't want Shawn to learn about God or discover God's power to break Satan's hold on him through his wrong thoughts and feelings. Satan insinuated doubts about God, and Shawn took in those thoughts and acted upon them. The parents' misconceptions allowed Satan to work freely. But Jesus has the remedy. It is never too late to begin doing right. The best time to correct wrong ways is as soon as you see them. Go to God to learn the way out. Make a plan with Him, defining the wrong behavior and the underlying wrong thought that is likely driving the behavior and plan the replacement thought and behavior you want. Then begin to restrain the wrong and cultivate the right. *True discipline is to allow no wrong habit to go uncorrected that must be changed later.* Giving your infant nothing for which he cries is the beginning of this process.

Discipline is subduing your child's passions and temper

It was early evening, and Abigail arrived at the home of two-year-old Aaron to get her babysitting directions before his parents left for their "date night."

In the midst of giving her instructions, Aaron's mother said, "Don't even bother putting him to bed. He won't go to sleep for anyone but me. Anyone else who tries has a terrible battle, and it's just not worth it. I'll put him down when I get home."

The parents left. Abigail and Aaron got along well at first, but as the evening grew longer and longer, Aaron became more tired and cranky. He became an Angry Aaron. Abigail prayed for direction and felt that God was encouraging her to put Aaron to bed—that this was his real need. Abigail wrestled with that thought as she recalled the mother's warnings, but she decided to try it anyway. She snuggled the fussing little boy in her arms with his favorite blanket and started toward his bedroom. He saw where she was taking him and dissolved in tears. She looked in his eyes and saw fear overwhelming him. He clung desperately to her as if she were about to consign him to a bed of flames.

Abigail retreated to the living room to calm him down, hoping that some quiet play would let sleepiness take over. She laid down the boundaries, "You may have your blanket only when you are in my lap." He wanted the blanket, so he sat in her lap momentarily. But he was restless and got up to pace back and forth on the couch. He pulled on the blanket, hoping to carry it with him. "You may not have the blanket unless you are in my lap." And she smiled, holding out her hand to him while breathing a silent prayer that the blanket would be an incentive for him to relax in her arms.

He threw a little tantrum at first, stomping his feet and yelling angrily, but then he submitted. He looked so tired. Abigail turned off the light, sang a lullaby, cuddled him, and prayed—but he did not rest. He got up again and paced back and forth restlessly. Abigail turned the light back on. He wanted to get off the couch, but Abigail restrained him with a gentle but firm "No." The parents called, saying they'd be much later than expected.

Abigail picked up a favorite storybook. "Come here, Aaron. I'll read you a story." He grabbed the book and threw it across the room. Abigail corrected him and prayed with him. He folded his hands for prayer and then let her rock him and sing him lullabies again. He was getting sleepy, but fought going to sleep with all his might. He wanted down again, and when Abigail restrained him, he lashed out at her in frustration.

"No, you don't want to hit." Abigail kindly held his hand, looking directly into his eyes and smiled. "You want to sit down and be still. You are so tired. Come sit here." He did.

After about twenty minutes of this, God impressed upon Abigail, *Now try to put him to bed again. He so needs his sleep.*

At first she argued with God. "This is ridiculous! The mother said— The experience was—" But still, going to bed was so reasonable. She chose to act upon God's suggestion. Carrying Aaron gently to his bedroom, she said soothingly, "You are such a tired boy. It's a good time to sleep now. God is with you. The angels are with you. Jesus, help him settle into sweet sleep." She laid him down in his crib, saying, "Nighty night, pumpkin."

To her shock and joy, he relaxed willingly in his bed. He squirmed around a bit, but seemed resigned to settle into sleep. Back in the living room, Abigail listened silently, but there was no fuss from the little guy. Watching him over the monitor, she saw him rub his blanket on his cheek and turn this way and that very quietly for about twenty minutes; then he went off to sleep. Later she learned that this tossing was his normal routine.

In the midst of the situation, Abigail didn't know for certain that the ideas she had were God's inaudible voice directing her. But in hindsight, she saw clearly that it was God, because everything good comes from God. Self-surrender was one of the biggest evidences of God's involvement. He reached into Aaron's heart and gave him the freedom to go to bed without Mommy. God's divine power redeemed him from obeying his passionate emotions. My God is the God of the impossible!

Why do parents pray so little for God's help in raising their children, in helping them to change wrong thoughts and behaviors? Shouldn't we be teaching our little ones to follow God and right instead of their flesh and wrong habits? God still awaits each of us to come to Him in this way.

It was God who made the difference here in this situation, and mild discipline was all that was needed to redeem Aaron from his resistance to going to sleep without Mommy. It's best to use the mildest measures possible, but if these don't work, we must be willing to resort to firmer measures—not to hurt the child, but to redeem the child.

THE LONE EMBRACE
A SPECIAL WORD OF ENCOURAGEMENT FOR SINGLE PARENTS

Perhaps you thought that discipline meant spanking, and that was the extent of your view of discipline. Maybe you had no clue that discipline is calling self into control under God's Holy Spirit. You may have tried to force obedience and thought this was parenting. Or you may have been like Shawn's parents and didn't require any obedience at all from your child.

Are you seeing a bigger picture of discipline? Do you want the kind of success that God can give you? Do you fear to go forward and also fear to do nothing and stay in your current experience?

Be of good courage. God has overcome the world. He has overcome our flesh, and in Him we can overcome whatever besets us. As we learn this core of the Christian life, we can impart it under God's leadership to our infant or toddler. Christ says, "Perfect love casteth out fear."[5] In Christ we can say "No" to our fear and past history of responding in the flesh and can say "Yes" to God instead. We can trust He will be there for us and that He can subdue all things that have ruled over us in our life. That is what a Redeemer does. Then He re-creates you and your toddler into His image as you cooperate with Him. Trust God in a new and deeper way, starting today.

---

5. 1 John 4:18.

Matthew and Andrew Hohnberger.
True discipline in Christ
delivers us from self-rule and
instills self-control.

Chapter 17

Discipline to Deliver:
Firmer Measures

A wise son heeds his father's instruction,
But a scoffer does not listen to rebuke.
—Proverbs 13:1

I was out for an early morning walk in the countryside. It was late spring, and the sun was just peeking over the distant hills, flooding the valley with gold and making the dewdrops sparkle like diamonds. I was pondering Jesus' words: "I am the vine, ye are the branches." Just then, I spied an ancient grape vine climbing an old fence along the road. Its trunk was thick and gnarled, and its green leafy branches spread in profusion along the old fencerow, tiny tendrils clinging to splinters of wood. I stepped over to have a closer look. I discovered dozens of tiny grape buds tucked under the leaves. "I am the vine, ye are the branches: He that abideth in me, and I in him, the same bringeth forth much fruit: for without me ye can do nothing."[1]

We all know that no branch can produce fruit if it is severed from the vine. The branch is utterly dependent on the life coming from the vine. We would think someone very foolish to try to get fruit from a disconnected branch—and yet we often expect to find the fruits of the Spirit in our children without first connecting them to Christ. How foolish! Both they and we are utterly dependent on the life that comes from Christ.

What is that life? "The words that I speak unto you," Jesus said, "they are life."[2] Christ communicates to us through His Word, through nature, through providence, and through the impressions of the Holy Spirit upon our heart. When we grasp His thoughts and act upon them, He supplies the power to make them real for us from the inside out. Inspiring our children to do this is the real purpose of discipline—for when the child is connected with Christ he will bear lovely, sweet fruit.

When a child is stuck in stubbornness, arguing, or rebellion, it is evident that he is feeding on the wrong kinds of thoughts. For him to be delivered there must be a disconnection from self and Satan and a reconnection to Christ. This is not always an easy matter. When mild measures do not bring reform and surrender to God and right, what are we to do? Does God sometimes direct us to use firmer measures? Is firmness love? Let's see.

---

1. John 15:5.
2. John 6:63.

Discipline is using firmer measures when mild measures do not work

Two-year-old Fussy Frank hunched down in his high chair, a scowl on his face. His mother offered him a bite of peas, and he shook his little head and said, "No!" His mother was very conscientious and wanted Frank to develop good eating habits and healthy tastes.

"Frank, you must eat your vegetables. They are good for you. Jesus will help you." This is teaching—telling the child what is right.

Was teaching enough motivation for Fussy Frank to eat his vegetables? No! He was uncooperative in disposition, thought, and response to his mother. He would not pray to God or surrender to eat his vegetables. The meal passed without Frank eating his vegetables.

Frank's mother started feeling helpless. Then she remembered that God was there to help her. "Lord, what should I do? Should I just let this go?" she cried out in her heart. As the afternoon progressed, she prayed and thought as she worked.

Something she had read recently came to her mind. "When you have gained the confidence of your child and taught him to love and obey you, you have given him the first lessons in obeying God. Selfishness and the desire for supremacy will flee when Christ comes in and takes possession of the thoughts and feelings."

"Lord, I see that Frank needs to obey me in order to learn to obey You and that he will obey when You take possession of his thoughts and feelings. But how can I bring this about? How do I get him to that point? Telling him what to do is not working."

"Mother, when mild measures do not work, go to the firmest means necessary with Me as your General. I know how to get and motivate his heart so he can experience Me in him making this change possible."

A couple of scriptures came to her mind and confirmed her direction. "Because sentence against an evil work is not executed speedily, therefore the heart of the sons of men is fully set in them to do evil."[3] "I will punish them for their ways, and reward them their doings."[4] Another scripture cautioned her, "Children obey your parents *in the Lord.*"[5]

Frank's mother reflected, "I must first be in Jesus, surrendered to Him, cling to Him, communicate with Him so that He can guide me how to implement some consequences without harshness or anger. In the past, I'd ask Frank many times to do something until I lost my temper and punished him harshly." Turning to God again, she prayed, "Help me Lord! I can't let Frank have the authority over what he will or will not eat. I need You to bring my words and consequences to the level of Fussy Frank's understanding and motivate him to eat good food. You will work on his heart to obey. I am not in this alone. I need to do my

---

3. Ecclesiastes 8:11.
4. Hosea 4:9.
5. Ephesians 6:1; emphasis added.

part—give the consequence in a matter-of-fact fashion, so You can do Your part—transform his disposition. I'm willing to do more than teach him. I'm willing also to train his will to engage with You. Oh, Lord, give me the courage of a hero rescuing him, rather than the force of a controlling parent. Okay, Lord, let's go face this together."

Suppertime came, and Mother placed a small serving of green beans and corn on Frank's plate. "Frank, this is very special food. It is so good—yum, yum! Let's begin by thanking Jesus for this good food." Frank scowled but folded his hands to pray. As soon as prayer was over, he tried to shove the food off his tray. Mother picked up his plate.

"No, Frank, you may not do that. You must eat your vegetables before you can have anything else. There is no other way." Frank fussed at this restraint of self.

"Then you need to go to Jesus and pray for a willing heart." And they prayed on their knees. Frank cooperated, but as soon as he got back in his high chair he did the same thing again.

Mother's soft heart was about to give in and let him have something else.

"Mother, if you give in to him, he is the one in charge. He will do it next time and expect you to surrender to him again. Is this how you want to train his will?"

"No, I don't want to do that," Mother said to herself. "Well then, I need to give Frank some consequences now for being uncooperative, rather than trying six times and becoming autocratic."

Out loud she said, "Frank, you may not eat then. You can go play." And she picked him up in a matter-of-fact manner and set him down by his playbox. Frank was surprised. He wasn't used to this! He was hungry and wanted to eat, so he followed his mother right back to the kitchen.

Constantly in prayer, Mother asked the Lord, "What shall I do now?"[6] *"Use the law of the mind until he is convinced there is no other way."*

Mother had read about the law of the mind and knew that Frank skipping his vegetables must be denied so firmly that he would lose all hope of gaining his objective. Then he would surrender. This was difficult on this soft mother, but she was convinced this was God's direction, this was love, so she followed it. Putting him up into the high chair, she offered him his vegetables again.

"No," he said and covered his mouth.

Again she returned Frank to his toy basket to play; he protested loudly, wrapping himself around her legs.

"Frank, you must choose to pray to Jesus and cling to Him like you are holding on to me right now. Jesus will help you change inside here," and his mother pointed to his heart. "Jesus can take away stubbornness and bad feelings when you let Him. Let's pray!"

Frank said, "No" and swung his hand gently at his mother.

Without losing her temper, Mother said firmly, "Frank, that is very naughty."

---

6. Acts 9:6.

And she gave him a motivational spank on the backside. "You will need to sit here on the steps for five minutes and think about how you are acting. Mother will come when your time is done."

Mother went to the table to help serve the rest of the family, but she was praying, "Lord, help my son yield and come to You. I'm willing to do whatever it takes, but this is hard. You know that was the first spanking I ever gave without anger. Wow! I didn't really think that could be done."

God encouraged her in the course she took, *"And I will punish them for their ways, and reward them their doings."*[7]

After five minutes, Mother returned to Fussy Frank and found that he was now willing to pray. He looked up at Mother with soft eyes and said, "I'm sorry for hitting you, Mommy." She gave him a warm hug and put him back in his high chair.

"You can choose to eat your green beans and corn, and Mother will gladly help you."

"No, Mommy. I don't want to," he insisted—but this No lacked the strong spirit of former No's.

"Then you need to get down and play since you won't eat." So she put him down.

His mother could hear him fuss to himself while he played. She wondered if he were talking things over with Jesus. It turned out that he was still feeding on his selfish thoughts and required one more spanking. This time, after they cuddled and prayed, Frank came to the kitchen table with a sweet spirit and simply asked, "Mommy, eat?"

She returned him to the high chair and explained, "Mommy will help you by cutting these green beans smaller for you. They taste so good." And she put some rice with the small pieces of green beans. To her amazement and joy, he ate it all. What a difference it makes when we bring God with us and aim to connect our child to Him! Stubbornness is dethroned and replaced with willing obedience. The change is so remarkable once your child yields to obey Jesus and right.

Mother built on this victory day after day with small pieces of veggies mixed with rice or potatoes. Then she made the vegetable pieces larger and larger. After six months, Frank ate his trees (broccoli) and clouds (cauliflower), as well as his other vegetables with great relish saying, "Yum, yum!"

What if this mother had not consulted with God or taken the steps that were hard for her soft personality? What if she hadn't given motivational consequences in a consistent, prayerful, Christlike spirit? The outcome would have been very different.

You see, we differ from the branches of the grape vine in that we are not passive recipients of the life of the Vine; neither are we automatically connected to the Vine. We are naturally disconnected from God and independent from

---

7. Hosea 4:9.

Him. We carry with us resistance to the fruits of the Spirit.

So Christ needs to do more than just give us right instructions. He has to restructure our inner life. The habits and inclinations that produce sour fruit must be eliminated and replaced with those that bear sweet fruit. Sour thoughts, unwilling feelings, stubbornness, and selfishness must all be yielded up to Christ for Him to cleanse so that we can bear the fruits of the Spirit—love, joy, peace, patience, and so forth. Thus, redemption includes both a cleansing from wrong and a restoration to what is right. Christ's cleansing and restorative work occur simultaneously, but we need to see both parts of this process.

In parenting, God sometimes directs us to implant right thoughts and behaviors. At other times, He will have us focus on bringing the child to give up that sour fruit so the sweet fruit can replace it. Sometimes mild measures can bring that about, and other times firmer measures are necessary. Firmness can be love!

Lawyer Larry

Larry, age two, didn't like Mother's lovely meal of mashed potatoes, gravy, peas, and salad. But he did like Mother's homemade zucchini bread. Pushing his vegetables this way and that, he ate his zucchini bread and asked, "Bread, Mama?"

"What do you say, Son?"

"Pwease," he said, and Mother gave him more bread. After three pieces of bread, Mother realized what was happening.

"No more bread until you have eaten your potatoes and peas. Then you can have some more."

Larry began to cry and whine, "More bread. More bread. I want more bread."

Mother explained to Larry why he needed to eat his other food first, but Lawyer Larry continued to ask over and over. "Mommy, you need to listen to me. I don't need potatoes, I need only bread."

Mother said, "Larry, don't ask me again!" But he did anyway. Three times his mother said, "Don't ask again." Yet nothing happened to Larry for asking.

Larry said, "Mommy, I need bread. I want bread." And he began to cry.

"Okay," Mother said, "you leave me no choice. You must get down from the table. No more discussion." Larry's cries grew louder. But Mother didn't take him down from the table.

Larry turned to his father and asked, "Bread, Daddy?"

"What did your mother say?" Father responded.

Larry sat quietly for a few moments and then started begging in a singsong way again and again, "Bread, Mommy! More bread!"

Mother threatened again to take him down from the table but hesitated to follow through. She'd much prefer for him to obey than to have to discipline him. Oh, how she hated spanking! It was hard for her even to tell him to get down from the table, but God encouraged her to do so.

"Because sentence against an evil [selfish] work is not executed speedily, therefore the heart of the sons of men is fully set in them to do evil." [8]

Mother wrestled with her own soft heart. She could see the love involved in firmer measures, but she knew they still wouldn't be easy for her or for Larry. Finally, without saying another word, she lifted him out of his high chair and set him down in the living room with instructions that he was finished eating.

Larry cried, wailed, and fussed. "I'm soooo hungry, Mommy!" She put him back in the high chair, but he still wanted only the zucchini bread. That text rehearsed itself in her mind again and again. She tried praying with Larry, but he still demanded zucchini bread. She tried another time-out, but that didn't work either. She threatened to spank him, hoping against hope that the threat would be enough to motivate him to eat his meal. Nothing changed.

Finally, she implemented the spanking. Larry seemed devastated, and his mother's heart almost broke. Mother took him to prayer again, and this time Lawyer Larry surrendered. He willingly ate his potatoes and peas and then had one more piece of zucchini bread.

"Why didn't I do this sooner?" Mother wondered. "I could have saved us all of this."

Sometimes firmer measures are necessary. Under God, firmness works the reformation of wrong thoughts and actions and restrains insistent behavior. It stopped the lawyerlike arguments, and it connected Larry to God. When he chose to obey, God enabled him to follow through. If we are too soft on sin, it will grow and reign in our children.

A spanking is not to be used as an excuse for the parent to vent his or her anger or to hurt the child, but as a motivator for the child to choose to do the right. It makes the wrong way uncomfortable. It promotes a decision toward the right. When the child yields to God, he can experience God changing his thoughts and emotions. God has a thousand ways of motivating our toddlers. Go to him for just one idea to meet your situation right now and see that He is there for you. It isn't the method that changes our toddler. It is God behind the method that transforms the life.

Give a spanking in Christ—not in self. Gain a full surrender—not a partial surrender. Our toddlers need to be convinced that they are not in charge and they will be much happier. Until they are convinced, they will continue trying to exert their will over you. When they are convinced, they cease to long for their way and will yield to yours, bringing peace to the home. God will lead you in this warfare. Convince your child in a matter-of-fact fashion, not a dominating manner. We don't want to use Satan's tactics of force and anger. Instead, in Christ, and in self-control, demonstrate to them the way to go.

The Vine and the branch

That spring morning, as I examined that old vine and thought on the words

---

8. Ecclesiastes 8:11.

of Christ, the tendrils of that plant seemed especially significant. They were so small and fragile looking, and yet they clung to those old splinters of wood with a tenacity that lifted the branches heavenward. I thought of our relation to Christ. Clinging to Him, we, too, can climb heavenward and live His life. Apart from this dependence on Him, we naturally trail earthward.

Adam and Eve sowed the seeds of disobedience that gave us an inheritance of independence from God. We naturally want our own way; we want to be in charge. This is the root of every wrong trait of character. When parents, under God, challenge these bad habits and traits, they often feel like they've gone to war, and to a degree, at times they have. As most of us have seen, bad habits are more easily formed than good ones and are given up with more difficulty. One neglect on the part of a parent, daily repeated, forms self-serving habits in our toddlers. Self naturally grows like a brambly blackberry bush. These habits learned in the early years of life become deeply engrained upon their minds. Coming out of them often requires a wrestling and a decision before the fruit is seen.

Abiding in Christ is learning how to be a clinging tendril that receives its life from the Vine. We need to educate our infants and toddlers to learn how to abide in Christ. This is a discipline for both parent and toddler, but it needs to become our ultimate goal and direction in parenting by the Spirit. It goes right back to the root of Adam's and Eve's sin and meets the challenge of determining who is in charge—God or self.

Who is in charge?

Ruling Ryan, age three, was grumbling. "I'm tired. It's too far. I can't walk anymore. I want to go home." Over and over, becoming more and more whiney, he repeated his complaints.

"Ryan, honey," his mother, Mary, cajoled, "it's such a pretty day, and we are going to see a beautiful lake with our friends. You've looked forward to this all morning. Did you notice the snowcapped mountains? Look at the pretty trees and flowers and listen to the birds sing. They are so happy!"

All of this was lost on Ryan. He was so caught up in his grumbles that he didn't notice four-year-old Sweet Sarah take her older sister's hand in excitement. He didn't notice Fearful Frank take his father's hand and let his fears melt away. He didn't notice the other children of various ages entering into the adventure. All he could think of was how tired he was.

Mother tried to reason with him without success. She had three other children to watch over, including the baby in her backpack. After the fourth round of the same scenario, Ryan's mother was getting frustrated.

Ruling Ryan began to tug at her skirt to hold her back. When that didn't work, he sat down on the path, unwilling to go one more step. Mother reasoned; she threatened; she coaxed; she even carried him for a while. But when she finally put him down, he fussed more than before. He didn't care how tired Mother was. He didn't care that he was interrupting her from talking with the other adults. He didn't care if they missed the fun hike. He was unwilling to join the other children and change his attitude. Now his mother was under his cloud with him.

My husband, Jim, watched what was happening. God spoke inaudibly to his heart, *"Can you help?"*

After a little wrestling, he decided to offer to help. Mary was delighted and gave Jim permission to do whatever was necessary with Ryan; she even told Ryan that Mr. Hohnberger had permission to spank him if need be.

Ruling Ryan knew Jim, and he loved to play with him. Jim could be so much fun! But now, with the thought of being disciplined by Jim, he clung to his mother. Jim sat down on the ground beside Ryan. "So tell me what the problem is here."

"The walk is too long. It's too hard, and I don't want to go any farther."

Jim sent up a prayer to heaven for wisdom. He knew that Ryan was physically capable of hiking to this lake. The situation wasn't as bad as Ryan saw it. There were several two-year-olds walking and enjoying it. So first, Jim tried to reason with Ryan. Ryan wasn't listening. Then he tried to pray with him, but Ryan wouldn't cooperate. Third, he threatened a spanking, but Ryan wasn't moved at all.

As he sought God again, the thought came to his mind, *"Without Me he will not change. Bring him to Me, and I'll work with you."*

Jim said firmly, "Well, Ryan, everyone has left us. Do you see that? We can't stay up on the mountain forever, and we need to finish going up before we can go down. You have no choice but to begin walking. God will help you choose to walk and be happy. You need to ask God to help you, so let's pray right now."

Ryan looked around and saw that everyone else had disappeared around the bend in the trail. More out of fear than surrender, he prayed. His words were defiant, and his heart was not in it.

"Son, that is not good enough. You leave me no choice but to give you an educational spanking. You must obey to pray and begin walking." Jim knew this straight talk was using the law of the mind. He wanted Ryan to lose all hope of getting his way, so that he'd cooperate. Jim had to follow through and spank Ryan. Then he said, "I didn't want to do that. I'm sorry you chose the spanking. Ryan, if you go to God and let go of these wrong thoughts and feelings you hold so firmly, God can bring you out of this misery you are in."

Ryan prayed respectfully then got up and walked with his hand in Jim's. But after a few hundred yards, he again gave into despair asserting, "I can't go any farther. My legs are worn-out!"

Jim examined his legs and pronounced, "You have fine, strong legs. You can go farther." Ryan went five minutes farther and stopped again saying, "I can't. You'll have to carry me."

Jim recognized that Ryan was trying to rule, and that was not good for him. Consulting again with God, he prayed with Ryan and gave him an inspiring courageous talk. Ruling Ryan accepted some of what was said, and God gave him proportionate freedom. Not even God would force Ryan against his will. Until he willingly surrendered the wrong, God could not take it from him. Walking with a quicker step now, they reached the lake. Oh, it was so beautiful! Even Ryan got excited. Unfortunately, he had taken so long to arrive that everyone else had already started down the return loop of the trail.

Jim took him to the lake's edge, and the two of them threw some stones into the lake. Jim visited pleasantly with him and shared an object lesson, "Every thought you have has its influence upon your legs—just like the pebble going into the water influences the ripples on the lake. God wants to take away your negative thoughts, while Satan wants you to keep them and be miserable. God wants to set you free so you can have fun running like a man." Ruling Ryan was listening but fought stubbornly to hold on to his negative thoughts.

"Okay, Ryan, it's time for us to start heading back. The others will be waiting for us at the cars." Ryan would not walk. He plopped down on a log and refused to get up. "You'll have to carry me," he whined.

This stubbornness earned him another motivational spanking, and Jim prayed with him again to connect him to God. Jim encouraged him, and he made a right choice. He was beginning to trust Jim. Each time Ryan chose to walk, he gained a little more freedom from his negative, lying thoughts.

"Let's run down the mountain, Ryan!" Jim challenged cheerfully. "It's fun!" Ryan took his hand and began to run, giggling as they went. Then out of the blue, he sat down and started pouting. Poor Ruling Ryan wrestled between happiness and sadness. He obeyed first one, then the other.

He would not go forward anymore, so Jim told him he had to sit right there until he decided to move. Jim went down the trail a little ways, out of sight, and stopped to wait and pray. The minutes ticked by. Jim began to wonder if Ryan would ever choose to follow him. So he prayed again in faith for God to help. A few more minutes passed, and a little figure came trudging around the corner. When Ryan reached Jim, he asked, "Will you pray with me again. I don't want to be so miserable. I want to have fun. Do you think Jesus will forgive me for being so naughty?"

"He sure will, Son. Let's pray."

After that, everything changed. The sitting apart, the spanking, the reasoning all had entered into his free will decision to cry out to God for help. Jim and Ryan skipped and then ran together hand in hand down the hill. Ruling Ryan wasn't ruling anymore. He was listening to Jim and following him instead of his feelings. In his childlike way he recognized that Satan hurt him with sadness and that God wanted to help him. But it took his choice to cross over to God's side. Then his feelings and emotions changed from negative to positive. Running became fun. They caught up with the rest of the group just before everyone got to the end of the trail.

Ryan was no longer the same boy his mother had left with Jim. He was happy, cheerful, enjoying the hike, and his legs didn't hurt. Neither did his mind hurt anymore with all those former negative thoughts.

"So, Ryan, there is your mother. What is God asking you to say to her?"

Three-year-old Ryan ran to Mother, wrapped his arms around her legs, and looked into her eyes saying, "Mother, I'm sorry. I was a naughty boy. I could walk. I just didn't want to. Jesus helped me want to walk."

A week later Mary called our home to tell us the far-reaching effects of that surrender on the hill. Ryan was much more cooperative at home and asked for help when he felt so negative. He would ask for prayer to get rid of ugly thoughts and feelings. But her greatest joy was in relating what Ryan said of that discipline time on the hill when firmer measures had to be given him.

"Mother, Mr. Hohnberger really loves me."

"Oh, why do you say that?" Mother asked.

"He loves me so much he won't let me disobey."

Difficulties will arise; children will reveal their selfishness, their wanting to be the one in charge. They will show a hatred of restraint and discipline, an independent spirit. Instead of punishing children for these faults, too many parents make themselves blind, not wanting to discern the true meaning of these things. Therefore the children continue forming characters that God cannot approve, while Satan tightens his hold and control over them. So when mild measures do not work, we need to go to firmer measures led of God to demonstrate to our toddlers what they can be and do in Jesus! Is the effort worth it?

Discipline is changing masters

"I don't want to get dressed! I want to stay in my pajamas!" sassed Sassy Susie.

"No, it's time to get dressed, and it's cold today. Let's put on some warm clothes."

Susie ran out of the bedroom yelling, "No, I won't!"

Mother took a deep breath. "Now, Lord?"

"Yes now, Mother. Don't be afraid. I'm with you."

Mother mentally reviewed what God had been teaching her in her quiet time with Him. Her Susie was sassy when she could be sweet. Her mother had refrained from restraining her, because she feared the conflict that would ensue, but she so longed for change. A friend had shared with her the flowchart you will find at the end of this chapter. As she studied the chart, a longing rose within her that her Susie could be free from sassiness. Would it work for her? As she mulled over her hopes and fears, two verses came to her mind. "I am with you always" and "I will instruct thee and teach thee in the way which thou shalt go."[9]

"Lord, please give me a plan for what to do the next time Susie is sassy." She took out a pencil and paper and began writing down her ideas. She reasoned that she needed to replace the wrong thoughts with the right ones. She needed

---

9. Matthew 28:20; Psalm 32:8.

PARENTING YOUR INFANT/TODDLER BY THE SPIRIT

to restrain the wrong and cultivate in the right like gardening. "Well then, I need to interrupt Sassy Susie's sassiness. That's restraining the wrong. I can usually tell by the look on her face when she is going to be sassy. Lord, help me be sensitive to this. Direct me in what to say and how to say it. Then I must tell her what to do instead of the wrong."

Mother was pleased with the wording of her thoughts and wrote them down to reread so she would know what to say at the time of correction. "No, Susie you don't want to be sassy like that. Instead you want to be sweet and work through your problem calmly without anger. Jesus says a soft answer turns away wrath. Jesus will help you do that. Let's pray to Him to help you make the right choices."

Next she thought, "What if Susie fusses and argues? What then? She'll need some kind of consequence. What would an appropriate consequence be for a three-year-old to gain a little surrender to Mother and God's will? Hmm, I could have her take a five-minute time-out when she can't talk. Or she could scrub the sink or sweep a reasonable section of the floor. Or we could take a 'grizzly run' around the house or around the kitchen island. After that, I should call her to a decision to pray and do the right. Choosing God is changing masters. She must learn it would be easier to obey than disobey. I'll stay in this corrective circle until Susie chooses to surrender and obey. Her demeanor must show Jesus is abiding there. She will be calm and sweet, not agitated and sassy. Once she agrees to obey she must act it out. When she does the right she will be rewarded with a happy heart from Jesus, and a hug or praise from me."

"Lord, attend me as I try this new way," prayed Mother silently as she went to pick up Susie. Mother sat her on her lap saying, "Susie there will be no more sassy talk. Jesus will help Mother be firm and teach you how to say 'No' to sassiness and Satan and 'Yes' to God and sweetness instead. God, you and I will be very happy doing this."

"No Mommy! Let me go! I will not pray. I don't like Jesus!"

Mother consulted with God moment by moment, and God directed her faithfully as she saw in hindsight. At the time, it seemed the mother was putting all the effort into reasoning and planning, rather than executing. In hindsight, it was basically what she had put on her paper that led her now. It was the principle of connection to God she laid out as her purpose in reasoning, giving consequences, and calling for a decision. They were all for the purpose of connecting Sassy Susie to Jesus so that God could empower her to do the right and be sweet instead of sassy. Susie didn't have to obey Satan any more.

Mother had Susie sweep the kitchen floor because she would not pray to Jesus. But Susie refused. She plopped down in the middle of the floor. Mother carried her to a quiet spot alone in the house for a quiet time. Susie didn't like that because she was very social, but she still refused to pray. Then Mother took her for a miniature "grizzly run" which started to break through her stubbornness.

Susie decided to pray. She was convinced there was no other way. During this prayer, her heart was softened some. Then she went to sweep the floor. She did the first half well then got sassy again. She didn't want to complete the task even though it was a small kitchen floor. Another time-out, prayer, and another call to a decision got the entire kitchen floor swept good for a three-year-old. Then back to getting dressed. Susie was pouting, so Mother gave her a spanking for being unkind and uncooperative. Prayer followed, and Susie was much different.[10]

Sweet Susie now had a calm countenance, a sweet smile, and a heart willing to get dressed. This was a real surrender from the inside out. It was not outward domination, but a cleansed heart that wanted to be sweet and Christlike. The branch was connected to the Vine and bore sweet fruit. Mother swung Sweet Susie up in the air, pointing out how good it is for Jesus to be in our hearts. Satan only makes us miserable and unhappy. We can choose Jesus over Satan any time, and God will help us do the right.

Later that day, the old nature returned for supremacy—in not wanting to go potty before leaving in the car. Mother followed the same pattern under God's direction, and the situation was resolved much faster. Mother had to give only one consequence, and Susie chose to cooperate. Prayer, submission, and connection to God are the vital parts of this heart change. Truly, subjection to God is restoration to one's self. Self-control brings happiness from the inside out.

When mild measures fail to work, use the firmest means necessary under God's direction, and you will gain a pleasant child who contributes to a pleasant home. Taking your toddler to Christ is disconnecting him from Satan. Tell him he doesn't have to follow Satan or sassiness and be unhappy anymore. When he chooses Jesus, he can be happy again. Jesus is a good Master whereas Satan is a nasty master. Tell Satan you are no longer under his control, for Jesus is your Master instead. When your child chooses to obey Christ, he connects. The Holy Spirit flows through him, giving life to a seemingly dead branch. You will know your child has surrendered by his fruits. So it can be with you!

THE LONE EMBRACE
A SPECIAL WORD OF ENCOURAGEMENT FOR SINGLE PARENTS

I can hear some of you saying, "The firmer virtues of force, perseverance, and determination scare me. Yes, I come from the too soft side, and I see that I, too, am unbalanced as you illustrated. You see, I was abused physically and emotionally as a child and youth. My experience was devastating. I've never seen a spanking given without harshness and anger. I vowed I'd never hurt my child by spanking him. I equate spanking with hurting—not as a motivator to find freedom in Christ. Until reading this chapter and seeing the love of taking my toddler out of Satan's hand I would never have consented to spank. Can

10. See Proverbs 13:24.

God take someone like me and teach me how to work with Him and use firmness properly?"

Most assuredly. God wants to call us out of a life of serving fear or our past history.[11] God is with each of us to call to our hearts to give up our wrong ways, to be willing to try a new and better way directed by Him. First He must gain the parent, then the child. God wants us to come unto Him, to take His hand, for He knows we cannot do it of ourselves, or by methods that do not involve Him. We need divine power attending our human effort. He invites you and me to come to Him with all our perplexities and history issues so He can direct our steps, our thoughts, and our responses and enable us to direct our little ones in the right spirit. Day by day, we form characters that can place our little ones as well-disciplined soldiers under Prince Emmanuel's banner—not as rebels under the banner of the prince of darkness. God wants to re-create us into His image! We just need to connect with Him as the branch is connected to the Vine.

Landon Hohnberger.
Discipline is teaching the toddler that he can
obey when he's sure he can't.

---

11. Luke 1:74, 75.

Sally and Jesse.
"Being a grandparent is great fun!"

Jesse and Landon Hohnberger.
"I love my brother!"

Bringing My Child's Heart to a Surrender

My child listens to "the flesh" and disobeys, acts ugly, whines, or wrongs someone and needs corrective guidance.

Parent searches his or her own heart.
"Is my heart surrendered to Jesus right now?"
"Am I willing to follow the Lord's leading to lead my child to Him?"

Parent's heart
is not fully surrendered.

Come apart and pray.
"Father, give me the right spirit
and a willing heart to do your will
concerning my child."

Parent's heart is fully surrendered.
"By the grace of God, I'm prepared
to see this battle, small or great,
through to the end
without indulging harshness or anger."

Call your child to surrender.
"You can not complain."

Tell the child what he is to do instead.
"You can choose to be happy."

Encourage the child that through Christ he can obey and do right.
*"Let's go to Jesus, your best Friend,
so He can help you...I love you too much
to let you disobey...You can choose to stop
complaining and be happy with Jesus."*

What is the child's decision?
The child has now been called to a decision:
a call to self-denial and self-control.

The child shows repentance
and a desire to have a changed heart.
*You can see a real desire
and effort on his part.
He is willing to accept
the consequences of his actions
and perform any restitution cheerfully.*

Once the surrender is made,
the child must cheerfully do right,
correcting the wrong that required
this corrective procedure.
*Wash the dishes.
*Speak kind words to the person
they spoke unkindly to.
*Apologize to the person they hit
and serve him by doing a chore for him.

Pray and thank Jesus for
giving the child victory
over self!

Make the child aware
of the happy heart he now has.
Verbally give God the credit
Sometime during the day (as God directs),
point out the contrast of the joy
that comes from surrendering to Jesus
and dying to self
with the misery of listening to the flesh
and living for self.

The child makes no effort to change.
*Does not portray true repentance
in words, actions, or expressions.*

Send up a silent petition.
"Lord, what will Thou have me to do?"

**Administer discipline in love,
without harshness or anger,
and with the intention of helping
the child surrender to God.**

Take the child to prayer.
*Assure him a connection with
Christ is needed to do right.*
(Be prepared—self resists being crossed.)
*Parent, surrender your child's will
to God in their stead.*
*Have the child speak his sin to God,
then ask for grace to choose to do right.*

Chapter 18

"Slaying the Giants"

How we shall order the child, and how we shall do unto him?
—Judges 13:12

God inspired Israel of old to go up and possess the Land of Promise. He led them out of the slavery of Egypt, which represents our slavery to sin, self, and Satan. He freed them for the purpose of serving Him. As they made the great Exodus they stopped at Mount Sinai to meet their God, to learn of Him, to learn His voice, to bow before Him in gratitude for their deliverance, and to learn more of what it means to follow Him. They had experienced evidence of His power to deliver, but now He wanted to make that deliverance practical in their everyday lives by teaching them to turn to Him in the trials they faced.

In God's wisdom, He led Israel to the bitter water so that they would turn to Him for the solution, but they did not. Instead, they murmured. So God had to repeat this lesson out of love to help them learn how to solve problems. He wanted to teach them of His love, wisdom, and power. God has the solution for every trial, no matter how impossible it might appear. The people ran out of water, but God supplied water when Moses sought Him.

Our spiritual sojourn is very similar to the journey of Israel of old. God calls us to follow Him and then leads us through a wilderness of trials designed to teach us to depend upon Him. Afflictions, crosses, temptations, adversity, and our varied trials are all used by God to refine us. Our trials reveal giants in the land of our characters that need to be evicted; because it is in a crisis that our true character is revealed.

Parenting a disobedient child can be a trial. Some trials are bigger than others. We must see our trials as God's workmen and turn to Him for the answer to our present problems.

Encountering giants

Israel scouted out the Land of Promise and found giants living there who had to be dispossessed before the land could be occupied. Two spies were of good courage and trusted God and His promise to give them the land, while ten spies buckled to despair and hopelessness. "The giants are too large and strong," they whined.

We want to go up and possess the Promised Land too—the land of Christ-in-me, the land of an upright character.[1] There are giants in this land—the giant, Fear; the giant, Despair; the giant, Selfishness; the giant, "I Can't"; and

---

1. Psalm 143:10.

many others. God can slay these giants. He awaits our calling upon Him. He promises to be our General in this warfare. He will give us all the wisdom, ideas, directions, and strength we need so that we are freed to serve God and right instead of self and Satan. There is a pattern to this warfare that we must learn, as God personally directs us in how to slay the giants in our hearts and homes.

As in the days of Israel, God promises, "I have given you this land. Go up and possess it." Of ourselves, we are not strong enough to slay the giants, but in Christ we are. It is His wisdom and strength that will slay those giants, and we must do our part, wielding the sword of the Spirit and following Christ, until at last the giants fall dead before us by His grace. One by one, the giants can be evicted from our character as we join hands with Christ and go out to do this warfare under Him. At times it is a hand-to-hand battle with the giants. It takes every ounce of effort and decision to remain in the battle. Like Israel of old, we, too, must believe God's word and go up to possess this land.

Large and small giants

Some giants are small and fall easier. They are God's training ground to develop our muscles of faith, trust, and communion with our General so that we have the strength to wield that sword courageously. Our muscles strengthen in the action of slaying the small giants in our character. But not all giants are small—just ask David! Some are very large and intimidating. As you know, David took one stone for the giant Goliath, and the other four stones were for Goliath's four brothers who might come out when they saw Goliath dying. David didn't doubt God would make his aim hit the mark. David was experienced because he had been through God's training program in smaller trials—facing bears and lions—as a shepherd boy. He learned of the great I Am just as we may on our battlefield.

As good soldiers of Christ we are in a training program to learn of Him, to trust, and to experience His presence and care for us. We need to be led by Him to know what course to pursue when giants present themselves. We need to call forth the firmer virtues when we come face to face with these big giants. These giants don't fall by the milder means of discipline. The Christian life is more than many take it to be. It does not consist wholly in gentleness, patience, meekness, and kindliness. These graces are essential, but there is need also of courage, force, energy, and perseverance. We need the firmer virtues to press on through difficulties and discouragements. This requires men and women who are more than weaklings. In Christ, we are sufficient for whatever task that presents itself to us.[2]

The hand-to-hand battle against our habits or those of our toddlers is fought in our thoughts, feelings, habits, inclinations, and history. Yes, even our toddlers have a history caused by our lack of training or our inheritance to them. If we win the battle at the level of our thoughts in Christ, we win the character

---

2. Hebrews 2:8; Jeremiah 32:27; Jude 24.

and behavior too. In parenting, we face and must evict the giant Self and his brothers: the giant, Habit; the giant, Lying Thoughts; the giant, Driving Emotions; and the giant, Fear, in order that Christ may abide there in their place. Like David, we, too, need five stones, showing our willingness to enter the battlefield.

Parenting requires persevering firmness to change masters

Tearful Tommy, age four, was crying uncontrollably. He had banged on the wall with his toy hammer, and his mother had just taken it away. "You naughty boy!" she scolded. "How many times do I have to tell you not to bang on the wall? Will you ever learn? Now go to your room until you get control of yourself. Don't come out until you stop crying."

Poor Tearful Tommy! Off he went to his room, his little shoulders rounded in despair. He didn't know how to stop crying. His mother, Timid Tamara, had tried everything she knew to help him, but he was always crying in despair. He was very hard to please and would break down in tears at the most reasonable request or command. A "No" was devastating to him, and he'd cry and cry. Mother recalled that this behavior had started when he was about a year old, but now he'd cry for as much as four hours no matter what she did to console him.

She was not inclined to spank him—she felt it would crush or hurt him—so she continued to apply the mild measures that didn't change or help his behavior. She had been sending him to his room like this for over a year without any improvement in his disposition or behavior. "Where is God?" she wondered. "I've prayed from the beginning for God to take away this giving-up attitude, fear, and despondency. God isn't doing anything about it. I need help," she resolved. And God began to answer her prayer by opening up an opportunity for her and her children to visit our home for a few days. She hoped to gain some insights into parenting—specifically what she could do to help her son. As of yet, I knew nothing about Tearful Tommy's uncontrollable tears.

Timid Tamara arrived late one evening, and after we welcomed them and settled them into the guest cabin, we all went to bed for the night. The next morning my boys and I were preparing breakfast when Timid Tamara knocked so quietly at the door that I didn't even hear her knock. My sons made me aware of it.

I opened the door and found a very anxious Tamara. "Oh Sally, I have a real problem on my hands with my Tommy. I asked him to get dressed, and no matter what I do, he won't do it. Can you help me? I know it's not a good time," she apologized, "but I just don't know what else to do. I've been trying to get him to obey for an hour already. I brought Timmy hoping the boys could watch him while we deal with Tommy."

My head swam with the responsibilities of getting breakfast for our two families. This wasn't a good time at all, and I didn't feel like dealing with Tommy right then. Couldn't I defer it for later—surely I could. "Lord" I cried, "What shall I do?"

"Sally, you need to help her now. I'll be with you. The boys [then ages ten and twelve] *can prepare the meal for you."*

I wrestled with the decision. Inner turmoil argued against God's request. My emotions arose strongly against going, but my soul sensed that this was God calling me. I must say "Yes" to God. Once I made my decision to help, all the confusing thoughts and feelings found rest. My mind focused on what I needed to do. I didn't like not knowing a child or his background before I began disciplining, but God knew the situation, and I could trust He'd teach me as it developed.

"Okay, Tamara, I'll come now." I told Jim where I was going and gave the boys directions for breakfast. Tamara told Timmy to mind Jim and the boys, and we were off.

"Tamara, I don't have the wisdom to help your son, but God does. We need to connect with Him first before we get there. Let's pray." Stopping on the roadway, we prayed.

"Lord, You are our wisdom, our strength, and we put ourselves into Your keeping and care. We ask for wisdom to deal with Tommy, to understand why he isn't obeying, and to show him how he can obey. We need a Power outside of ourselves to bring him and ourselves under control in You. We put Tommy and his brother, Timmy, into Your hands to call them unto You. Take Tommy's will and make it Yours. We trust You, Lord, to answer our prayers."

"So Tamara, tell me what happened this morning."

"I asked Tommy to get dressed, and he just refused. I deal with this at home all the time. He just refuses to obey me. He is so stubborn and willful. I need you to show me how to bring him to obedience."

Arriving at the cabin, we entered to find Tommy sitting on the floor in his pajamas with his shoes and clothes before him, crying.

"Lord, what do I do? Where do I begin?" I cried out again.

"Begin with what you know."

"All right, what would that be?" I reasoned. "I need to call self into control through a connection with Jesus. Give simple instructions easy for a four-year-old to understand."

"Good morning, Tommy. Mother asked me to come and help you get dressed. I'm your helper to show you how you can obey and be happy. First, you have to stop crying." Little did I know how important this directive was! "I want to take you to Jesus for power to obey. Jesus will come inside you to take away all the icky feelings you have right now, but you must do God's will not yours. Come kneel before God with me."

To my utter shock, he came running to me willing and wanting to pray although he was still crying. Getting a toddler to pray is usually the biggest battle. I mistakenly thought, "Oh, this is a simple problem. We'll be done shortly." The truth I didn't know was that there was a giant behind this crying that needed to be slain, and I didn't perceive the depth of Tommy's bondage to him. It was a good thing that Jesus was my General in this warfare. He wouldn't be caught off guard. He knew the battle accurately.

"Dear Jesus, come into Tommy's heart and cleanse away all the yucky feelings he has inside. Give him freedom to stop crying. Help him choose to obey and give him wisdom and power to do so." Tommy was still crying in a whimpering way.

Wiping his eyes with a Kleenex, I smiled at him. "Tommy, I can help you to stop crying and get dressed. But you need to do whatever I tell you to do, and you need to do what I say right away without thinking about it. Whatever I tell you to do, do it. Do you understand what I am asking you to do?"

Tommy nodded, Yes.

"Do you feel any different after prayer, Tommy?"

"No."

"That's Okay. Jesus is there inside you, because you asked Him in. You can't feel the difference, but God is still there. Trust God and me—not your feelings."

"Tearful Tommy, I want you to stop crying right now. I want you to smile instead. When you obey to do this, God will change you inside, and even your heart will be happy. But you must choose to obey exactly what I said. Okay, choose to smile!"

"I don't know—" he grimaced and continued crying. "I can't stop crying!" And the tears poured forth in greater torrents.

"Oh my, what a strong reaction! He looks fearful, despairing, and hopeless. What does he mean, 'I can't stop crying?' I need to tell him unequivocally that in Christ he can," I reasoned. In hindsight, the outcome made it clear to me that God was leading my reasoning, but I couldn't feel Him at the time.

"Tearful Tommy, you must choose to believe me, not your feelings. In Jesus you can stop crying. You are free not to cry. God cannot change you inside until you choose to believe He can and cooperate to put on the best smile you can. Then God will begin to cleanse the fear from inside you. Do you understand this?"

"Yes," he sniffled.

I tried the process of instructing and praying to make God as real as possible, and then calling him to a decision—but it appeared that he didn't even try to smile. Every call to smile only escalated his tears and fears. "Lord, this doesn't look very hopeful. I can read despair and fear all over this boy. May You help him understand what is expected of him and give him power to choose."

"I am with you. You'll need to be very firm. Bring him to Me."

"Tommy! Look at me." And I turned his head to look into my eyes. "I love you. I want to help you, but I can't help you unless you cooperate with me. I can't choose for you—only you can choose. This is your part. Obey God and me. We will direct you out of this awful misery you are in. With Jesus, you can stop crying. But you must choose."

I could see him hesitate, fearful of trying. "Tommy, choose to put that smile on right now before it feels right. Jesus will make it feel right in time. Trust me."

He not only refused to decide, he also pulled away from me, threw himself on the floor in total despair, and cried even harder. I was tempted to become frustrated, to give up, and not expect obedience this time. But God was there too.

"Sally, you are facing giants in the land of his character. Let's slay them together," God directed and encouraged me.

"That is right," I agreed. "This *is* a giant. This is God's problem, not mine. I just need to stay close to my General and communicate with Him. He wants to win this battle more than I do. I choose to think courageous thoughts instead of following my feelings. This is what I need to show Tommy."

Turning to the boy, I said, "Tommy, you are believing the lie that you can't stop crying. It is a lie of the devil. Satan doesn't want you to be free from crying. He is your giant enemy. Jesus wants to help you find happiness, but He can't unless you cooperate with Him. You must say 'Yes' to God, believing you can be happy. And then you can say 'No' to Satan and crying. Making no choice leaves you in Satan's land of sadness. You have all the power of heaven to choose not to believe Satan's lie and believe that God can do this in you." Tommy was listening, looking into my eyes; I saw a flicker of hope there in his eyes.

"Tommy, just smile. It's simple. Jesus is with you! You can do it." But he didn't.

"Tommy," I said more firmly, but not harshly. "If you don't choose right now, I'm going to have to give you a consequence for disobeying. Not to decide is to decide."

He grimaced with enough self-control to put on a partial smile, but it faded as quickly and momentarily as it came. My hope was dashed. I was so disappointed that he didn't go forward with courage, force, and determination.

"Lord, help me! This is not easy. We aren't getting anywhere. What do I do?"

"Weary not in well doing. Don't absorb his despair. Demonstrate more courage, hope, and faith to him. He needs consequences to motivate his decision. Realize that he is very weak. He has been raised to give up, so have pity on him and show him the way."

As soon as I felt pity for Tommy, my despair vanished. God freed me just as I knew He would free Tommy. I must motivate him to connect vitally to God. It would not be love to leave him under Satan's bondage. Love would be working with God to do whatever it took to free him. If it took firmer measures, so be it. I wanted his freedom in Jesus. If he didn't connect with God, I'd be leaving him to be whipped and beaten with the giant Despair's lying thoughts.

"Tamara, do I have your permission to give Tommy a spanking?"

Now Tamara was put in a tough position. She had watched me trying all the mild measures and had seen that they did not work a change, yet she feared spanking. She didn't want her son hurt. Her misconception and lack of balance were her giant enemies. God was calling to her heart and reasoning with her, but the emotional battle was great. She stood up, walked around, and didn't answer for several minutes. I began to pray for her, for I knew by experience that without some undesirable motivation we would leave her son in Satan's hands.

"Tamara, I'm not going to spank or give consequences in harshness and anger. I'm going to use whatever measure God leads me to use, but I'll do it in a Christlike spirit. Satan's lying thoughts have a choke hold on your son. If we don't implement firmer consequences, Tommy will remain Satan's victim and will be hurt terribly by these lying thoughts. He will have no self-control. Satan will increase his hold on him unless we put him in God's hands. But it must be Tommy's free will choice to go to Jesus—to trust Him—before Jesus will extricate him from Satan's service. It is love to motivate our child to take Jesus' hand to experience freedom. Try it."

"I don't believe in spanking because I was spanked harshly as a child. I suppose I'm too soft. This is hard for me. Okay, let's try it," Mother decided, thinking this was God's leading.

"Tell your son simply that I have your permission to spank him. Tell him to obey me—that I have your authority." And she did.

I gave him a moderate education on his backside and then reassured him that I loved him.

"Okay, Tommy. Trust me. Do what I say and put on that smile. You certainly don't want another spanking. Smiling is a little thing. You don't want Satan to hurt you anymore. Run to Jesus, take His hand, and believe God by putting on a smile."

He put on a semblance of a smile—a good move, weak though it was. He was still crying softly. "Good boy," I encouraged him, "keep going. You can do it. Jesus is with you."

Then Tommy gave up the effort, and his smile dissolved into a big frown, furrowed brow, despairing eyes, and loud crying again. He reminded me of a weak-limbed child learning to walk.

"Oh, Tommy, you were doing so well! Choose again!" But he gave into despair again and lay down on the floor, crying uncontrollably.

"I can't stop crying. I can't smile!" he said over and over.

This battle against the giant Self is a strong foe, but Jesus is stronger. "Okay Tommy, I'm going to spank you again for not obeying me. I'm so sorry. I tried my best to encourage you in your choices, and you didn't even try. You must believe God and smile. You chose this spanking. I don't want to do this, but because I love you I will do it."

He wrestled against me and cried very loudly before I ever touched him. I gave him a firm, but not an abusive, spanking for the purpose of motivating him to choose and connect with God. Then I cuddled him and told him I loved him. I told him he was free—in Jesus' power—to choose to smile and that Jesus' power is strong enough to help us do anything. "You don't want Satan to hurt you anymore, so you need to choose to be under God instead. You can do that by smiling right now!" And I smiled a big, friendly smile to encourage him.

Again, he put forth an effort to smile, and this attempt was better than the last, but it continued only five seconds. I repeated my encouragement, education, and call to surrender. Several more times he refused, and the consequence was given. Tamara was pacing the floor, watching this—very anxiously.

"Lord, what shall I do now? We don't seem to be getting anywhere."

"Keep going. I'm directing. The giant is weakening. Soon we will swing the final blow. Take courage and trust Me regardless of appearances. This is a battle, but you are winning." [3]

"Okay, Lord, I'll trust You rather than my senses."

"Tamara, are you all right? Shall I still proceed?"

"Yes, go ahead." She was seeing progress and had hope. "Tommy, I want you to say this truth out loud: 'Jesus can save me now. I'm free to stop crying in Jesus.' " And Tommy did so amidst his continuous tears.

"Look at me, Tommy. Do I love you?"

He nodded.

"I want you to smile to chase away the frown and sadness you have right now. You have seen Jesus empower you to smile when you chose to trust Him. Keep the smile on longer this time."

He smiled a pretty good smile. His mother clapped her hands—this was a miracle, and she was so pleased. But Tommy's furrowed brow remained. His crying remained. His eyes were pitiful and sad. "Okay, Lord, is this good enough?"

"No, Sally. We want a full surrender, not a partial surrender. Keep going."

Despair was at my heart's door. We had already spent forty minutes in this warfare. The mother was happy. We needed to stay on a schedule. But God asked me for a full surrender. I chose to go with God rather than my convenience or my feelings. What could I do differently?

"Okay, Tommy. You are doing better. When you put forth the effort to surrender and obey, God makes your smile possible. When you don't try to obey God, your lying thoughts take over, you believe them, and you are sad and cry. You need to let go and let God take your sad feelings now. Don't hang onto them." We knelt in prayer together.

"Now, I want you to smile so big that it overflows and sparkles into your eyes. Then you will see how strong and wonderful God is."

The thought that he hadn't yet done enough was too much for Tommy. He broke down into tears of severe despair. I felt that we were back at the beginning. I could feel despair pulling me down. An idea popped into my head—a good one—and I chose to follow it.

Picking Tommy up, I cuddled him and assured him that this was love and

---

3. Read Leviticus 26 to see what God did with erring Israel.

that he would realize very soon what love was really like. "Tommy, look at me. You can stop crying! Jesus is here. You know it's true."

Tommy exercised some self-control, and we were back to mere whimpering. "That's good, Tommy. You want to get rid of the rest of those tears, don't you?" I questioned.

"Yes."

"Do you see the corner of the ceiling over there?"

He nodded.

"I want you to blow all your tears to Jesus just as hard as you can. He will take them away." And Tommy did—oh, so willingly! A few moments passed. The whimpering became a little less.

"Well, Jesus took what you let go. Do you still have some crying left?" Tommy was now in a short breathing pattern, followed by a sigh which is common at the end of a long cry.

"Yes, I still have more," he admitted.

"Blow them to Jesus again." And he willingly did so. He blew harder and harder to get rid of them, believing that God was taking them with each breath.

After blowing five times, he stood before me with no crying whatsoever! Oh what a miracle for this lad! But his face was still very sad and his brow was so heavily furrowed that it went across his entire forehead.

"Lord, are we finished?"

"Go the full distance. Didn't you say 'sparkle in his eyes'?"

I was actually sad I had said that! Again, I wanted to stop and settle for what had been accomplished—but I didn't.

"Jesus takes away every wrong thing you give to him doesn't He, Tommy? He gave you this victory."

"Yes."

"Now, I want you to show that Satan is no longer your master, but that Jesus is. In Jesus, you are free to smile until your smile sparkles all the way into your eyes. In Jesus, you can do this. Believe Him. So let us see that smile of freedom." And I smiled a big smile at him.

His mother and I saw him wrestling, the mouth pouting to cry in despair. But then we could see him decide to believe God, and his smile got bigger and bigger and bigger! It became so full and free that it went all the way into a sparkle in his eyes. He stood up straight, his shoulders were back, and he was free, truly free. This four-year-old child stood before us in the full freedom of manhood under Christ. He was free from Satan's lying thoughts, free from his pushy negative emotions, and free to be happy in Jesus!

The transformation was so marked that this little child physically looked like a different child! I was shocked and sat back to enjoy gazing at him. Instead of appearing fearful, worried, and hurt, he looked so sweet, innocent, and calm. The thick brow of fear was gone! He was truly free! The giant had been slain through Christ!

We rejoiced with Tommy. Both Tamara and I hugged him individually, congratulating him on his success.

"Now Tommy, you are free to get dressed as Mommy asked you to do earlier. Jesus will be with you, giving you the freedom to obey." Cheerfully, Tommy dressed and stood proudly before his mother. The most attractive piece of clothing was his award-winning smile. Is Jesus big enough to care for your needs with your "Tommy"?

Every step toward this freedom was an exercise of weak faith muscles. Tommy exercised these muscles by believing the truth in place of the lies that formerly occupied the land of his character. God's blessings upon that exercise brought life. There are blessings that result from obedience and believing God. And there are curses that come from disobedience and not believing God. It was the consequences that tipped Tommy over to God's side and allowed him to experience God's power working in him to give him freedom. How much better is this than being Satan's victim!

Notice that Tearful Tommy's victory was progressive. First, we used all the milder measures of instruction, correction, prayer, and a call to decide to obey the right. When mild measures were exhausted, we progressed to firmer measures, consistently given, until he chose Jesus. Finally, in a motivated surrender, he gained the experience of a connection with God that gave him power to obey. This is true love!

What if we would not have used firmer measures to motivate Tommy to choose to try and to experience God? Is there a place for firmer measures? Can they be manifestations of love? Can they be given in a Christlike manner? Most assuredly, yes.

Well, the story doesn't end there. We went in for a lovely breakfast, telling everyone of Tommy's victories over crying. Satan had put lying thoughts into his mind, and he believed them—but not anymore! He was free to serve God and be happy now. The giant Despair was slain that day, and if he rises again tomorrow, Tommy now knows how to come to Jesus to slay him again.

After breakfast, Tommy's eighteen-month-old brother, Timmy, was denied an object he wanted that wasn't safe for him to play with. Timmy began crying and crying inconsolably. *Tempered* Tommy came over to me and led me by the hand to his mother and brother and said, "Mrs. Hohnberger, can you please teach Timmy how he doesn't have to cry anymore—that Jesus can help him be a happy boy!"

The gospel according to a four-year-old boy! Did Tommy learn to obey? Did he learn a lot more than just how to get dressed? Did firmness and calling him to reach higher than he was comfortable with trying to reach bring about fear in his heart toward me? No! He loved me more for showing him a better way even though it had been a tough road for him.

Every parent today needs to answer these questions and seek God for balance —whether they are too soft or too firm. Without knowing all the whys and wherefores, trust God to direct you with your child just as He did me with

Tearful Tommy. God has miracles for you in your home—with your disposition, with your infant and toddler. Come to God for your blessing and fear not the giants to be slain in your land. Instead, see Jesus as bigger than all that Satan can toss at you or your child. In Him, go up and possess the Land of Promise!

THE LONE EMBRACE
A SPECIAL WORD OF ENCOURAGEMENT FOR SINGLE PARENTS

The secret to my success and yours is Christ in you, our hope of glory. Go out courageously to slay—or at least to mortally wound—the giants in your land today. We must eventually utterly slay each giant in our character or that of our infant or toddler if we want to be free to serve God wholly. Don't settle for a partial surrender. Ask God if you are done, and He will direct you in the logic of your mind.

Whether you are widowed, divorced, or a single parent, God will direct your steps. If you are a single parent, God has double watch care over you. You are not at a disadvantage as Satan may insinuate. Or perhaps you are married, but in reality you are just as alone as a single parent. You, too, can claim God's promise with power. Read Exodus 22:22–24; Deuteronomy 10:18; 27:19; Psalm 146:9; and Proverbs 15:25. God is there for you!

Nathan Hohnberger.
Let us dress for the cold war
to slay the giants—it's a good work!

Left to right:
Sarah, Andrew, Jesse, Landon,
Sally, Jim, Angela, Nathan, Matthew.

Appendix

Resources for Parenting Your Infant/Toddler

Baby Management

Chapter 3, Me—a Parent?

By citing the references below, I'm not suggesting that you follow the concepts of human psychology they may contain. However, understanding the growth and development of your child can help to prepare you to cooperate with God in the task before you. You can get similar simplified versions of this list at any Borders bookstore too.

Gary Ezzo and Robert Bucknam, *On Becoming Baby Wise: Giving Your Infant the Gift of Nighttime Sleep* (Sisters, Ore.: Parent-Wise Solutions, November, 2001). A valuable guide that includes what to expect from your infant at what age, feeding, scheduling, and more.

Gladys Hendrick, *My First 300 Babies* (Goleta, Calif.: Hurst Publishing, 1964). Includes organizational tips, information on scheduling, how to deal with fussy times, etc. Author's e-mail address: hurstpub@silcom.com.

Tracy Hogg and Melinda Blau, *Secrets of the Baby Whisperer: How to Calm, Connect, and Communicate With Your Baby* (New York: Ballantine Publishing, 2001). Very sound scheduling ideas.

Steven P. Shelov, et. al, eds., *Caring for Your Baby and Young Child: Birth to Age 5* (New York: Bantam Books, 1993).

Character Development

Chapter 3, Me—a Parent?; Chapter 9, Toddling On to Victory

Etta B. Degering, *My Bible Friends,* 5 vols. (Hagerstown, Md.: Review and Herald® Publishing Association, 1977.) A five-book series of colorful Bible stories.

Janell Garey, *Secrets to Parenting* (Columbia Falls, Mont.: Empowered

Living Ministries, 2004), CD seminar. Visit our online store at www .EmpoweredLivingMinistries.org for information.

General Conference of Seventh-day Adventists, Office of Education, Ladder of Life (Hagerstown, Md.: Review and Herald® Publishing Association, 1996). Eight coloring storybooks with activities, songs, and a teacher's manual.

Sally Hohnberger, "How to Bring My Child to Surrender," Empowered Living Ministries, www.EmpoweredLivingMinistries.org. A step-by-step guide. Available on the article section of our Web site. Choose the link to "Free Resources" and then select "Articles."

Sally Hohnberger, *Parenting Your Child by the Spirit* (Nampa, Idaho: Pacific Press® Publishing Association, 2005).

Sally Hohnberger, *Parenting Your Teen by the Spirit* (Nampa, Idaho: Pacific Press® Publishing Association, 2007).

Sally Hohnberger, *The Indulgent Parent Delivered* (Columbia Falls, Mont.: Empowered Living Ministries, 1993), CD seminar. Visit our online store at www.EmpoweredLivingMinistries.org for information.

Other sources for materials

My Bible First! Ministries, 706-517-2428 or www.mybiblefirst.org. Bible stories, pictures, memory verse cards, songs, etc.

Rod & Staff Publishers, 606-522-4348. Character-building stories with no cartoons that illustrate the price of disobedience and the joys of obedience to God.

Faith Building

Chapter 12, Faith Building

General Conference of Seventh-day Adventists, Office of Education, Ladder of Life (Hagerstown, Md.: Review and Herald® Publishing Association, 1996). Eight storybooks with activities, songs, and a teacher's manual.

Ellen G. White, *Christ's Object Lessons* (Hagerstown, Md.: Review and Herald® Publishing Association, 1900). An excellent book to start you on the road to seeing object lessons in nature and with the everyday things in your life and home.

Financial Management

Chapter 7, Day Care Destruction

Crown Financial Ministries, 770-534-1000, toll-free 800-722-1976 www .crown.org. Offers a wide array of resources and tools to gain personal financial freedom within the model of faithful stewardship under God.

Personal Preparation for Parents

Chapter 1, Wonderfully Wrought

Jim Hohnberger, *Empowered Living* (Nampa, Idaho: Pacific Press® Publishing Association, 2002). Available in book, CD, or DVD editions.

Jim Hohnberger, *Escape to God* (Nampa, Idaho: Pacific Press® Publishing Association, 2001). Available in book, CD, or DVD editions.

Jim Hohnberger, *Men of Power* (Nampa, Idaho: Pacific Press® Publishing Association, 2007).

Sally Hohnberger, *Parenting by the Spirit* (Nampa, Idaho: Pacific Press® Publishing Association, 2004). Available in book, CD, or DVD editions.

Ellen G. White, *The Desire of Ages* (Nampa, Idaho: Pacific Press® Publishing Association, 1940). An excellent work on the life of Christ!

Other resources

CD or DVD seminars available on our Web site: www.EmpoweredLivingMinistries.org

Marriage & Family, CD seminar by Jim Hohnberger
A Personal Walk, CD and DVD seminar by Sally Hohnberger
Back to the Basics, CD seminar by Jim Hohnberger
Mastering the Basics, CD seminar by Jim Hohnberger
Christ All and In All, CD seminar by Jim Hohnberger

Potty Training

Chapter 9, Toddling On to Victory

Teri Crane, *Potty Train Your Child in Just One Day: Proven Secrets of the Potty Pro* (New York: Fireside, 2006).

Gary Ezzo and Ann Marie Ezzo, *Potty Training 1-2-3: What Works, How it Works, Why it Works* (Sisters, Ore.: Hawks Flight & Association, 2004). Very simple concepts.

Alona Frankel, *Once Upon a Potty* (Richmond Hill, Ont.: Firefly Books, 2007). This book for small children is available at Wal-Mart.

It's Potty Time (Carlsbad, Calif.: Penton Overseas, 2000).

Prenatal Influences

Chapter 1, Wonderfully Wrought

Thomas Verny and John Kelly, *The Secret Life of the Unborn Child: How You Can Prepare Your Baby for a Happy, Healthy Life* (New York: Dell Publishing, 1994).

Storknet, "Storknet's Pregnancy Week-by-Week Guide" Storknet, http://www.pregnancyguideonline.com.

Scheduling

Chapter 11, A Predictable Home

Sally Hohnberger, *Parenting by the Spirit* (Nampa, Idaho: Pacific Press® Publishing Association, 2004). See especially chapter 9, "Does Your Schedule Match Your Priorities?"

Sally Hohnberger, *The Making of a Woman* (Columbia Falls, Mont.: Empowered Living Ministries, n.d.), CD seminar. A CD series available online at www.EmpoweredLivingMinistries.org.

Schedules for Newborns

Chapter 11, A Predictable Home

Tracy Hogg and Melinda Blau, *Secrets of the Baby Whisperer: How to Calm, Connect, and Communicate With Your Baby* (New York: Ballantine Publishing,

2001). Discusses how to be calm, connect, and communicate with your baby. Also deals with how to get your infant to sleep through the night in the first months. A happy baby sleeps through the night. Wouldn't this help your schedule?

Gary Ezzo and Robert Bucknam, *On Becoming Baby Wise: Giving Your Infant the Gift of Nighttime Sleep* (Sisters, Ore.: Parent-Wise Solutions, 2001). Read this excellent book prayerfully to educate yourself about your infant, his needs, his problems, solutions to consider, and ideas for scheduling your life during this critical time.

Work

Chapter 14, I Can Help!

Watty Piper, *The Little Engine That Could* (New York: Platt & Munk, 1978).

Worships

Chapter 13, Worshiping God

Resources for Personal Worship in Addition to the Scriptures

Webster's Dictionary of the English Language, 1828 facsimile edition (San Francisco, Calif.: Foundation for American Christian Education, 1967.) Webster's 1828 edition is good for a deeper understanding of words.

James Strong, *The Exhaustive Concordance of the Bible* (Iowa Falls, Ia.: Riverside Book and Bible House). Necessary for word or topical studies in the Scriptures.

Safe Christian books. We don't need to be restricted to just denominational reading, but our extra reading needs to measure up to the Bible principles and the character of God. Test it by Isaiah 8:20. We don't want to accept "anything goes," but neither do we want to be unwilling to rightly challenge our present views.

Resources for Toddler's Quiet Time

Scripture Songs
Thy Word Creations has a selection available at their Web site, http://www

.thywordcreations.com/Childrens.htm. A source for whole chapters of the Bible sung on CD with an illustrative coloring book. It's lovely!

Check out http://www.ScriptureSongs.com or call 403-845-2839.

My Bible First! Ministries, 706-517-2428 or http://www.mybiblefirst.org. Memory verse songs and other resources.

Bible Stories on CD or tape
Check out http://www.Bibleinlivingsound.org.

Felt Books of Bible stories
These are available at most Christian bookstores.

Resources for Family Worship in Addition to the Scriptures

Books

Etta B. Degering, *My Bible Friends,* 5 vols. (Hagerstown, Md.: Review and Herald® Publishing Association, 1977). A lovely set of illustrative Bible stories to read and re-read. Available in print, CD, and DVD.

Arthur S. Maxwell, *The Bible Story,* 10 vols. (Nampa, Idaho: Pacific Press® Publishing Association, n.d.).

General Conference of Seventh-day Adventists, Office of Education, Ladder of Life (Hagerstown, Md.: Review and Herald® Publishing Association, 1996). Eight coloring storybooks with activities, songs, and a teacher's manual.

Want to Know MORE About the Hohnbergers?

E mpowered Living Ministries is the outgrowth of Jim and Sally's experience with God. Located near Glacier National Park, the ministry office is here to serve your needs, whether it is to book a speaking engagement, request a media appearance, or order any of a large variety of resource materials, including books, booklets, and seminars on CD or DVD. For more information, contact:

Empowered Living Ministries
3945 North Fork Road
Columbia Falls, MT 59912

EMPOWEREDLIVINGMINISTRIES.ORG

Phone 406-387-4333
Orders 877-755-8300
Fax 406-387-4336

*Y*OUR INFANT WON'T BE AN INFANT FOR LONG.

*I*F YOU'VE APPRECIATED THIS BOOK YOU'LL WANT TO READ THESE OTHER BOOKS IN HER FOUR-BOOK SERIES FOR THE NEXT STAGES OF YOUR CHILD'S GROWTH:

Parenting by the Spirit
Sally Hohnberger

Sally's first book on parenting reveals the principles she learned—on her knees. She discovered being a stay-at-home mom was more difficult than her nursing career. She needed help! And she got it, not from a talk-show host or the latest psychological guru. She learned—sometimes painfully—what it meant to parent her children by the Spirit. This book will show you how to be the parent God designed you to be.
Paperback, 160 pages.   ISBN 10: 0-8163-2031-4

Parenting Your Child by the Spirit (ages 5-12)
Sally Hohnberger

In this book, Sally teaches child-rearing principles from the context of personal time spent with Jesus. You'll meet some colorful characters with names like "Sassy Susie," and "Lying Larry." You'll learn the replacement principle of exchanging unwanted traits for Christian character traits.
Paperback, 304 pages.   ISBN 10: 0-8163-2070-5

Parenting Your Teen by the Spirit (ages 13-19)
Sally Hohnberger

The turbulent teens is a time period more dreaded by namy parents than the terrible twos! And yet this critical bridge between childhood and maturity should be some of the most rewarding years of parenting—and they can be, when we take hold of certain very important keys. Sally illustrates with many real-life stories how, with Jesus, our teens can be all that God intends them to be!
Paperback, 224 pages.   ISBN 10: 0-8163-2162-0

3 Ways to Order:
1. Local Adventist Book Center®
2. Call 1-800-765-6955
3. Shop AdventistBookCenter.com